W9-BZA-655

Legal Notice

ISBN-13: 978-1519617378
ISBN-10: 1519617372

BOOKS FROM THE GET 800 COLLECTION FOR COLLEGE BOUND STUDENTS

28 SAT Math Lessons to Improve Your Score in One Month
  Beginner Course
  Intermediate Course
  Advanced Course

320 SAT Math Problems Arranged by Topic and Difficulty Level

320 SAT Math Subject Test Problems Arranged by Topic and Difficulty Level
  Level 1 Test
  Level 2 Test

The 32 Most Effective SAT Math Strategies

SAT Prep Official Study Guide Math Companion

SAT Vocabulary Book

320 ACT Math Problems Arranged by Topic and Difficulty Level

320 AP Calculus AB Problems Arranged by Topic and Difficulty Level

320 AP Calculus BC Problems Arranged by Topic and Difficulty Level

555 Math IQ Questions for Middle School Students

555 Advanced Math Problems for Middle School Students

555 Geometry Problems for High School Students

Algebra Handbook for Gifted Middle School Students

CONNECT WITH DR. STEVE WARNER

www.facebook.com/SATPrepGet800

www.youtube.com/TheSATMathPrep

www.twitter.com/SATPrepGet800

www.linkedin.com/in/DrSteveWarner

www.pinterest.com/SATPrepGet800

plus.google.com/+SteveWarnerPhD

28 New SAT Math

Lessons to Improve Your Score in One Month

Advanced Course

For Students Currently Scoring Above 600
in SAT Math and Want to Score 800

Dr. Steve Warner

Table of Contents

Actions to Complete After You Have Read This Book 302

About the Author   *303*

Books by Dr. Steve Warner   304

V

ACTIONS TO COMPLETE BEFORE YOU READ THIS BOOK

1. Purchase a TI-84 or equivalent calculator

It is recommended that you use a TI-84 or comparable calculator for the SAT. Answer explanations in this book will always assume you are using such a calculator.

2. Take a practice SAT from the Official Guide to get your preliminary SAT math score

Your score should be at least a 600. If it is lower, you should begin with the Beginner or Intermediate book in this series.

3. Claim your FREE bonuses

Simply visit the following webpage and enter your email address to receive solutions to all the supplemental problems in this book and other materials.

www.thesatmathprep.com/28Les800.html

4. 'Like' my Facebook page

This page is updated regularly with SAT prep advice, tips, tricks, strategies, and practice problems. Visit the following webpage and click the 'like' button.

www.facebook.com/SATPrepGet800

INTRODUCTION
STUDYING FOR SUCCESS

*T*his book was written specifically for the student currently scoring more than 600 in SAT math. Results will vary, but if you are such a student and you work through the lessons in this book, then you will see a substantial improvement in your score.

If your current SAT math score is below 600 or you discover that you have weaknesses in applying more basic techniques (such as the ones reviewed in the first lesson from this book), you may want to go through the intermediate course before completing this one.

The book you are now reading is self-contained. Each lesson was carefully created to ensure that you are making the most effective use of your time while preparing for the SAT. It should be noted that a score of 700 can usually be attained without ever attempting a Level 5 problem. Readers currently scoring below a 700 on practice tests should not feel obligated to work on Level 5 problems the first time they go through this book.

The optional material in this book contains what I refer to as "Level 6" questions and "Challenge" questions. Level 6 questions are slightly more difficult than anything that is likely to appear on an actual SAT, but they are just like SAT problems in every other way. Challenge questions are theoretical in nature and are much more difficult than anything that will ever appear on an SAT. These two types of questions are for those students that really want an SAT math score of 800.

There are two math sections on the SAT: one where a calculator is allowed and one where it is not. I therefore recommend trying to solve as many problems as possible both with and without a calculator. If a calculator is required for a specific problem it will be marked with an asterisk (*).

1. Using this book effectively

- Begin studying at least three months before the SAT
- Practice SAT math problems twenty minutes each day
- Choose a consistent study time and location

You will retain much more of what you study if you study in short bursts rather than if you try to tackle everything at once. So try to choose about a twenty minute block of time that you will dedicate to SAT math each day. Make it a habit. The results are well worth this small time commitment. Some students will be able to complete each lesson within this twenty minute block of time. If it takes you longer than twenty minutes to complete a lesson, you can stop when twenty minutes are up and then complete the lesson the following day. At the very least, take a nice long break, and then finish the lesson later that same day.

- Every time you get a question wrong, **mark it off, no matter what your mistake**.
- Begin each lesson by first redoing the problems from previous lessons on the same topic that you have marked off.
- If you get a problem wrong again, **keep it marked off**.

As an example, before you begin the third "Heart of Algebra" lesson (Lesson 9), you should redo all the problems you have marked off from the first two "Heart of Algebra" lessons (Lessons 1 and 5). Any question that you get right you can "unmark" while leaving questions that you get wrong marked off for the next time. If this takes you the full twenty minutes, that is okay. Just begin the new lesson the next day.

Note that this book often emphasizes solving each problem in more than one way. Please listen to this advice. The same question is never repeated on any SAT (with the exception of questions from the experimental sections) so the important thing is learning as many techniques as possible. Being able to solve any specific problem is of minimal importance. The more ways you have to solve a single problem the more prepared you will be to tackle a problem you have never seen before, and the quicker you will be able to solve that problem. Also, if you have multiple methods for solving a single problem, then on the actual SAT when you "check over" your work you will be able to redo each problem in a different way. This will eliminate all "careless" errors on the actual exam. In this book the quickest solution to any problem will always be marked with an asterisk (*).

2.   Calculator use.

- Use a TI-84 or comparable calculator if possible when practicing and during the SAT.
- Make sure that your calculator has fresh batteries on test day.
- You may have to switch between DEGREE and RADIAN modes during the test. If you are using a TI-84 (or equivalent) calculator press the MODE button and scroll down to the third line when necessary to switch between modes.

Below are the most important things you should practice on your graphing calculator.

- Practice entering complicated computations in a single step.
- Know when to insert parentheses:
    - Around numerators of fractions
    - Around denominators of fractions
    - Around exponents
    - Whenever you actually see parentheses in the expression

Examples:

We will substitute a 5 in for x in each of the following examples.

Expression	Calculator computation
$\dfrac{7x+3}{2x-11}$	(7*5 + 3)/(2*5 – 11)
$(3x-8)^{2x-9}$	(3*5 – 8)^(2*5 – 9)

- Clear the screen before using it in a new problem. The big screen allows you to check over your computations easily.
- Press the **ANS** button (**2ND (-)**) to use your last answer in the next computation.
- Press **2ND ENTER** to bring up your last computation for editing. This is especially useful when you are plugging in answer choices, or guessing and checking.
- You can press **2ND ENTER** over and over again to cycle backwards through all the computations you have ever done.
- Know where the $\sqrt{\ }$, π, and **^** buttons are so you can reach them quickly.
- Change a decimal to a fraction by pressing **MATH ENTER ENTER**.

9

- Press the **MATH** button - in the first menu that appears you can take cube roots and nth roots for any n. Scroll right to **NUM** and you have **lcm(** and **gcd(**.
- Know how to use the **SIN**, **COS** and **TAN** buttons as well as **SIN^{-1}**, **COS^{-1}** and **TAN^{-1}**.

You may find the following graphing tools useful.

- Press the **Y=** button to enter a function, and then hit **ZOOM 6** to graph it in a standard window.
- Practice using the **WINDOW** button to adjust the viewing window of your graph.
- Practice using the **TRACE** button to move along the graph and look at some of the points plotted.
- Pressing **2ND TRACE** (which is really **CALC**) will bring up a menu of useful items. For example selecting **ZERO** will tell you where the graph hits the x-axis, or equivalently where the function is zero. Selecting **MINIMUM** or **MAXIMUM** can find the vertex of a parabola. Selecting **INTERSECT** will find the point of intersection of 2 graphs.

3. Tips for taking the SAT

Each of the following tips should be used whenever you take a practice SAT as well as on the actual exam.

Check your answers properly: When you go back to check your earlier answers for careless errors *do not* simply look over your work to try to catch a mistake. This is usually a waste of time.

- When "checking over" problems you have already done, **always redo the problem from the beginning** without looking at your earlier work.
- If possible use a different method than you used the first time.

For example, if you solved the problem by picking numbers the first time, try to solve it algebraically the second time, or at the very least pick different numbers. If you do not know, or are not comfortable with a different method, then use the same method, but do the problem from the beginning and do not look at your original solution. If your two answers do not match up, then you know that this is a problem you need to spend a little more time on to figure out where your error is.

10

This may seem time consuming, but that is okay. It is better to spend more time checking over a few problems, than to rush through a lot of problems and repeat the same mistakes.

Take a guess whenever you cannot solve a problem: There is no guessing penalty on the SAT. Whenever you do not know how to solve a problem take a guess. Ideally you should eliminate as many answer choices as possible before taking your guess, but if you have no idea whatsoever do not waste time overthinking. Simply put down an answer and move on. You should certainly mark it off and come back to it later if you have time.

Pace yourself: After you have been working on a question for about 30 seconds you need to make a decision. If you understand the question and think that you can get the answer in another 30 seconds or so, continue to work on the problem. If you still do not know how to do the problem or you are using a technique that is going to take a long time, mark it off and come back to it later if you have time.

Feel free to take a guess. But you still want to leave open the possibility of coming back to it later. Remember that every problem is worth the same amount. Do not sacrifice problems that you may be able to do by getting hung up on a problem that is too hard for you.

Now, after going through the test once, you can then go through each of the questions you have marked off and solve as many of them as you can. You should be able to spend 5 to 7 minutes on this, and still have 7 minutes left to check your answers. If there are one or two problems that you just cannot seem to get, let them go for a while. You can come back to them intermittently as you are checking over other answers.

Grid your answers correctly: The computer only grades what you have marked in the bubbles. The space above the bubbles is just for your convenience, and to help you do your bubbling correctly.

Never mark more than one circle in a column or the problem will automatically be marked wrong. You do not need to use all four columns. If you do not use a column just leave it blank.

The symbols that you can grid in are the digits 0 through 9, a decimal point, and a division symbol for fractions. Note that there is no negative symbol. So answers to grid-ins *cannot* be negative. Also, there are only four slots, so you cannot get an answer such as 52,326.

Sometimes there is more than one correct answer to a grid-in question. Simply choose one of them to grid-in. *Never* try to fit more than one answer into the grid.

If your answer is a whole number such as 2451 or a decimal that only requires four or less slots such as 2.36, then simply enter the number starting at any column. The two examples just written must be started in the first column, but the number 16 can be entered starting in column 1, 2 or 3.

Note that there is no zero in column 1, so if your answer is 0 it must be gridded into column 2, 3 or 4.

Fractions can be gridded in any form as long as there are enough slots. The fraction 2/100 must be reduced to 1/50 simply because the first representation will not fit in the grid.

Fractions can also be converted to decimals before being gridded in. If a decimal cannot fit in the grid, then you can simply *truncate* it to fit. But you must use every slot in this case. For example, the decimal .167777777... can be gridded as .167, but .16 or .17 would both be marked wrong.

Instead of truncating decimals you can also *round* them. For example, the decimal above could be gridded as .168. Truncating is preferred because there is no thinking involved and you are less likely to make a careless error.

12

Here are three ways to grid in the number $\frac{8}{9}$.

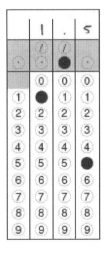

Never grid-in mixed numerals. If your answer is $2\frac{1}{4}$, and you grid in the mixed numeral $2\frac{1}{4}$, then this will be read as $\frac{21}{4}$ and will be marked wrong. You must either grid in the decimal 2.25 or the improper fraction $\frac{9}{4}$.

Here are two ways to grid in the mixed numeral $1\frac{1}{2}$ correctly.

13

LESSON 1
HEART OF ALGEBRA

In this lesson we will be reviewing four very basic strategies that can be used to solve a wide range of SAT math problems in all topics and all difficulty levels. Throughout this book you should practice using these four strategies whenever it is possible to do so. You should also try to solve each problem in a more straightforward way.

Start with Choice (B) or (C)

In many SAT math problems you can get the answer simply by trying each of the answer choices until you find the one that works. Unless you have some intuition as to what the correct answer might be, then you should always start in the middle with choice (B) or (C) as your first guess (an exception will be detailed in the next strategy below). The reason for this is simple. Answers are usually given in increasing or decreasing order. So very often if choice (B) or (C) fails you can eliminate one or two of the other choices as well.

Try to answer the following question using this strategy. **Do not** check the solution until you have attempted this question yourself.

LEVEL 2: HEART OF ALGEBRA

$$x - 3 = \sqrt{x + 3}$$

1. What is the solution set of the equation above?

    (A) $\{1\}$
    (B) $\{6\}$
    (C) $\{1,6\}$
    (D) There are no solutions.

See if you can answer this question by starting with choice (B) or (C).

14

Solution by starting with choice (B): Let's start with choice (B) and guess that the answer is {6}. We substitute 6 for x into the given equation to get

$$6 - 3 = \sqrt{6 + 3}$$
$$3 = \sqrt{9}$$
$$3 = 3$$

Since this works, we have eliminated choices (A) and (D). But we still need to check to see if 1 works to decide if the answer is (B) or (C).

We substitute 1 for x into the given equation to get

$$1 - 3 = \sqrt{1 + 3}$$
$$-2 = \sqrt{4}$$
$$-2 = 2$$

So 1 is not a solution to the given equation and we can eliminate choice (C). The answer is therefore choice (B).

Important note: Once we see that $x = 6$ is a solution to the given equation, it is **very important** that we make sure there are no answer choices remaining that also contain 6. In this case answer choice (C) also contains 6 as a solution. We therefore <u>must</u> check if 1 is a solution too. In this case it is not.

Solution by starting with choice (C): Let's start with choice (C) and guess that the answer is {1,6}. We begin by substituting 1 for x into the given equation to get the false equation $-2 = 2$ (see the previous solution for details). So 1 is not a solution to the given equation and we can eliminate choice (C). Note that we also eliminate choice (A).

Let's try choice (B) now and guess that the answer is {6}. So we substitute 6 for x into the given equation to get the true equation $3 = 3$ (see the previous solution for details).

Since this works, the answer is in fact choice (B).

Important note: Once we see that $x = 6$ is a solution to the given equation, it is **very important** that we make sure there are no answer choices remaining that also contain 6. In this case we have already eliminated choices (A) and (C), and choice (D) does not contain 6 (in fact choice (D) contains no numbers at all).

15

Before we go on, try to solve this problem algebraically.

Algebraic solution:

$$x - 3 = \sqrt{x + 3}$$
$$(x - 3)^2 = \left(\sqrt{x + 3}\right)^2$$
$$(x - 3)(x - 3) = x + 3$$
$$x^2 - 6x + 9 = x + 3$$
$$x^2 - 7x + 6 = 0$$
$$(x - 1)(x - 6) = 0$$
$$x - 1 = 0 \text{ or } x - 6 = 0$$
$$x = 1 \text{ or } x = 6$$

When solving algebraic equations with square roots we sometimes generate extraneous solutions. We therefore need to check each of the *potential* solutions 1 and 6 back in the original equation. As we have already seen in the previous solutions 6 <u>is</u> a solution, and 1 <u>is not</u> a solution. So the answer is choice (B).

Notes: (1) Do not worry if you are having trouble understanding all the steps of this solution. We will be reviewing the methods used here later in the book.

(2) Squaring both sides of an equation is not necessarily "reversible." For example, when we square each side of the equation $x = 2$, we get the equation $x^2 = 4$. This new equation has two solutions: $x = 2$ and $x = -2$, whereas the original equation had just one solution: $x = 2$.

This is why we need to check for **extraneous solutions** here.

(3) Solving this problem algebraically is just silly. After finding the potential solutions 1 and 6, we still had to check if they actually worked. But if we had just glanced at the answer choices we would have already known that 1 and 6 were the only numbers we needed to check.

When NOT to Start with Choice (B) or (C)

If the word **least** appears in the problem, then start with the smallest number as your first guess. Similarly, if the word **greatest** appears in the problem, then start with the largest number as your first guess.

Try to answer the following question using this strategy. **Do not** check the solution until you have attempted this question yourself.

LEVEL 2: HEART OF ALGEBRA

2. What is the greatest integer x that satisfies the inequality $2 + \frac{x}{5} < 7$?

   (A) 20
   (B) 22
   (C) 24
   (D) 25

See if you can answer this question by starting with choice (A) or (D).

Solution by plugging in answer choices: Since the word "greatest" appears in the problem, let's start with the largest answer choice, choice (D). Now $2 + \frac{25}{5} = 2 + 5 = 7$ This is just barely too big, and so the answer is choice (C).

Before we go on, try to solve this problem algebraically.

* Algebraic solution: Let's solve the inequality. We start by subtracting 2 from each side of the given inequality to get $\frac{x}{5} < 5$. We then multiply each side of this inequality by 5 to get $x < 25$. The greatest integer less than 25 is 24, choice (C).

Take a Guess

Sometimes the answer choices themselves cannot be substituted in for the unknown or unknowns in the problem. But that does not mean that you cannot guess your own numbers. Try to make as reasonable a guess as possible, but do not over think it. Keep trying until you zero in on the correct value.

Try to answer the following question using this strategy. **Do not** check the solution until you have attempted this question yourself.

LEVEL 3: HEART OF ALGEBRA

3.   Dana has pennies, nickels and dimes in her pocket. The number of dimes she has is three times the number of nickels, and the number of nickels she has is 2 more than the number of pennies. Which of the following could be the total number of coins in Dana's pocket?

   (A) 15
   (B) 16
   (C) 17
   (D) 18

See if you can answer this question by taking guesses.

* Solution by taking a guess: Let's take a guess and say that Dana has 3 pennies. It follows that she has $3 + 2 = 5$ nickels, and $(3)(5) = 15$ dimes. So the total number of coins is $3 + 5 + 15 = 23$. This is too many. So let's guess that Dana has 2 pennies. Then she has $2 + 2 = 4$ nickels, and she has $(3)(4) = 12$ dimes for a total of $2 + 4 + 12 = 18$ coins. Thus, the answer is choice (D).

Before we go on, try to solve this problem the way you might do it in school.

Attempt at an algebraic solution: If we let x represent the number of pennies, then the number of nickels is $x + 2$, and the number of dimes is $3(x + 2)$. Thus, the total number of coins is

$$x + (x + 2) + 3(x + 2) = x + x + 2 + 3x + 6 = 5x + 8.$$

So some possible totals are 13, 18, 23,... which we get by substituting 1, 2, 3,... for x. Substituting 2 in for x gives 18 which is answer choice (D).

Warning: Many students incorrectly interpret "three times the number of nickels" as $3x + 2$. This is not right. The number of nickels is $x + 2$, and so "three times the number of nickels" is $3(x + 2) = 3x + 6$.

18

Pick a Number

A problem may become much easier to understand and to solve by substituting a specific number in for a variable. Just make sure that you choose a number that satisfies the given conditions.

Here are some guidelines when picking numbers.

(1) Pick a number that is simple but not too simple. In general you might want to avoid picking 0 or 1 (but 2 is usually a good choice).
(2) Try to avoid picking numbers that appear in the problem.
(3) When picking two or more numbers try to make them all different.
(4) Most of the time picking numbers only allows you to eliminate answer choices. So do not just choose the first answer choice that comes out to the correct answer. If multiple answers come out correct you need to pick a new number and start again. But you only have to check the answer choices that have not yet been eliminated.
(5) If there are fractions in the question a good choice might be the least common denominator (lcd) or a multiple of the lcd.
(6) In percent problems choose the number 100.
(7) Do not pick a negative number as a possible answer to a grid-in question. This is a waste of time since you cannot grid a negative number.
(8) If your first attempt does not eliminate 3 of the 4 choices, try to choose a number that's of a different "type." Here are some examples of types:
  (a) A positive integer greater than 1.
  (b) A positive fraction (or decimal) between 0 and 1.
  (c) A negative integer less than -1.
  (d) A negative fraction (or decimal) between -1 and 0.
(9) If you are picking pairs of numbers try different combinations from (8). For example you can try two positive integers greater than 1, two negative integers less than -1, or one positive and one negative integer, etc.

Remember that these are just guidelines and there may be rare occasions where you might break these rules. For example sometimes it is so quick and easy to plug in 0 and/or 1 that you might do this even though only some of the answer choices get eliminated.

Try to answer the following question using this strategy. **Do not** check the solution until you have attempted this question yourself.

LEVEL 3: HEART OF ALGEBRA

$$\frac{x+y}{x} = \frac{2}{9}$$

4. If the equation shown above is true, which of the following must also be true?

(A) $\dfrac{x}{y} = \dfrac{9}{11}$

(B) $\dfrac{x}{y} = -\dfrac{9}{7}$

(C) $\dfrac{x-y}{x} = \dfrac{11}{9}$

(D) $\dfrac{x-y}{x} = -\dfrac{9}{7}$

See if you can answer this question by picking numbers.

Solution by picking numbers: Let's choose values for x and y, say $x = 9$ and $y = -7$. Notice that we chose these values to make the given equation true.

Now let's check if each answer choice is true or false.

(A) $\dfrac{9}{-7} = \dfrac{9}{11}$ False

(B) $\dfrac{9}{-7} = -\dfrac{9}{7}$ True

(C) $\dfrac{9-(-7)}{9} = \dfrac{11}{9}$ or $\dfrac{16}{9} = \dfrac{11}{9}$ False

(D) $\dfrac{9-(-7)}{9} = -\dfrac{9}{7}$ or $\dfrac{16}{9} = -\dfrac{9}{7}$ False

Since (A), (C), and (D) are each False we can eliminate them. Thus, the answer is choice (B).

Before we go on, try to solve this problem the way you might do it in school.

Algebraic solution 1: $\frac{x+y}{x} = \frac{x}{x} + \frac{y}{x} = 1 + \frac{y}{x}$. So the given equation is equivalent to $1 + \frac{y}{x} = \frac{2}{9}$. Therefore $\frac{y}{x} = \frac{2}{9} - 1 = \frac{2}{9} - \frac{9}{9} = -\frac{7}{9}$, and so $\frac{x}{y} = -\frac{9}{7}$, choice (B).

Note: Most students have no trouble at all adding two fractions with the same denominator. For example,

$$\frac{x}{x} + \frac{y}{x} = \frac{x+y}{x}$$

But these same students have trouble reversing this process.

$$\frac{x+y}{x} = \frac{x}{x} + \frac{y}{x}$$

Note that these two equations are **identical** except that the left and right hand sides have been switched. Note also that to break a fraction into two (or more) pieces, the original denominator is repeated for **each** piece.

Algebraic solution 2: We cross multiply the given equation to get

$$9(x + y) = 2x$$

We now distribute the 9 on the left to get

$$9x + 9y = 2x$$

Now we subtract $2x$ from each side of this last equation to get

$$7x + 9y = 0$$

We subtract $9y$ from each side to get $7x = -9y$.

We can get $\frac{x}{y}$ to one side by performing **cross division.** We do this just like cross multiplication, but we divide instead. Dividing each side of the equation by $7y$ will do the trick (this way we get rid of 7 on the left and y on the right).

$$\frac{x}{y} = \frac{-9}{7} = -\frac{9}{7}$$

This is choice (B).

You're doing great! Let's just practice a bit more. Try to solve each of the following problems by using one of the four strategies you just learned. Then, if possible, solve each problem another way. The answers to these problems, followed by full solutions are at the end of this lesson. **Do not** look at the answers until you have attempted these problems yourself. Please remember to mark off any problems you get wrong.

LEVEL 1: HEART OF ALGEBRA

5. If $3z = \frac{y-5}{2}$ and $z = 5$, what is the value of y ?

    (A) 20
    (B) 25
    (C) 30
    (D) 35

6. If $x > 0$ and $x^4 - 16 = 0$, what is the value of x ?

LEVEL 2: HEART OF ALGEBRA

7. If $\frac{5x}{y} = 10$, what is the value of $\frac{8y}{x}$?

    (A) 4
    (B) 3
    (C) 2
    (D) 1

LEVEL 3: HEART OF ALGEBRA

8. The cost of 5 scarves is d dollars. At this rate, what is the cost, in dollars of 45 scarves?

    (A) $\frac{9d}{5}$

    (B) $\frac{d}{45}$

    (C) $\frac{45}{d}$

    (D) $9d$

22

9. Bill has cows, pigs and chickens on his farm. The number of chickens he has is four times the number of pigs, and the number of pigs he has is three more than the number of cows. Which of the following could be the total number of these animals?

    (A) 28
    (B) 27
    (C) 26
    (D) 25

LEVEL 4: HEART OF ALGEBRA

10. For all real numbers x and y, $|x - y|$ is equivalent to which of the following?

    (A) $x + y$
    (B) $\sqrt{x - y}$
    (C) $(x - y)^2$
    (D) $\sqrt{(x - y)^2}$

11. If $k \neq \pm 1$, which of the following is equivalent to $\dfrac{1}{\frac{1}{k+1} + \frac{1}{k-1}}$.

    (A) $2k$
    (B) $k^2 - 1$
    (C) $\dfrac{k^2 - 1}{2k}$
    (D) $\dfrac{2k}{k^2 - 1}$

12. In the real numbers, what is the solution of the equation $4^{x+2} = 8^{2x-1}$?

    (A) $-\dfrac{7}{4}$
    (B) $-\dfrac{1}{4}$
    (C) $\dfrac{3}{4}$
    (D) $\dfrac{7}{4}$

23

Answers

1. B	5. D	9. B
2. C	6. 2	10. D
3. D	7. A	11. C
4. B	8. D	12. D

Note: The full solution for question 9 has been omitted because its solution is very similar to the solution for question 3.

Full Solutions

8.

Solution by picking numbers: Let's choose a value for d, say $d = 10$. So 5 scarves cost 10 dollars, and therefore each scarf costs 2 dollars. It follows that 45 scarves cost $(45)(2) = $ **90** dollars. **Put a nice big, dark circle around this number so that you can find it easily later.** We now substitute 10 in for d into **all** four answer choices (we use our calculator if we're allowed to).

(A) 90/5 = 18
(B) 10/45
(C) 45/10 = 4.5
(D) 9*10 = 90

Since (D) is the only choice that has become 90, we conclude that (D) is the answer.

Important note: (D) is **not** the correct answer simply because it is equal to 90. It is correct because all 3 of the other choices are **not** 90.

* Solution using ratios: We begin by identifying 2 key words. In this case, such a pair of key words is "scarves" and "dollars."

scarves	5	45
dollars	d	x

Notice that we wrote in the number of scarves next to the word scarves, and the cost of the scarves next to the word dollars. Also notice that the cost for 5 scarves is written under the number 5, and the (unknown) cost for 45 scarves is written under the 45. Now draw in the division symbols and equal sign, cross multiply and divide the corresponding ratio to find the unknown quantity x.

$$\frac{5}{d} = \frac{45}{x}$$
$$5x = 45d$$
$$x = 9d$$

So 45 scarves cost $9d$ dollars, choice (D).

10.

Solution by picking numbers: Let's choose values for x and y, let's say $x = 2$ and $y = 5$. Then $|x - y| = |2 - 5| = |-3| = \mathbf{3}$.

Put a nice big dark circle around **3** so you can find it easily later. We now substitute $x = 2$ and $y = 5$ into each answer choice:

(A) 7
(B) $\sqrt{-3}$
(C) $(-3)^2 = 9$
(D) $\sqrt{(-3)^2} = \sqrt{9} = 3$

Since A, B and C each came out incorrect, we can eliminate them. Therefore the answer is choice (D).

* Solution using the definition of absolute value: One definition of the absolute value of x is $|x| = \sqrt{x^2}$. So $|x - y| = \sqrt{(x - y)^2}$, choice (D).

Note: Here we have simply replaced x by $x - y$ on both sides of the equation $|x| = \sqrt{x^2}$.

11.

Solution by picking a number: Let's choose a value for k, say $k = 2$. Then

$$\frac{1}{\frac{1}{k+1} + \frac{1}{k-1}} = \frac{1}{\frac{1}{2+1} + \frac{1}{2-1}} = \frac{1}{\frac{1}{3} + 1} = \frac{1}{\frac{1}{3} + \frac{3}{3}} = \frac{1}{\frac{4}{3}} = \frac{3}{4}$$

Put a nice big, dark circle around this number so that you can find it easily later. We now substitute 2 in for k into **all** four answer choices (we use our calculator if we're allowed to).

(A) $2 * 2 = 4$
(B) $2{\char`\^}2 - 1 = 3$
(C) $(2{\char`\^}2 - 1)/(2 * 2) = 3/4$
(D) $(2 * 2)/(2{\char`\^}2 - 1) = 4/3$

25

Since (C) is the only choice that has become $\frac{3}{4}$, we conclude that (C) is the answer.

Important note: (C) is **not** the correct answer simply because it is equal to $\frac{3}{4}$. It is correct because all 3 of the other choices are **not** $\frac{3}{4}$.

*Algebraic solution: We multiply the numerator and denominator of the complex fraction by $(k + 1)(k - 1)$ to get

$$\frac{1}{\frac{1}{k+1} + \frac{1}{k-1}} \cdot \frac{(k+1)(k-1)}{(k+1)(k-1)} = \frac{(k+1)(k-1)}{(k-1) + (k+1)} = \frac{k^2 - 1}{2k}$$

This is choice (C).

Notes: (1) The three simple fractions within this complex fraction are $1 = \frac{1}{1}, \frac{1}{k+1}$, and $\frac{1}{k-1}$.

The least common denominator (LCD) of these three fractions is

$$(k + 1)(k - 1)$$

Note that the least common denominator is just the least common multiple (LCM) of the three denominators. In this problem the LCD is the same as the product of the denominators.

(2) To simplify a complex fraction we multiply each of the numerator and denominator of the fraction by the LCD of all the simple fractions that appear.

(3) Make sure to use the distributive property correctly here.

$$\left(\frac{1}{k+1} + \frac{1}{k-1}\right) \cdot (k+1)(k-1)$$
$$= \left(\frac{1}{k+1}\right) \cdot (k+1)(k-1) + \left(\frac{1}{k-1}\right) \cdot (k+1)(k-1)$$
$$= (k-1) + (k+1)$$

This is how we got the denominator in the second expression in the solution.

(4) Do not worry too much if you are having trouble understanding all the steps of this solution. We will be reviewing the methods used here later in the book.

12.

Solution by starting with choice (C) and using our calculator: Let's start with choice (C) and guess that $x = \frac{3}{4}$. We type in our calculator:

$$4\wedge(3/4 + 2) \approx 45.255 \quad \text{and} \quad 8\wedge(2 * 3/4 - 1) \approx 2.828$$

Since these two numbers are different we can eliminate choice (C).

Let's try choice (D) next:

$$4\wedge(7/4 + 2) \approx 181.019 \quad \text{and} \quad 8\wedge(2 * 7/4 - 1) \approx 181.019$$

Since they came out the same, the answer is choice (D).

* Algebraic solution: The numbers 4 and 8 have a common base of 2. In fact, $4 = 2^2$ and $8 = 2^3$. So we have $4^{x+2} = (2^2)^{x+2} = 2^{2x+4}$ and we have $8^{2x-1} = (2^3)^{2x-1} = 2^{6x-3}$. Thus, $2^{2x+4} = 2^{6x-3}$, and so $2x + 4 = 6x - 3$. We subtract $2x$ from each side of this equation to get $4 = 4x - 3$. We now add 3 to each side of this last equation to get $7 = 4x$. Finally we divide each side of this equation by 4 to get $\frac{7}{4} = x$, choice (D).

Note: For a review of the laws of exponents see lesson 13.

Download additional solutions for free here:

www.thesatmathprep.com/28Les800.html

LESSON 2
GEOMETRY

Computation of Slopes

Slope formulas are not given on the SAT. You should make sure that you know the following.

$$\text{Slope} = m = \frac{rise}{run} = \frac{y_2 - y_1}{x_2 - x_1}$$

Note: Lines with positive slope have graphs that go upwards from left to right. Lines with negative slope have graphs that go downwards from left to right. If the slope of a line is zero, it is horizontal. Vertical lines have **no** slope (this is different from zero slope). We may also use the expressions **undefined** or **infinite** to describe the slope of vertical lines.

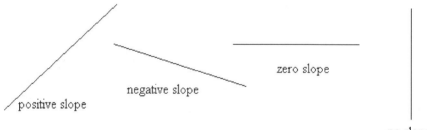

positive slope

negative slope

zero slope

no slope

The **slope-intercept form of an equation of a line** is $y = mx + b$ where m is the slope of the line and b is the y-coordinate of the y-intercept, i.e. the point $(0, b)$ is on the line. Note that this point lies on the y-axis.

Technical note: The SAT sometimes contains an abuse of language with regard to intercepts. A problem may talk about the y-intercept b. Technically a y-intercept is a point of the form $(0, b)$, but many people identify this point with the number b.

The **point-slope form of an equation of a line** is $y - y_0 = m(x - x_0)$ where m is the slope of the line and (x_0, y_0) is any point on the line.

Try to answer the following question using this strategy together with the strategy of picking numbers from Lesson 1. **Do not** check the solution until you have attempted this question yourself.

LEVEL 4: GEOMETRY

1. If $a > 1$, what is the slope of the line in the xy-plane that passes through the points (a^2, a^4) and (a^3, a^6)?

    (A) $-a^3 + a^2$
    (B) $-a^3 - a^2$
    (C) $\quad a^3 - a^2$
    (D) $\quad a^3 + a^2$

Solution by picking a number: Let's pick a number for a, say $a = 2$. So the two points are (4,16) and (8,64). The slope of the line passing through these two points is

$$m = \frac{64-16}{8-4} = \frac{48}{4} = 12$$

Put a nice big, dark circle around the number 12. We now plug $a = 2$ into each answer choice.

    (A) $-8 + 4 = -4$
    (B) $-8 - 4 = -12$
    (C) $\quad 8 - 4 = 4$
    (D) $\quad 8 + 4 = 12$

Since choices (A), (B), and (C) all came out incorrect, the answer is (D).

Remark: We could have also gotten the slope geometrically by plotting the two points, and noticing that to get from (4,16) to (8,64) we need to travel up 48 units and right 4 units. So the slope is

$$m = \frac{rise}{run} = \frac{48}{4} = 12.$$

Before we go on, try to solve this problem directly (without plugging in numbers).

* Algebraic solution: Using the slope formula we have

$$m = \frac{a^6-a^4}{a^3-a^2} = \frac{a^4(a^2-1)}{a^2(a-1)} = \frac{a^2(a+1)(a-1)}{a-1} = a^2(a+1) = a^3 + a^2.$$

This is choice (D).

Note: Do not worry if you have trouble following this solution. The algebra performed here will be reviewed later in the book.

Plug in the Given Point

If the graph of a function or other equation passes through certain points, plug those points into the equation to eliminate answer choices.

Try to answer the following question using this strategy. **Do not** check the solution until you have attempted this question yourself.

LEVEL 4: GEOMETRY

2. Which of the following is an equation of the line in the xy-plane that passes through the point $(4, -2)$ and is perpendicular to the line $y = -4x + 7$?

   (A) $y = -4x - 3$
   (B) $y = -4x + 3$
   (C) $y = \frac{1}{4}x - 3$
   (D) $y = \frac{1}{4}x + 6$

* Solution by plugging in the point: Since the point $(4, -2)$ lies on the line, if we substitute 4 in for x, we should get -2 for y. Let's substitute 4 in for x in each answer choice.

   (A) $-4 * 4 - 3 = -16 - 3 = -19$
   (B) $-4 * 4 + 3 = -16 + 3 = -13$
   (C) $(1/4) * 4 - 3 = 1 - 3 = -2$
   (D) $(1/4) * 4 + 6 = 1 + 6 = 7$

We can eliminate choices (A), (B) and (D) because they did not come out to -2. The answer is therefore choice (C).

Important note: (C) is **not** the correct answer simply because y came out to -2. It is correct because all 3 of the other choices did **not** give -2 for y.

Before we go on, try to solve this problem using geometry.

Geometric solution: Note that the given line has a slope of -4. Since **perpendicular lines have slopes that are negative reciprocals of each other**, $m = \frac{1}{4}$.

30

Also, we are given that the point $(x_0, y_0) = (4, -2)$ is on the line. We use the point-slope form for the equation of a line $\boldsymbol{y - y_0 = m(x - x_0)}$ to get $y - (-2) = \frac{1}{4}(x - 4)$. Let's solve this equation for y.

$$y + 2 = \frac{1}{4}(x - 4)$$
$$y + 2 = \frac{1}{4}x - 1$$
$$y = \frac{1}{4}x - 3$$

Therefore the answer is choice (C).

Note: To get the reciprocal of a number we interchange the numerator and denominator. The number -4 has a "hidden" denominator of 1, so the reciprocal of -4 is $-\frac{1}{4}$. Now to get the negative reciprocal, we simply change the sign of the reciprocal. Thus, the negative reciprocal of -4 is $\frac{1}{4}$.

Now try to solve each of the following problems by plugging in the given points if possible. Then, if possible, solve each problem another way. The answers to these problems, followed by full solutions are at the end of this lesson. **Do not** look at the answers until you have attempted these problems yourself. Please remember to mark off any problems you get wrong.

LEVEL 1: GEOMETRY

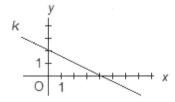

3.   What is the equation of line k in the figure above?

    (A) $y = -2x + 2$
    (B) $y = -2x + 4$
    (C) $y = -\frac{1}{2}x + 2$
    (D) $y = -\frac{1}{2}x + 4$

LEVEL 2: GEOMETRY

4. A line in the xy-plane passes through the origin and has a slope of $-\frac{2}{3}$. Which of the following points lies on the line?

   (A) $(-6,4)$
   (B) $(3,-3)$
   (C) $(3,2)$
   (D) $(0,\frac{2}{3})$

LEVEL 3: GEOMETRY

5. Which of the following equations represents a line that passes through the point $(0,-5)$ and is parallel to the line with equation $y = -4x + 7$?

   (A) $4x + y = -7$
   (B) $4x + y = -5$
   (C) $x + 4y = 20$
   (D) $x + 4y = 28$

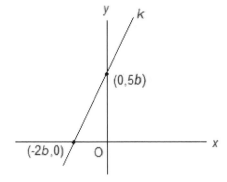

6. In the figure above, what is the slope of line k ?

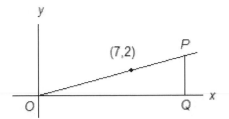

7. Line k (not shown) passes through O and intersects $\overline{PQ}$ between P and Q. What is one possible value of the slope of line k?

8. The line m in the xy-plane contains points from each of Quadrants I, III, and IV, but no points from Quadrant II. Which of the following must be true?

   (A) The slope of line m is positive.
   (B) The slope of line m is negative.
   (C) The slope of line m is zero.
   (D) The slope of line m is undefined.

9. In the xy-coordinate plane, line n passes through the points $(0,5)$ and $(-2,0)$. If line m is perpendicular to line n, what is the slope of line m?

   (A) $-\dfrac{5}{2}$
   (B) $-\dfrac{2}{5}$
   (C) $\dfrac{2}{5}$
   (D) $\dfrac{5}{2}$

LEVEL 4: GEOMETRY

10. Which of the following is the equation of a line in the xy-plane that is perpendicular to the line with equation $y = 3$?

    (A) $y = -3$
    (B) $y = -\dfrac{1}{3}$
    (C) $x = -2$
    (D) $y = -3x$

33

11. In the xy-plane, the line determined by the points $(c, 5)$ and $(10, 2c)$ passes through the origin. Which of the following could be the value of c?

(A) 0
(B) 5
(C) 10
(D) 25

LEVEL 5: GEOMETRY

12. In the xy-plane, the points $(5, e)$ and $(f, 7)$ are on a line that is perpendicular to the graph of the line $y = -\frac{1}{5}x + 12$. Which of the following represents e in terms of f?

(A) $5f + 32$
(B) $-5f + 32$
(C) $-\frac{1}{5}f + 32$
(D) $\frac{1}{5}f + 32$

Answers

1. D	5. B	9. B
2. C	6. 5/2 or 2.5	10. C
3. C	7. $0 < m < .259$	11. B
4. A	8. A	12. B

Full Solutions

5.

* **Solution by plugging in the point:** Since the point $(0, -5)$ lies on the line, if we substitute 0 in for x and -5 in for y we should get a true equation.

(A) $0 + (-5) = -7$ ⠀⠀⠀⠀False
(B) $0 + (-5) = -5$ ⠀⠀⠀⠀True
(C) $0 + 4(-5) = 20$ ⠀⠀⠀False
(D) $0 + 4(-5) = 28$ ⠀⠀⠀False

We can eliminate choices (A), (C) and (D) because they came out False. The answer is therefore choice (B).

34

Solution by starting with choice (B): The given line is written in the form $y = mx + b$, where m is the slope of the line. Note that the slope of the given line is $m = -4$. Since **parallel lines have the same slope**, we are looking for an equation in the answer choices that represents a line with slope -4.

Let's start with choice (B) and put the equation into slope-intercept form. We do this by subtracting $4x$ from each side of the equation to get $y = -4x - 5$. The slope is -4. Now note that the y-intercept of this line is $(0, -5)$. So the answer is choice (B).

Notes: (1) The equation in choice (A) also has a slope of -4, but it has the wrong y-intercept. To see this we add $-4x$ to each side of the equation to get $y = -4x - 7$. The y-intercept of this line is $(0, -7)$.

(2) It is very important that you understand this solution. On the SAT you could be asked to identify a line parallel to a given line without being given a point. In that case, this is the only solution of these three that would work.

Algebraic solution: We start by writing an equation of the line in the slope-intercept form $y = mx + b$.

$(0, -5)$ is the y-intercept of the point. Thus, $b = -5$. The slope of the given line is -4. Since the new line is parallel to this line, its slope is also $m = -4$, and the equation of the new line is $y = -4x - 5$.

We now simply add $4x$ to each side of this equaton to get $4x + y = -5$, choice (B).

6.
Solution by picking a number: Let's choose a value for b, let's say $b = 3$. Then the two points are $(-6, 0)$ and $(0, 15)$. Therefore the slope of line k is $\frac{15 - 0}{0 - (-6)} = \frac{15}{6} = \mathbf{2.5}$.

Remarks: (1) Here we have used the slope formula $m = \frac{y_2 - y_1}{x_2 - x_1}$.
(2) $0 - (-6) = 0 + 6 = 6$

(3) We could have also found the slope graphically by plotting the two points and observing that to get from $(-6, 0)$ to $(0, 15)$ we need to move up 15 and right 6. Thus the slope is $m = \frac{rise}{run} = \frac{15}{6} = 2.5$.

35

* Solution using the slope formula: $\frac{5b-0}{0-(-2b)} = \frac{5b}{2b}$ = **5/2 or 2.5.**

7.

* Solution by picking a line: Let's choose a specific line k. The easiest choice is the line passing through $(0,0)$ and $(7,1)$. Now plug these two points into the slope formula to get $\frac{1-0}{7-0}$ = **1/7.**

Remark: If the line j passes through the origin (the point $(0,0)$) and the point (a,b) with $a \neq 0$, then the slope of line j is simply $\frac{b}{a}$.

Complete geometric solution: The slope of line $\overline{OP}$ is $\frac{2}{7} \approx .2587$ (see the Remark above) and the slope of line $\overline{OQ}$ is 0. Therefore we can choose any number strictly between 0 and $.259$ that fits in the answer grid.

8.

* Solution by drawing a picture: Let's draw a picture of a line satisfying the given condition.

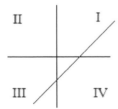

We see that this line has a slope which is positive, choice (A).

Notes: (1) A line with a positive slope must have points in exactly 3 of the four quadrants: either quadrants I, III, and IV, or quadrants I, II, and III. See if you can draw a picture for the latter situation.

(2) Each of the other three choices also have two possibilities. Here are pictures of one possibility for each of them. See if you can draw the other possibility for each.

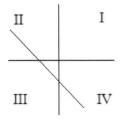

9.

* Solution using the definition of slope: We first compute the slope of line n. We can do this by plotting the two points, and computing $\frac{rise}{run} = \frac{5}{2}$ (to get from $(-2,0)$ to $(0,5)$ we go up 5 and right 2). Since line m is perpendicular to line n, the slope of line m is the negative reciprocal of the slope of line n. So the answer is $-\frac{2}{5}$, choice (B).

Remark: We can also find the slope of line n by using the slope formula $m = \frac{y_2 - y_1}{x_2 - x_1} = \frac{5 - 0}{0 - (-2)} = \frac{5}{2}$.

10.

* Any equation of the form $y = a$ for some real number a is a horizontal line. Any equation of the form $x = c$ for some real number c is a vertical line. Vertical lines are perpendicular to horizontal lines. Therefore the answer is choice (C).

11.

* Solution by starting with choice (B): Let's guess that $c = 5$ so that the two points are $(5,5)$ and $(10,10)$. It is pretty easy to see that $(0,0)$ is on this line (see notes below). So the answer is choice (B).

Notes: (1) Since $(5,5)$ and $(10,10)$ are both on the line, it follows that the line consists of all points for which the x and y-coordinates are equal. In particular, the origin $(0,0)$ is on the line.

(2) Since both points have the same x and y-coordinates, the equation of the line is $y = x$. The origin $(0,0)$ is a point on this line because $0 = 0$ is in fact true.

(3) We can formally find the slope of the line passing through $(5,5)$ and $(10,10)$ using the slope formula: $m = \frac{y_2 - y_1}{x_2 - x_1} = \frac{10 - 5}{10 - 5} = \frac{5}{5} = 1$.

Alternatively, we can plot the two points and observe that to get from $(5,5)$ to $(10,10)$ we need to move up 5 and right 5. Thus the slope is $m = \frac{rise}{run} = \frac{5}{5} = 1$.

(4) Using the slope $m = 1$ and the point $(5,5)$, we can write an equation of the line in point-slope form as $y - 5 = 1(x - 5)$, or equivalently $y = x$.

* Quick solution: Since we want the origin $(0,0)$ to be on the line we must have $\frac{5}{c} = \frac{2c}{10}$. Cross multiplying gives $2c^2 = 50$. We divide each side of this last equation by 2 to get $c^2 = 25$. So $c = 5$, choice (B).

37

Notes: (1) If the line j passes through the origin and the point (a, b) with $a \neq 0$, then the slope of line j is simply $\frac{b}{a}$.

So in this problem we can compute the slope as $\frac{5}{c}$ or $\frac{2c}{10}$. Since both of these quantities are equal to the slope, it follows that they are equal to each other.

(2) The equation $c^2 = 25$ actually has two solutions $c = \pm 5$. So $c = -5$ would also be an acceptable answer if it were a choice.

12.

* **Geometric solution:** The given line has a slope of $-\frac{1}{5}$. Since **perpendicular lines have slopes that are negative reciprocals of each other**, we have that the slope of the line containing points $(5, e)$ and $(f, 7)$ is 5 or $\frac{5}{1}$. So $\frac{e-7}{5-f} = \frac{5}{1}$. Cross multiplying (or simply multiplying by $5 - f$) yields $e - 7 = 5(5 - f) = 25 - 5f = -5f + 25$. Adding 7 to each side of this equation gives $e = -5f + 32$, choice (B).

Download additional solutions for free here:

www.thesatmathprep.com/28Les800.html

LESSON 3
PASSPORT TO ADVANCED MATH

Direct Variation

The following are all equivalent ways of saying the same thing:

(1) y varies directly as x
(2) y is directly proportional to x
(3) $y = kx$ for some constant k
(4) $\frac{y}{x}$ is constant
(5) the graph of $y = f(x)$ is a nonvertical line through the origin.

For example, in the equation $y = 5x$, y varies directly as x. Here is a partial table of values for this equation.

x	1	2	3	4
y	5	10	15	20

Note that we can tell that this table represents a direct relationship between x and y because $\frac{5}{1} = \frac{10}{2} = \frac{15}{3} = \frac{20}{4}$. Here the **constant of variation** is 5.

Here is a graph of the equation.

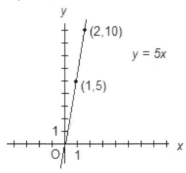

Note that we can tell that this graph represents a direct relationship between x and y because it is a nonvertical line through the origin. The constant of variation is the slope of the line, in this case $m = 5$.

The various equivalent definitions of direct variation lead to several different ways to solve problems.

39

LEVEL 1: ADVANCED MATH

1.   If $y = kx$ and $y = 5$ when $x = 8$, then what is y when $x = 24$?

Solutions

(1) We are given that $y = 5$ when $x = 8$, so that $5 = k(8)$, or $k = \frac{5}{8}$. Therefore $y = \frac{5x}{8}$. When $x = 24$, we have $y = \frac{5(24)}{8} = \mathbf{15}$.

(2) Since y varies directly as x, $\frac{y}{x}$ is a constant. So we get the following ratio: $\frac{5}{8} = \frac{y}{24}$. Cross multiplying gives $120 = 8y$, so that $y = \mathbf{15}$.

(3) The graph *of* $y = f(x)$ is a line passing through the points (0,0) and (8,5) The slope of this line is $\frac{5-0}{8-0} = \frac{5}{8}$. Writing the equation of the line in slope-intercept form we have $y = \frac{5}{8}x$. As in solution 1, when $x = 24$, we have $y = \frac{5(24)}{8} = \mathbf{15}$.

* (4) To get from $x = 8$ to $x = 24$ we multiply x by 3. So we have to also multiply y by 3. We get $3(5) = \mathbf{15}$.

Inverse Variation

The following are all equivalent ways of saying the same thing:

(1) y varies inversely as x
(2) y is inversely proportional to x
(3) $y = \frac{k}{x}$ for some constant k
(4) xy is constant

The following is a consequence of (1), (2) (3) or (4).

(5) The graph of $y = f(x)$ is a hyperbola

Note: (5) is not equivalent to (1), (2), (3) or (4).

For example, in the equation $y = \frac{12}{x}$, y varies inversely as x. Here is a partial table of values for this equation.

x	1	2	3	4
y	12	6	4	3

Note that we can tell that this table represents an inverse relationship between x and y because $(1)(12) = (2)(6) = (3)(4) = (4)(3) = 12$. Here the **constant of variation** is 12.

Here is a graph of the equation. On the left you can see the full graph. On the right we have a close-up in the first quadrant.

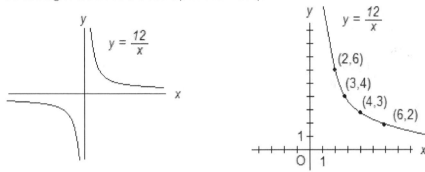

The various equivalent definitions of inverse variation lead to several different ways to solve problems.

LEVEL 2: ADVANCED MATH

2. If $y = \frac{k}{x}$ and $y = 8$ when $x = 3$, then what is y when $x = 6$?

Solutions

(1) We are given that $y = 8$ when $x = 3$, so that $8 = \frac{k}{3}$, or $k = 24$. Thus, $y = \frac{24}{x}$. When $x = 6$, we have $y = \frac{24}{6} = $ **4**.

(2) Since y varies inversely as x, xy is a constant. So we get the following equation: $(3)(8) = 6y$ So $24 = 6y$, and $y = \frac{24}{6} = $ **4**.

* **(3)** $\frac{(8)(3)}{6} = $ **4**.

41

Functions

A function is simply a rule that for each "input" assigns a specific "output." Functions may be given by equations, tables or graphs.

Note about the notation $f(x)$: The variable x is a placeholder. We evaluate the function f at a specific value by substituting that value in for x. For example, if $f(x) = x^3 + 2x$, then

$$f(-2) = (-2)^3 + 2(-2) = -12$$

LEVEL 4: ADVANCED MATH

x	$p(x)$	$q(x)$	$r(x)$
-2	-3	4	-3
-1	2	1	2
0	5	-1	-6
1	-7	0	-5

3. The functions p, q and r are defined for all values of x, and certain values of those functions are given in the table above. What is the value of $p(-2) + q(0) - r(1)$?

* To evaluate $p(-2)$, we look at the row corresponding to $x = -2$, and the column corresponding to $p(x)$. We see that the entry there is -3. Therefore $p(-2) = -3$. Similarly, $q(0) = -1$ and $r(1) = -5$. Finally, we have that $p(-2) + q(0) - r(1) = -3 - 1 - (-5) = -4 + 5 = \mathbf{1}$.

Try to solve each of the following problems. The answers to these problems, followed by full solutions are at the end of this lesson. **Do not** look at the answers until you have attempted these problems yourself. Please remember to mark off any problems you get wrong.

LEVEL 2: ADVANCED MATH

$$f(x) = 7x - 3$$
$$g(x) = x^2 - 2x + 6$$

4. The functions f and g are defined above. What is the value of $f(11) - g(4)$?

$$g(x) = \frac{2}{5}x + b$$

5. In the function above, b is a constant. If $g(10) = 7$, what is the value of $g(-5)$?

   (A) -1
   (B) 0
   (C) 1
   (D) 2

LEVEL 3: ADVANCED MATH

6. A function f satisfies $f(3) = 7$ and $f(7) = 1$. A function g satisfies $g(7) = 3$ and $g(1) = 4$. Find the value of $f(g(7))$.

7. If $g(x) = -3x - 7$, what is $g(-4x)$ equal to?

   (A) $12x^2 + 28x$
   (B) $12x + 7$
   (C) $12x - 7$
   (D) $-12x + 7$

LEVEL 4: ADVANCED MATH

8. For all real numbers x, let the function f be defined as $f(x) = 5x - 10$. Which of the following is equal to $f(3) + f(5)$?

   (A) $f(4)$
   (B) $f(6)$
   (C) $f(7)$
   (D) $f(20)$

43

x	$p(x)$	$q(x)$	$r(x)$
-2	-6	-2	-9
-1	-1	5	-10
0	-2	7	-3
1	5	-11	-6
2	-6	0	3

9. The functions p, q and r are defined for all values of x, and certain values of those functions are given in the table above. If the function u is defined by $u(x) = 3p(x) + q(x) - r(x)$ for all values of x, what is the value of $u(-1)$?

$$P(x) = \frac{20x}{98 - x}$$

10. * The function P above models the monthly profit, in thousands of dollars, for a company that sells x percent of their inventory for the month. If \$90,000 is earned in profit during the month of April, what percent of April's inventory, to the nearest whole percent, has been sold?

(A) 25%
(B) 42%
(C) 56%
(D) 80%

k	-1	1	2
$f(k)$	-5	3	7

11. The table above shows some values of the linear function f. Which of the following defines f?

(A) $f(k) = k - 4$
(B) $f(k) = k - 8$
(C) $f(k) = 2k - 4$
(D) $f(k) = 4k - 1$

LEVEL 5: ADVANCED MATH

12. For all positive integers x, the function f is defined by $f(x) = (\frac{1}{b^5})^x$, where b is a constant greater than 1. Which of the following is equivalent to $f(3x)$?

(A) $\sqrt[3]{f(x)}$
(B) $(f(x))^3$
(C) $3f(x)$
(D) $\frac{1}{3}f(x)$

Answers

1. 15	5. C	9. 12
2. 4	6. 7	10. D
3. 1	7. C	11. D
4. 60	8. B	12. B

Full Solutions

6.

* $f\big(g(7)\big) = f(3) = \mathbf{7}$.

Note: $g(7)$ is given to be 3. So we replace $g(7)$ by 3 in the expression $f(g(7))$.

Do you see that we have $f(\boxed{\text{something}})$ where $\boxed{\text{something}}$ is $g(7)$? Since $g(7)$ is 3, we can replace $\boxed{\text{something}}$ by 3 to get $f(3)$. Finally $f(3)$ is given to be 7.

7.

* $g(-4x) = -3(-4x) - 7 = 12x - 7$, choice (C).

Note: This problem can also be solved by picking a number for x. I leave the details to the reader.

8.

Solution by starting with choice (C): First note $f(3) = 5(3) - 10 = 5$ and $f(5) = 5(5) - 10 = 15$, so that $f(3) + f(5) = 5 + 15 = \mathbf{20}$.

Now, beginning with choice (C) we see that $f(7) = 5(7) - 10 = 25$.

This is a bit too big. So let's try choice (B). Then $f(6) = 5(6) - 10 = 20$. This is correct. Thus, the answer is choice (B).

Warning: Many students will compute $f(3) + f(5) = 20$ and immediately choose choice (D). Do not fall into this trap!

* Algebraic solution: As in the previous solution, direct computation gives $f(3) + f(5) = 20$. Setting $f(x) = 20$ yields $5x - 10 = 20$, so that $5x = 30$, and thus, $x = \frac{30}{5} = 6$. In other words, we have

$$f(6) = 20 = f(3) + f(5).$$

This is choice (B).

9.
* $u(-1) = 3p(-1) + q(-1) - r(-1) = 3(-1) + (5) - (-10)$

$$= -3 + 5 + 10 = \mathbf{12}.$$

10.
Solution by starting with choice (C): We are given that $P(x) = 90$, and being asked to approximate x. So we have $\frac{20x}{98-x} = 90$. Let's begin with choice (C) and plug in 56 for x. We have $20(56)/(98 - 56) \approx 26.67$, too small.

Let's try choice (D) next. So $20(80)/(98 - 80) \approx 88.89$. This is close, so the answer is probably choice (D). To be safe we should check the other answer choices.

(A) $20(25)/(98 - 25) \approx 6.85$
(B) $20(42)/(98 - 42) = 15$

So the answer must be choice (D).

* Algebraic solution:
$$\frac{20x}{98-x} = 90$$
$$20x = 90(98 - x)$$
$$20x = 8820 - 90x$$
$$110x = 8820$$
$$x = \frac{8820}{110} \approx 80.18$$

The final answer, to the nearest percent, is 80%, choice (D).

11.

* Quick solution: The last two columns tell us that the slope of the line is $7 - 3 = 4$. So the answer can be only choice (D).

Notes: (1) The table is telling us that the following points are on the line: $(-1, -5)$, $(1, 3)$, and $(2, 7)$.

(2) We can find the slope by using any two of the above points and then either using the slope formula, or plotting the points and computing $\frac{rise}{run}$. Both of these methods were covered in Lesson 2.

Since the x-coordinates of the last two points are one unit apart, we can get the slope by simply subtracting the y-coordinates: $7 - 3 = 4$.

(3) If we needed to find the y-intercept of the line, we could formally write the equation as we learned in Lesson 3, or we could use the following trick:

Since the function f is linear, "**equal jumps in k lead to equal jumps in $f(k)$.**" But the jumps in k are **not** equal. We can make them equal however if we just slip in the number 0. The "new" table looks like this.

k	-1	0	1	2
$g(k)$	-5		3	7

Now the jumps in k are equal: x keeps increasing by 1 unit. Therefore the jumps in $g(k)$ must be equal. It is not hard to see that the jumps in $g(k)$ need to be 4, so that the y-intercept is $g(0) = -1$.

(4) This problem could also be solved by plugging in the given points. I leave the details of this solution to the reader.

12.

Solution by picking numbers: Let's let $b = 2$. Then $f(x) = \left(\frac{1}{32}\right)^x$. Now let's plug in a value for x, say $x = 1$. Then

$$f(3x) = f(3) = \left(\frac{1}{32}\right)^3 \approx .00003.$$

Put a nice, big, dark circle around this number, and now plug $x = 1$ into each answer choice.

47

(A) $\sqrt[3]{f(1)} = \sqrt[3]{\frac{1}{32}} \approx .315$

(B) $(f(1))^3 = \left(\frac{1}{32}\right)^3 \approx .00003$

(C) $3f(1) = 3\left(\frac{1}{32}\right) = .09375$

(D) $\frac{1}{3}(f(1)) = \frac{1}{3}\left(\frac{1}{32}\right) \approx .0104.$

We eliminate (A), (C), and (D), and therefore the answer is choice (B).

* **Algebraic solution:** $f(3x) = \left(\frac{1}{b^5}\right)^{3x} = \left(\left(\frac{1}{b^5}\right)^x\right)^3 = \left(f(x)\right)^3$, (B).

OPTIONAL MATERIAL

LEVEL 6: ADVANCED MATH

1. Suppose that z varies directly as x^2 and inversely as y^3. If $z = 9$ when $x = 3$ and $y = 2$, what is y when $z = 4.5$ and $x = 6$?

Solution

1.

* We are given that $z = \frac{kx^2}{y^3}$ for some constant k. Since $z = 9$ when $x = 3$ and $y = 2$, we have $9 = \frac{k(3)^2}{2^3} = \frac{9k}{8}$. So $k = 8$, and $z = \frac{8x^2}{y^3}$. We now substitute $z = 4.5$, $x = 6$ to get $4.5 = \frac{8(6)^2}{y^3}$. So $y^3 = \frac{8(36)}{4.5} = 64$, and therefore $y = \mathbf{4}$.

Download additional solutions for free here:

www.thesatmathprep.com/28Les800.html

LESSON 4
STATISTICS

Change Averages to Sums

A problem involving averages often becomes much easier when we first convert the averages to sums. We can easily change an average to a sum using the following simple formula.

Sum = Average · Number

Many problems with averages involve one or more conversions to sums, followed by a subtraction.

Try to answer the following question using this strategy. **Do not** check the solution until you have attempted this question yourself.

LEVEL 3: STATISTICS

1. The average of x, y, z, and w is 15 and the average of z and w is 11. What is the average of x and y?

* Solution by changing averages to sums: The Sum of x, y, z, and w is $15 \cdot 4 = 60$. The Sum of z and w is $11 \cdot 2 = 22$. Thus, the Sum of x and y is $60 - 22 = 38$. Finally, the Average of x and y is $\frac{38}{2} = \mathbf{19}$.

Notes: (1) We used the formula "**Sum = Average · Number**" twice here.
(2) More formally we have the following.

$$x + y + z + w = 60$$
$$\underline{z + w = 22}$$
$$x + y = 38$$

Thus, $\frac{x+y}{2} = \frac{38}{2} = \mathbf{19}$.

Before we go on, try to solve this problem in two other ways.

(1) By "Picking Numbers"
(2) Algebraically (the way you would do it in school)

Solution by picking numbers: Let's let $z = w = 11$ and $x = y = 19$. Note that the average of x, y, z, and w is 15 and the average of z and w is 11. Now just observe that the average of x and y is **19**.

Remarks: (1) If all numbers in a list are all equal, then the average of these numbers is that number as well.

(2) When choosing numbers to form a certain average, just "balance" these numbers around the average. In this example we chose z and w to be 11. Since 11 is 4 less than the average, we chose x and y to be 4 greater than the average.

Algebraic solution: We are given that $\frac{x+y+z+w}{4} = 15$ and $\frac{z+w}{2} = 11$. We multiply each side of the first equation by 4 and each side of the second equation by 2 to eliminate the denominators. Then we subtract the second equation from the first.

$$x + y + z + w = 60$$
$$\underline{\quad\quad\quad z + w = 22}$$
$$x + y \quad\quad\quad = 38$$

Finally, the average of x and y is $\frac{x+y}{2} = \frac{38}{2} = 19$.

Important note: You should avoid this method on the actual SAT. It is too time consuming.

Now try to solve each of the following problems. Change averages to sums whenever possible. The answers to these problems, followed by full solutions are at the end of this lesson. **Do not** look at the answers until you have attempted these problems yourself. Please remember to mark off any problems you get wrong.

LEVEL 1: STATISTICS

2. The average (arithmetic mean) of four numbers is 85. If three of the numbers are 17, 58 and 83, what is the fourth number?

LEVEL 2: STATISTICS

3. The average (arithmetic mean) of z, 2, 16, and 21 is z. What is the value of z?

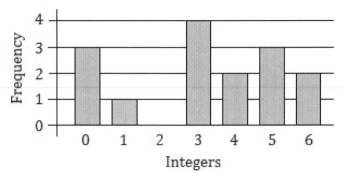

4. * The graph above shows the frequency distribution of a list of randomly generated integers between 0 and 6. What is the mean of the list of numbers?

LEVEL 3: STATISTICS

5. The mean length of a pop song released in the 1980's was 4 minutes and 8 seconds. The mean length of a pop song released in the 1990's was 4 minutes and 14 seconds. Which of the following must be true about the mean length of a pop song released between 1980 and 1999?

    (A) The mean length must be equal to 4 minutes and 11 seconds.
    (B) The mean length must be less than 4 minutes and 11 seconds.
    (C) The mean length must be greater than 4 minutes and 11 seconds.
    (D) The mean length must be between 4 minutes and 8 seconds and 4 minutes and 14 seconds.

LEVEL 4: STATISTICS

6. If the average (arithmetic mean) of a, b, and 23 is 12, what is the average of a and b?

    (A) 6.5
    (B) 11
    (C) 13
    (D) It cannot be determined from the information given.

7. The average (arithmetic mean) age of the people in a certain group was 35 years before one of the members left the group and was replaced by someone who is 12 years older than the person who left. If the average age of the group is now 37 years, how many people are in the group?

8. The average (arithmetic mean) of 11 numbers is j. If one of the numbers is k, what is the average of the remaining 10 numbers in terms of j and k?

(A) $\frac{k}{11}$

(B) $11j + k$

(C) $\frac{10j-k}{11}$

(D) $\frac{11j-k}{10}$

9. The average (arithmetic mean) of a, $2a$, b, and $4b$ is $2a$. What is b in terms of a?

(A) $\frac{a}{4}$

(B) $\frac{a}{2}$

(C) a

(D) $\frac{3a}{2}$

LEVEL 5: STATISTICS

10. If $h = a + b + c + d + e + f + g$, what is the average (arithmetic mean) of a, b, c, d, e, f, g and h in terms of h?

(A) $\frac{h}{2}$

(B) $\frac{h}{3}$

(C) $\frac{h}{4}$

(D) $\frac{h}{5}$

11. A group of students takes a test and the average score is 72. One more student takes the test and receives a score of 88 increasing the average score of the group to 76. How many students were in the initial group?

12. The average (arithmetic mean) salary of employees at an advertising firm with P employees in thousands of dollars is 53, and the average salary of employees at an advertising firm with Q employees in thousands of dollars is 95. When the salaries of both firms are combined, the average salary in thousands of dollars is 83. What is the value of $\frac{P}{Q}$?

Answers

1. 19	5. D	9. C
2. 182	6. A	10. C
3. 13	7. 6	11. 3
4. 16/5 or 3.2	8. D	12. 2/5 or .4

Full Solutions

5.

Solution by picking numbers: Let's suppose that there are 2 pop songs from the 80's each with length 4 minutes and 8 seconds, and 4 pops songs from the 90's each with length 4 minutes and 14 seconds. Note that the given conditions are satisfied, and the combined mean is 4 minutes and 12 seconds. This eliminates choices (A) and (B).

Now let's reverse the situation, and suppose that there are 4 pop songs from the 80's each with length 4 minutes and 8 seconds, and 2 pops songs from the 90's each with length 4 minutes and 14 seconds. Note once again that the given conditions are satisfied, and the combined mean is 4 minutes and 10 seconds. This eliminates choice (C).

Since we have eliminated choices (A), (B), and (C), the answer is choice (D).

Notes: (1) The combined mean length would only be equal to 4 minutes and 11 seconds if the same exact number of pops songs were released in both the 80's and 90's.

(2) It is not true, of course, that there were only 2 pop songs released in the 80's and 4 pop songs released in the 90's. Nonetheless, we can use these simple numbers to eliminate answer choices.

(3) To actually compute the means above we use the formula

$$\text{Mean} = \frac{\text{Sum}}{\text{Number}}$$

where "Sum" is the sum of all the data, and "Number" is the amount of data. In each of the examples above there are 6 pieces of data so that the Number is 6.

(4) When computing the various means in the solution above, we need only worry about the seconds since the minutes are the same. For example, in the first paragraph, we can pretend that our data is 8, 8, 14, 14, 14, 14. The mean of this data is $\frac{8+8+14+14+14+14}{6} = \frac{72}{6} = 12$. It follows that the combined mean is 4 minutes and 12 seconds.

* Direct solution: Let's let a be the mean length of a pop song released in the 1980's, and b be the mean length of a pop song released in the 1990's. Since $a < b$, it follows that the combined mean m must satisfy $a < m < b$. That is, the combined mean must be between 4 minutes and 8 seconds and 4 minutes and 14 seconds, choice (D).

6.

* Solution by changing averages to sums: The Sum of the 3 numbers is $12 \cdot 3 = 36$. Thus $a + b + 23 = 36$, and it follows that $a + b = 13$. So the Average of a and b is $\frac{13}{2} = 6.5$, choice (A).

Solution by picking numbers: Let's let $a = 1$ and $b = 12$. We make this choice because 1 and 23 are both 11 units from 12. Then the Average of a and b is $\frac{a+b}{2} = \frac{1+12}{2} = \frac{13}{2} = 6.5$, choice (A).

7.

* Solution by changing averages to sums: Let n be the number of people in the group. Then originally the sum of the ages of the people in the group was $35n$. After the replacement, the new sum became $37n$. So we have

$$37n = 35n + 12$$
$$2n = 12$$
$$n = \mathbf{6}.$$

8.

* Solution by changing averages to sums: The Sum of the 11 numbers is $11j$. The Sum of the remaining 10 numbers (after removing k) is $11j - k$. So the Average of the remaining 10 numbers is $\frac{11j-k}{10}$, choice (D).

9.

* Solution by changing averages to sums: Converting the Average to a Sum we have that $a + 2a + b + 4b = (2a)(4)$. That is $3a + 5b = 8a$. Subtracting $3a$ from each side of this equation yields $5b = 5a$. Finally, we divide each side of this last equation by 5 to get $b = a$, choice (C).

10.

* Solution by changing averages to sums: The average of $a, b, c, d, e, f,$ g and h is

$$\frac{a + b + c + d + e + f + g + h}{8}$$
$$= \frac{a + b + c + d + e + f + g + a + b + c + d + e + f + g}{8}$$
$$= \frac{2a + 2b + 2c + 2d + 2e + 2f + 2g}{8}$$
$$= \frac{2(a + b + c + d + e + f + g)}{8}$$
$$= \frac{2h}{8}$$
$$= \frac{h}{4}$$

This is choice (C).

Alternate solution by picking numbers: Let's let $a = 1$, $b = 2$, $c = 3$, $d = 4$, $e = 5$, $f = 6$, and $g = 7$. Then $h = 28$, and the average of a, b, c, d, e, f, g and h is $\frac{1 + 2 + 3 + 4 + 5 + 6 + 7 + 28}{8} = \frac{56}{8} = 7$. Put a nice big, dark circle around this number. Now plug $h = 28$ in to each answer choice.

(A) 14
(B) 9.3333...
(C) 7
(D) 5.6

Since (A), (B), and (D) are incorrect we can eliminate them. Therefore the answer is choice (C).

11.

* Solution by changing averages to sums: Let n be the number of students in the initial group. Then the Sum of the scores is $72n$.

When we take into account the new student, we can find the new sum in two different ways.

(1) We can add the new score to the old sum to get $72n + 88$.

(2) We can compute the new sum directly using the formula to get $76(n + 1) = 76n + 76$.

We now set these equal to each other and solve for n:

$$72n + 88 = 76n + 76$$
$$12 = 4n$$
$$n = \frac{12}{4} = \mathbf{3}.$$

12.

* Solution by changing averages to sums: The Sum of the salaries of employees at firm P (in thousands) is $53P$.

The Sum of the salaries of employees at firm Q (in thousands) is $95Q$.

Adding these we get the Sum of the salaries of all employees (in thousands): $53P + 95Q$.

We can also get this sum directly from the problem.

$$83(P + Q) = 83P + 83Q.$$

So we have that $53P + 95Q = 83P + 83Q$.

We get P to one side of the equation by subtracting $53P$ from each side, and we get Q to the other side by subtracting $83Q$ from each side.

$$12Q = 30P$$

We can get $\frac{P}{Q}$ to one side by performing **cross division.** We do this just like cross multiplication, but we divide instead. Dividing each side of the equation by $30Q$ will do the trick (this way we get rid of Q on the left and 30 on the right).

$$\frac{P}{Q} = \frac{12}{30} = \frac{2}{5}$$

So we can grid in **2/5** or **.4.**

LESSON 5
HEART OF ALGEBRA

Reminder: Before beginning this lesson remember to redo the problems from Lesson 1 that you have marked off. Do not "unmark" a question unless you get it correct.

Try a Simple Operation

Problems that ask for an expression involving more than one variable often look much harder than they are. By performing a single operation, the problem is often reduced to one that is very easy to solve. The most common operations to try are addition, subtraction, multiplication and division.

Try to answer the following question using this strategy. **Do not** check the solution until you have attempted this question yourself.

LEVEL 5: HEART OF ALGEBRA

1. If $rs = 4, st = 7, rt = 63$, and $r > 0$, then $rst =$

Solution by trying a simple operation: The operation to use here is multiplication.

$$rs = 4$$
$$st = 7$$
$$\underline{rt = 63}$$
$$(rs)(st)(rt) = 4 \cdot 7 \cdot 63$$
$$r^2 s^2 t^2 = 1764$$

Notice that we multiply all three left hand sides together, and all three right hand sides together. Now just take the square root of each side of the equation to get $rst = \mathbf{42}$.

Remark: Whenever we are trying to find an expression that involves multiplication, division, or both, **multiplying or dividing** the given equations usually does the trick.

* Quick computation: With a little practice, we can get the solution to this type of problem very quickly. Here, we multiply the three numbers together to get $4 \cdot 7 \cdot 63 = 1764$. We then take the square root of 1764 to get **42**.

Note: If a calculator is not allowed for this problem we can get the answer quickly by rewriting $4 \cdot 7 \cdot 63$ as $2^2 \cdot 3^2 \cdot 7^2$ (this is the prime factorization – note that $4 = 2^2$ and $63 = 3^2 \cdot 7$). We can then take the square root of this product by "forgetting" the exponents and multiplying the 2, 3, and 7: $\sqrt{2^2 \cdot 3^2 \cdot 7^2} = \sqrt{2^2}\sqrt{3^2}\sqrt{7^2} = 2 \cdot 3 \cdot 7 = 42$.

Before we go on, try to solve this problem by first finding r, s and t.

Important note: You should not solve this problem this way on the actual SAT.

Solving the first equation for s gives us $s = \frac{4}{r}$. Substituting this into the second equation gives us $\left(\frac{4}{r}\right)t = 7$, or equivalently $4t = 7r$. Therefore we have that $t = \frac{7r}{4}$. So the third equation becomes $r(\frac{7r}{4}) = 63$, or equivalently $\frac{7r^2}{4} = 63$. So $r^2 = \frac{63 \cdot 4}{7} = 36$, whence $r = 6$ (because $r > 0$). It follows that $t = \frac{7 \cdot 6}{4} = 10.5$, $s = \frac{4}{6} = \frac{2}{3}$, and $rst = 6 \cdot \left(\frac{2}{3}\right) \cdot 10.5 = \mathbf{42}$.

Systems of Linear Equations

There are many different ways to solve a system of linear equations. We will use an example to demonstrate several different methods.

LEVEL 5: HEART OF ALGEBRA

2.   If $2x = 7 - 3y$ and $5y = 5 - 3x$, what is the value of x?

* Method 1 – elimination: We begin by making sure that the two equations are "lined up" properly. We do this by adding $3y$ to each side of the first equation, and adding $3x$ to each side of the second equation.

$$2x + 3y = 7$$
$$3x + 5y = 5$$

We will now multiply each side of the first equation by 5, and each side of the second equation by -3.

$$5(2x + 3y) = (7)(5)$$
$$-3(3x + 5y) = (5)(-3)$$

Do not forget to distribute correctly on the left. Add the two equations.

$$10x + 15y = 35$$
$$\underline{-9x - 15y = -15}$$
$$x \qquad = \mathbf{20}$$

Remarks: (1) We chose to use 5 and -3 because multiplying by these numbers makes the y column "match up" so that when we add the two equations in the next step the y term vanishes. We could have also used -5 and 3.

(2) If we wanted to find y instead of x we would multiply the two equations by 3 and -2 (or -3 and 2). In general, if you are looking for only one variable, try to eliminate the one you are **not** looking for.

(3) We chose to multiply by a negative number so that we could add the equations instead of subtracting them. We could have also multiplied the first equation by 5, the second by 3, and subtracted the two equations, but a computational error is more likely to occur this way.

Method 2 – Gauss-Jordan reduction: As in method 1, we first make sure the two equations are "lined up" properly.

$$2x + 3y = 7$$
$$3x + 5y = 5$$

Begin by pushing the MATRIX button (which is 2ND x^{-1}). Scroll over to EDIT and then select [A] (or press 1). We will be inputting a 2×3 matrix, so press 2 ENTER 3 ENTER. We then begin entering the numbers 2, 3, and 7 for the first row, and 3, 5, and 5 for the second row. To do this we can simply type 2 ENTER 3 ENTER 7 ENTER 3 ENTER 5 ENTER 5 ENTER.

Note: What we have just done was create the **augmented matrix** for the system of equations. This is simply an array of numbers which contains the coefficients of the variables together with the right hand sides of the equations.

Now push the QUIT button (2ND MODE) to get a blank screen. Press MATRIX again. This time scroll over to MATH and select rref((or press B). Then press MATRIX again and select [A] (or press 1) and press ENTER.

Note: What we have just done is put the matrix into **reduced row echelon form**. In this form we can read off the solution to the original system of equations.

Warning: Be careful to use the rref(button (2 r's), and not the ref(button (which has only one r).

The display will show the following.

$$[\,[1\ 0\ 20]$$
$$[0\ 1 - 11]]$$

The first line is interpreted as $x = 20$ and the second line as $y = -11$. In particular, $x = \mathbf{20}$.

Method 3 – substitution: We solve the second equation for y and substitute into the first equation.

$5y = 5 - 3x$ implies $y = \frac{5-3x}{5} = \frac{5}{5} - \frac{3x}{5} = 1 - \frac{3x}{5}$. So now using the first equation we have

$$2x = 7 - 3y = 7 - 3\left(1 - \frac{3x}{5}\right) = 7 - 3 + \frac{9x}{5} = 4 + \frac{9x}{5}.$$

Multiply each side of this equation by 5 to get rid of the denominator on the right. So we have $10x = 20 + 9x$, and therefore $x = \mathbf{20}$.

Remark: If we wanted to find y instead of x we would solve the first equation for x and substitute into the second equation.

Method 4 – graphical solution: We begin by solving each equation for y.

$$2x = 7 - 3y \qquad\qquad 5y = 5 - 3x$$
$$2x - 7 = -3y \qquad\qquad y = 1 - \frac{3x}{5}$$
$$y = -\frac{2x}{3} + \frac{7}{3}$$

In your graphing calculator press the Y= button, and enter the following.

$$Y1 = -2X/3 + 7/3$$
$$Y2 = 1 - 3X/5$$

Now press ZOOM 6 to graph these two lines in a standard window. It looks like the point of intersection of the two lines is off to the right. So we will need to extend the viewing window. Press the WINDOW button, and change Xmax to 50 and Ymin to −20. Then press 2nd TRACE (which is CALC) 5 (or select INTERSECT). Then press ENTER 3 times. You will see that the x-coordinate of the point of intersection of the two lines is **20**.

Remark: The choices made for Xmax and Ymin were just to try to ensure that the point of intersection would appear in the viewing window. Many other windows would work just as well.

You're doing great! Let's just practice a bit more. Try to solve each of the following problems. Try a Simple Operation whenever you can. Then, if possible, solve each problem another way. The answers to these problems, followed by full solutions are at the end of this lesson. **Do not** look at the answers until you have attempted these problems yourself. Please remember to mark off any problems you get wrong.

LEVEL 2: HEART OF ALGEBRA

3.   If $x + 5y = 25$ and $x + 9y = 11$, what is the value of $x + 7y$?

$$2(x - 5) = y$$
$$\frac{y}{x} = 7$$

4.   If (x, y) is the solution to the system of equations above, what is the value of xy ?

LEVEL 3: HEART OF ALGEBRA

5.   If $x + y = 5$ and $z + w = 7$, then $xz + xw + yz + yw =$

$$5a + 2y + 3z = 23$$
$$5a + y + 2z = 15$$

6.   If the equations above are true, what is the value of $y + z$?

$$6z \qquad 2z$$
$$8 \qquad 8$$
$$2t \qquad w$$
$$3 \qquad 3$$
$$\underline{+9} \qquad \underline{+9}$$
$$52 \qquad 34$$

7. In the correctly worked addition problems above, what is the value of $4z + 2t - w$

8. If $ab = 7, bc = \frac{1}{9}, b^2 = 3$, what is the value of ac ?

LEVEL 4: HEART OF ALGEBRA

$$ax + by = 17$$
$$ax + (b + 1)y = 26$$

9. Based on the equations above, which of the following must be true?

    (A) $x = 13.5$
    (B) $x = 18$
    (C) $y = 4.5$
    (D) $y = 9$

LEVEL 5: HEART OF ALGEBRA

$$k = a - b + 12$$
$$k = b - c - 17$$
$$k = c - a + 11$$

10. In the system of equations above, what is the value of k?

11. If $x^{15} = \frac{2}{z}$ and $x^{14} = \frac{2y}{z}$ which of the following is an expression for x in terms of y ?

    (A) $3y$
    (B) $2y$
    (C) y
    (D) $\frac{1}{y}$

12. If $6x = 2 + 4y$ and $7x = 3 - 3y$, what is the value of x?

62

Answers

1. 42   5. 35   9. D
2. 20   6. 8   10. 2
3. 18   7. 18   11. D
4. 28   8. 7/27 or .259   12. 9/23 or .391

Full Solutions

5.

Solution by trying a simple operation: The operation to use here is multiplication.

$$x + y = 5$$
$$z + w = 7$$
$$(x + y)(z + w) = 35$$
$$xz + xw + yz + yw = \mathbf{35}$$

* Quick computation: Since $(x + y)(z + w) = xz + xw + yz + yw$, the answer is $(5)(7) = \mathbf{35}$.

Solution by picking numbers: Let's choose values for x, y, z, and w that satisfy the given conditions, say $x = 1$, $y = 4$, $z = 2$, $w = 5$. Then we have

$$xz + xw + yz + yw$$
$$= (1)(2) + (1)(5) + (4)(2) + (4)(5)$$
$$= 2 + 5 + 8 + 20 = \mathbf{35}.$$

6.

* Solution by trying a simple operation: The operation to use here is subtraction.

$$5a + 2y + 3z = 23$$
$$5a + y + 2z = 15$$
$$y + z = \mathbf{8}$$

Remark: Whenever we are trying to find an expression that involves addition, subtraction, or both, **adding or subtracting** the given equations usually does the trick.

7.

Solution by trying a simple operation: Let's rewrite the equations horizontally since that is how most of us are used to seeing equations.

$$6z + 8 + 2t + 3 + 9 = 52$$
$$2z + 8 + w + 3 + 9 = 34$$

63

The operation to use here is subtraction. Let's go ahead and subtract term by term.

$$6z + 8 + 2t + 3 + 9 = 52$$
$$\underline{2z + 8 + w + 3 + 9 = 34}$$
$$4z + (2t - w) \qquad = 18$$

So $4z + 2t - w = \mathbf{18}$.

* Visualizing the answer: You can save a substantial amount of time by performing the subtraction in your head (left equation minus right equation). Note that above the lines the subtraction yields $4z + 2t - w$. This is exactly what we are looking for. Thus, we need only subtract below the lines to get the answer: $52 - 34 = \mathbf{18}$.

Solution by picking numbers: If we choose any value for z, then t and w will be determined. So, let's set z equal to 0. Then

$$
\begin{array}{ll}
8 + 2t + 3 + 9 = 52 & \qquad 8 + w + 3 + 9 = 34 \\
20 + 2t = 52 & \qquad\qquad 20 + w = 34 \\
2t = 32 & \qquad\qquad\qquad w = 14 \\
t = 16 &
\end{array}
$$

So $4z + 2t - w = 0 + 2(16) - 14 = 32 - 14 = \mathbf{18}$.

Remark: Any choice for z will give us the same answer. We could have chosen a value for t or w as well. But once we choose a value for one of the variables the other two are determined.

8.

* Solution by trying a simple operation: The operation to use here is multiplication.

$$ab = 7$$
$$bc = \frac{1}{9}$$
$$\overline{\qquad\qquad\qquad\qquad}$$
$$(ab)(bc) = (7)\left(\frac{1}{9}\right)$$
$$ab^2c = \frac{7}{9}$$

Now substitute 3 in for b^2. So we have $a(3)c = \frac{7}{9}$. Dividing each side of the equation by 3 gives us $ac = \frac{1}{3} \cdot \frac{7}{9} = \mathbf{7/27}$ or $\mathbf{.259}$.

9.

* Solution by trying a simple operation: First multiply out the second term on the left hand side of the second equation to get

$$ax + by + y = 26.$$

Now subtract the first equation from the second equation.

$$\begin{aligned} ax + by + y &= 26 \\ \underline{ax + by \qquad} &= \underline{17} \\ y &= 9 \end{aligned}$$

We see that the answer is choice (D).

10.

* Solution by trying a simple operation: Notice that when we add the three given equations, all the variables on the right hand side add to zero. So we have $3k = 12 - 17 + 11 = 6$. Therefore $k = \mathbf{2}$.

11.

* Solution by trying a simple operation: The operation to use here is division. We divide the left hand sides of each equation, and the right hand sides of each equation. First the left: Recall that when we divide expressions with the same base we need to subtract the exponents. So $\frac{x^{15}}{x^{14}} = x^1 = x$. Now for the right: Recall that dividing is the same as multiplying by the reciprocal. So, $\frac{2}{z} \div \frac{2y}{z} = \frac{2}{z} \cdot \frac{z}{2y} = \frac{1}{y}$. Thus, $x = \frac{1}{y}$ and the answer is choice (D).

Alternate Solution: Multiply each side of each equation by z to get

$$zx^{15} = 2 \qquad\qquad zx^{14} = 2y$$

Multiplying each side of the second equation by x yields $zx^{15} = 2xy$. So $2xy = 2$, and thus, $xy = 1$, and therefore $x = \frac{1}{y}$, choice (D).

12.

* Solution using the elimination method: Since we are trying to find x, we want to make y go away. So we make the two coefficients of y "match up" by multiplying by the appropriate numbers. We will multiply the first equation by 3 and the second equation by 4.

$$\begin{aligned} 3(6x) &= (2 + 4y)(3) \\ 4(7x) &= (3 - 3y)(4) \end{aligned}$$

Don't forget to distribute on the right. Then add the two equations.

65

$$18x = 6 + 12y$$
$$\underline{28x = 12 - 12y}$$
$$46x = 18$$

Now divide each side by 46 to get $x = \mathbf{9/23}$ or $.\mathbf{391}$.

OPTIONAL MATERIAL

LEVEL 6: HEART OF ALGEBRA

1. If x and y are positive real numbers with $x^8 = \frac{z^3}{16}$ and $x^{12} = \frac{z^7}{y^4}$, what is the value of $\frac{xy}{z}$?

2. If $2x + 3y - 4z = 2$, $x - y + 5z = 6$ and $3x + 2y - z = 4$, what is the value of y ?

Solutions

1.

* $x^4 = \frac{x^{12}}{x^8} = \frac{z^7}{y^4} \div \frac{z^3}{16} = \frac{z^7}{y^4} \cdot \frac{16}{z^3} = \frac{16z^4}{y^4}$. So $x = \frac{2z}{y}$, and therefore $\frac{xy}{z} = \mathbf{2}$.

2.

* **Solution using Gauss-Jordan reduction:** Push the MATRIX button, scroll over to EDIT and then select [A] (or press 1). We will be inputting a 3×4 matrix, so press 3 ENTER 4 ENTER. Then enter the numbers 2, 3, −4 and 2 for the first row, 1, −1, 5 and 6 for the second row, and 3, 2, −1 and 4 for the third row.

Now push the QUIT button (2ND MODE) to get a blank screen. Press MATRIX again. This time scroll over to MATH and select rref((or press B). Then press MATRIX again and select [A] (or press 1) and press ENTER.

The display will show the following.

$$[\,[1\ 0\ 0\ -.4]$$
$$[0\ 1\ 0\ \ \ 3.6\,]$$
$$[0\ 0\ 1\ \ \ \ 2]\,]$$

The second line is interpreted as $y = \mathbf{3.6}$.

LESSON 6
GEOMETRY

Reminder: Before beginning this lesson remember to redo the problems from Lesson 2 that you have marked off. Do not "unmark" a question unless you get it correct.

Equations of Lines in General Form

The **general form of an equation of a line** is $ax + by = c$ where a, b and c are real numbers. If $b \neq 0$, then the slope of this line is $m = -\frac{a}{b}$. If $b = 0$, then the line is vertical and has no slope.

Let us consider 2 such equations.

$$ax + by = c$$
$$dx + ey = f$$

(1) If there is a number r such that $ra = d$, $rb = e$, and $rc = f$, then the two equations represent the **same line**. Equivalently, the two equations represent the same line if $\frac{a}{d} = \frac{b}{e} = \frac{c}{f}$. In this case the system of equations has **infinitely many solutions**.

(2) If there is a number r such that $ra = d$, $rb = e$, but $rc \neq f$, then the two equations represent **parallel** but distinct lines. Equivalently, the two equations represent parallel but distinct lines if $\frac{a}{d} = \frac{b}{e} \neq \frac{c}{f}$. In this case the system of equations has **no solution**.

(3) Otherwise the two lines intersect in a single point. In this case $\frac{a}{d} \neq \frac{b}{e}$, and the system of equations has a **unique solution**.

These three cases are illustrated in the figure below.

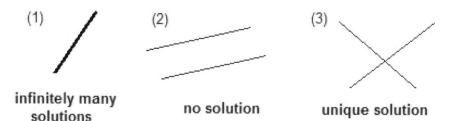

(1)   (2)   (3)

infinitely many solutions   **no solution**   **unique solution**

Example: The following two equations represent the same line.

$$2x + 8y = 6$$
$$3x + 12y = 9$$

To see this note that $\frac{2}{3} = \frac{8}{12} = \frac{6}{9}$.(or equivalently, let $r = \frac{3}{2}$ and note that $\left(\frac{3}{2}\right)(2) = 3$, $\left(\frac{3}{2}\right)(8) = 12$, and $\left(\frac{3}{2}\right)(6) = 9$).

The following two equations represent parallel but distinct lines.

$$2x + 8y = 6$$
$$3x + 12y = 10$$

This time $\frac{2}{3} = \frac{8}{12} \neq \frac{6}{10}$.

The following two equations represent a pair of intersecting lines.

$$2x + 8y = 6$$
$$3x + 10y = 9$$

This time $\frac{2}{3} \neq \frac{8}{10}$.

Try to answer the following question. **Do not** check the solution until you have attempted this question yourself.

LEVEL 4: GEOMETRY

$$2x - 7y = 12$$
$$kx + 6y = -17$$

1. For which of the following values of k will the system of equations above have no solution?

   (A) $-\frac{144}{17}$

   (B) $-\frac{12}{7}$

   (C) $\frac{12}{7}$

   (D) $\frac{144}{17}$

As mentioned above, the system of equations

$$ax + by = c$$
$$dx + ey = f$$

68

has no solution if $\frac{a}{d} = \frac{b}{e} \neq \frac{c}{f}$. So we solve the equation $\frac{2}{k} = \frac{-7}{6}$. Cross multiplying yields $12 = -7k$ so that $k = \frac{12}{-7} = -\frac{12}{7}$, choice (B).

Note: In this problem $\frac{b}{e} \neq \frac{c}{f}$. Indeed, $\frac{-7}{6} \neq \frac{12}{-17}$. This guarantees that the system of equations has no solution instead of infinitely many solutions.

* **Quick solution:** We multiply -7 by $-\frac{6}{7}$ to get 6. So we have $k = (2)\left(-\frac{6}{7}\right) = -\frac{12}{7}$, choice (B).

The Triangle Rule

The triangle rule states that the length of the third side of a triangle is between the sum and difference of the lengths of the other two sides.

Example: If a triangle has sides of length 2, 5, and x, then we have that $5 - 2 < x < 5 + 2$. That is, $3 < x < 7$.

The Pythagorean Theorem and its Converse

The Pythagorean Theorem says that if a right triangle has legs of length a and b, and a hypotenuse of length c, then $c^2 = a^2 + b^2$. Note that the Pythagorean Theorem is one of the formulas given to you in the beginning of each math section.

The converse of the Pythagorean Theorem is also true: If a triangle has sides with length a, b, and c satisfying $c^2 = a^2 + b^2$, then the triangle is a right triangle.

More specifically, we have the following.

$c^2 > a^2 + b^2$ if and only if the angle opposite the side of length c is greater than 90 degrees.

$c^2 < a^2 + b^2$ if and only if the angle opposite the side of length c is less than 90 degrees.

Try to answer the following question using the converse of the Pythagorean Theorem together with the Triangle Rule. **Do not** check the solution until you have attempted this question yourself.

LEVEL 4: GEOMETRY

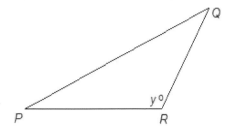

2. In the figure above, $PR = 12$ and $RQ = 9$. If $y > 90$, what is one possible length of $\overline{PQ}$?

We have $12 - 9 = 3$ and $12 + 9 = 21$. So by the **Triangle Rule**, $3 < PQ < 21$.

Using the **converse of the Pythagorean Theorem**, we have that $(PQ)^2 > (PR)^2 + (RQ)^2$. So we have

$$(PQ)^2 > 12^2 + 9^2 = 144 + 81 = 225,$$

and therefore $PQ > 15$.

Putting the two rules together we have **$15 < PQ < 21$**.

For example, we can grid in **16**.

The Generalized Pythagorean Theorem

The length d of the long diagonal of a rectangular solid is given by

$$d^2 = a^2 + b^2 + c^2$$

where a, b and c are the length, width and height of the rectangular solid.

Example: Find the length of the longest line segment with endpoints on a cube with side length 11.

70

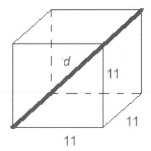

* In this example, our rectangular solid is a cube with a, b and c all equal to 11. So $d^2 = a^2 + b^2 + c^2 = 11^2 + 11^2 + 11^2 = 11^2 \cdot 3$.

So $d = \mathbf{11\sqrt{3}}$.

Now try to solve each of the following problems. The answers to these problems, followed by full solutions are at the end of this lesson. **Do not** look at the answers until you have attempted these problems yourself. Please remember to mark off any problems you get wrong.

LEVEL 3: GEOMETRY

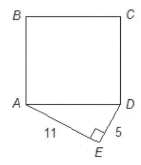

3.   In the figure above, what is the area of square $ABCD$?

Note: Figure not drawn to scale.

4.   In right triangle ABC above, what is the length of side $\overline{AB}$?

LEVEL 4: GEOMETRY

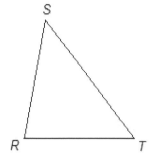

Note: Figure not drawn to scale.

5. In the triangle above, $RS = RT = 26$ and $ST = 20$. What is the area of the triangle?

6. In the xy-plane, line ℓ is the graph of $5x + ky = 8$, where k is a constant. The graph of $10x + 22y = 17$ is parallel to line ℓ. What is the value of k?

LEVEL 5: GEOMETRY

7. * A cube with volume 343 cubic inches is inscribed in a sphere so that each vertex of the cube touches the sphere. What is the length of the radius, in inches, of the sphere?

8. The lengths of the sides of a triangle are x, 16 and 31, where x is the shortest side. If the triangle is not isosceles, what is a possible value of x?

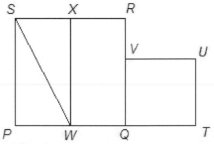

Note: Figure not drawn to scale.

9. In the figure above, $PQRS$ and $QTUV$ are squares, W and X are the midpoints of $\overline{PQ}$ and $\overline{RS}$, respectively, and $TW = SW$. If $RX = \frac{1}{2}$, what is the length of $\overline{UV}$?

    (A) $\dfrac{\sqrt{5}-1}{2}$

    (B) $\dfrac{\sqrt{3}-1}{2}$

    (C) $\dfrac{\sqrt{5}}{2}$

    (D) $\dfrac{\sqrt{3}}{2}$

10. Points Q, R and S lie in a plane. If the distance between Q and R is 18 and the distance between R and S is 11, which of the following could be the distance between Q and S?

    I. 7
    II. 28
    III. 29

    (A) I only
    (B) III only
    (C) I and III only
    (D) I, II, and III

73

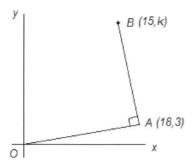

11. In the xy-plane above $OA = AB$. What is the value of k?

$$3x + 9y = 11$$
$$cx + dy = 55$$

12. In the system of equations above, c and d are constants. If the system has infinitely many solutions, what is the value of $\frac{c}{d}$?

Answers

1. B	5. 240	9. A
2. $15 < PQ < 21$	6. 11	10. D
3. 146	7. 6.06	11. 21
4. 8	8. $15 < x < 16$	12. 1/3 or .333

Full Solutions

3.

* Solution using the Pythagorean Theorem: Let x be the length of a side of the square. So $AD = x$. By the Pythagorean Theorem

$$x^2 = 11^2 + 5^2 = 121 + 25 = 146.$$

But x^2 is precisely the area of the square. Therefore the answer is **146**.

4.

* Solution using the Pythagorean Theorem:

$$c^2 = a^2 + b^2 = 23 + 41 = 64.$$

Therefore $AB = c = $ **8**.

5.

* We choose ST as the base, and draw altitude RP from vertex R to base ST.

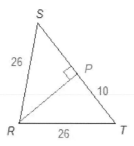

In an isosceles triangle the altitude is equal to the median. It follows that $TP = \frac{1}{2}ST = 10$. Note that $10 = 2 \cdot 5$ and $26 = 2 \cdot 13$. Using the Pythagorean triple 5, 12, 13, we have that $RP = 2 \cdot 12 = 24$.

Area $= (\frac{1}{2})bh = (\frac{1}{2})(20)(24) = \textbf{240}$.

Remarks:

(1) An **altitude** of a triangle is perpendicular to the base. A **median** of a triangle splits the base into two equal parts. In an isosceles triangle, the altitude and median are equal (when you choose the base that is **not** one of the equal sides).

(2) We chose ST to be the base because it is the side that is not one of the equal sides.

(3) 3, 4, 5 and 5, 12, 13 are the two most common Pythagorean triples. These sets of numbers satisfy the Pythagorean Theorem.

(4) If you do not remember the Pythagorean triples it is no big deal. Just use the Pythagorean Theorem. In this case,

$$10^2 + b^2 = 26^2$$
$$100 + b^2 = 676$$
$$b^2 = 676 - 100 = 576$$
$$b = 24.$$

    6.
* Since we multiply 5 by 2 to get 10, we multiply k by 2 to get 22. Therefore $k = \textbf{11}$.

    7.
* The diameter of the sphere is the long diagonal of the cube.

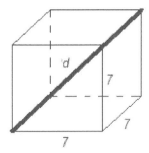

* Since the volume of the cube is 343, the length of a side of the cube is 7 (we get this by taking the cube root of 343). Thus, the diameter of the sphere is given by $d^2 = a^2 + b^2 + c^2 = 7^2 + 7^2 + 7^2 = 49 \cdot 3$.

So $d = 7\sqrt{3}$, and the radius is $r = \frac{d}{2} = \frac{7}{2}\sqrt{3}$.

Putting this in our calculator, we get that $r \approx 6.0621778$ which we truncate (or round) to **6.06**.

8.

* **Solution using the triangle rule:** By the triangle rule, x lies between $31 - 16 = 15$ and $31 + 16 = 47$. That is, we have $15 < x < 47$.

But we are also given that x is the length of the shortest side of the triangle. So $x < 16$. Therefore we can grid in any number between 15 and 16. For example, we can grid in **15.1**.

9.

* Let's label the given figure with what we know.

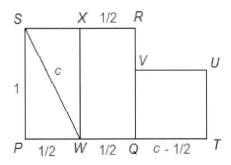

By the Pythagorean Theorem, $c^2 = 1^2 + \left(\frac{1}{2}\right)^2 = 1 + \frac{1}{4} = \frac{5}{4}$. So $c = \sqrt{\frac{5}{4}} = \frac{\sqrt{5}}{2}$. Then $UV = QT = c - \frac{1}{2} = \frac{\sqrt{5}}{2} - \frac{1}{2} = \frac{\sqrt{5}-1}{2}$, choice (A).

10.

* Solution using the triangle rule: If Q, R and S form a triangle, then the length of QS is between $18 - 11 = 7$ and $18 + 11 = 29$. The extreme cases 7 and 29 form straight lines. In this problem that is fine, so the distance between Q and S is between 7 and 29, inclusive. Thus, the answer is choice (D).

11.

* Geometric solution using slope: To get from O to A we go up 3 units, right 18 units. So the slope of OA is $\frac{3}{18} = \frac{1}{6}$. Since AB is perpendicular to OA, we have that the slope of AB is $-6 = -\frac{6}{1}$. Thus, for every unit we move right along AB, we must move down 6 units. Equivalently, for every unit we move left along AB, we must move up 6 units. To get from 18 to 15 we must move left 3 units. Therefore we must move up $3 \cdot 6 = 18$ units. Since we are starting at 3, $k = 3 + 18 = \mathbf{21}$.

Algebraic solution using slopes: We can do all of this algebraically using the slope formula as follows.

The slope of OA is $\frac{3}{18} = \frac{1}{6}$ (see the remark at the end of the first solution to problem 7 from Lesson 2). So the slope of AB is -6 because OA and AB are perpendicular. We can also compute the slope of AB using the slope formula as follows.

$$m_{AB} = \frac{k - 3}{15 - 18} = \frac{k - 3}{-3}$$

Now set these equal to each other and solve for k (or guess and check).

$$\frac{k - 3}{-3} = -6$$
$$k - 3 = 18$$
$$k = \mathbf{21}$$

A solution using two applications of the Pythagorean Theorem: We form two right triangles and use the given points to write down three lengths as shown in the picture below.

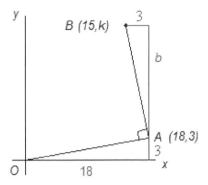

We can now find OA using the Pythagorean Theorem.

$$OA^2 = 18^2 + 3^2 = 333.$$

So $OA = \sqrt{333}$, and therefore $AB = \sqrt{333}$ also since $OA = AB$ is given. Finally, we can use the Pythagorean Theorem one more time to find b.

$$3^2 + b^2 = AB^2$$
$$9 + b^2 = 333$$
$$b^2 = 324$$
$$b = 18$$

So $k = 3 + 18 = \mathbf{21}$.

12.

The system of equations

$$3x + 9y = 11$$
$$cx + dy = 55$$

has infinitely many solutions if $\frac{3}{c} = \frac{9}{d} = \frac{11}{55}$. In particular, we must have $\frac{3}{c} = \frac{9}{d}$, or equivalently $\frac{c}{d} = \frac{3}{9} = \mathbf{1/3}$ or $\mathbf{.333}$.

Note: In this problem we did not need to find c and d themselves.

If we did need to find c we could solve the equation $\frac{3}{c} = \frac{11}{55}$ to get $11c = 3 \cdot 55$, and so $c = \frac{3 \cdot 55}{11} = 3 \cdot 5 = 15$.

Similarly we can find d by solving $\frac{9}{d} = \frac{11}{55}$ to get $11d = 9 \cdot 55$, and so $d = \frac{9 \cdot 55}{11} = 9 \cdot 5 = 45$.

OPTIONAL MATERIAL

CHALLENGE QUESTIONS

1. Draw a rectangular solid with sides of length a, b and c, and let the long diagonal have length d. Show geometrically that $d^2 = a^2 + b^2 + c^2$.

Solutions

1.

Let's begin by drawing a picture.

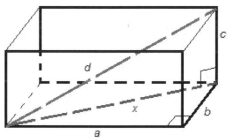

We first use the Pythagorean Theorem on the right triangle with sides of length a, b, and x to get $x^2 = a^2 + b^2$. Then we use the Pythagorean Theorem on the triangle with sides of length x, c, and d to get

$$d^2 = x^2 + c^2 = a^2 + b^2 + c^2.$$

Download additional solutions for free here:

www.thesatmathprep.com/28Les800.html

LESSON 7
PASSPORT TO ADVANCED MATH

Reminder: Before beginning this lesson remember to redo the problems from Lesson 3 that you have marked off. Do not "unmark" a question unless you get it correct.

Graphs of Functions

If f is a function, then

$f(a) = b$ is equivalent to "the point (a, b) lies on the graph of f."

Example 1:

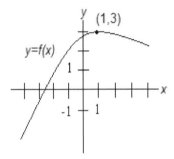

In the figure above we see that the point $(1,3)$ lies on the graph of the function f. Therefore $f(1) = 3$.

Try to answer the following question using this fact. **Do not** check the solution until you have attempted this question yourself.

LEVEL 4: ADVANCED MATH

1. In the xy-plane, the graph of the function h, with equation $h(x) = ax^2 - 16$, passes through the point $(-2, 4)$. What is the value of a?

* **Solution:** Since the graph of h passes through the point $(-2,4)$, $h(-2) = 4$. But by direct computation

$$h(-2) = a(-2)^2 - 16 = 4a - 16.$$

So $4a - 16 = 4$. Therefore $4a = 20$, and so $a = $ **5**.

Function Facts

Fact 1: The **y-intercept** of the graph of a function $y = f(x)$ is the point on the graph where $x = 0$ (if it exists). There can be at most one y-intercept for the graph of a function. A y-intercept has the form $(0, b)$ for some real number b. Equivalently, $f(0) = b$.

Fact 2: An **x-intercept** of the graph of a function is a point on the graph where $y = 0$. There can be more than one x-intercept for the graph of a function or none at all. An x-intercept has the form $(a, 0)$ for some real number a. Equivalently, $f(a) = 0$.

Example 2:

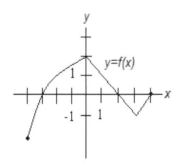

In the figure above we see that the graph of f has y-intercept $(0,2)$ and x-intercepts $(-3,0)$, $(2,0)$ and $(4,0)$.

The numbers -3, 2, and 4 are also called **zeros**, **roots**, or **solutions** of the function.

Fact 3: If the graph of $f(x)$ is above the x-axis, then $f(x) > 0$. If the graph of f is below the x-axis, then $f(x) < 0$. If the graph of f is higher than the graph of g, then $f(x) > g(x)$

Example 3: In the figure for example 2 above, observe that $f(x) < 0$ for $-4 \leq x < -3$ and $2 < x < 4$. Also observe that $f(x) > 0$ for $-3 < x < 2$.

Fact 4: As x gets very large, $\frac{1}{x}$ gets very small.

Example 4: Let $f(x) = \frac{3x^2 + \frac{1}{x}}{x^2}$. Then for large x, $f(x) \approx \frac{3x^2}{x^2} = 3$. So, for example $f(10^{100}) \approx 3$.

Even and Odd Functions

A function f with the property that $f(-x) = f(x)$ for all x is called an **even** function. For example, $f(x) = |x|$ is an even function because

$$f(-x) = |-x| = |x| = f(x).$$

A function f with the property that $f(-x) = -f(x)$ for all x is called an **odd** function. For example, $g(x) = \frac{1}{x}$ is odd because

$$g(-x) = \frac{1}{-x} = -\frac{1}{x} = -g(x).$$

A **polynomial function** is a function for which each **term** has the form ax^n where a is a real number and n is a positive integer.

Polynomial functions with only even powers of x are even functions. Keep in mind that a constant c is the same as cx^0, and so c is an even power of x. Here are some examples of polynomial functions that are even.

$$f(x) = x^2 \qquad g(x) = 4 \qquad h(x) = 3x^8 - 2x^6 + 9$$

Polynomial functions with only odd powers of x are odd functions. Keep in mind that x is the same as x^1, and so x is an odd power of x. Here are some examples of polynomial functions that are odd.

$$f(x) = x^3 \qquad g(x) = x \qquad h(x) = 3x^{11} - 2x^5 + 9x$$

A quick graphical analysis of even and odd functions: The graph of an even function is **symmetrical with respect to the y-axis**. This means that the y-axis acts like a "mirror," and the graph "reflects" across this mirror.

The graph of an odd function is **symmetrical with respect to the origin**. This means that if you rotate the graph 180 degrees (or equivalently, turn it upside down) it will look the same as it did right side up.

So another way to determine if $f(-x) = f(x)$ is to graph f in your graphing calculator, and see if the y-axis acts like a mirror. Another way to determine if $f(-x) = -f(x)$ is to graph f in your graphing calculator, and see if it looks the same upside down. This technique will work for **all** functions (not just polynomials).

Try to answer the following question about even functions. **Do not** check the solution until you have attempted this question yourself.

LEVEL 5: ADVANCED MATH

2. For which of the following functions is it true that $f(-x) = f(x)$ for all values of x?

   (A) $f(x) = x^2 + 5$
   (B) $f(x) = x^2 + 5x$
   (C) $f(x) = x^3 + 5x$
   (D) $f(x) = x^3 + 5$

Solution by picking numbers: Let's choose a value for x, say $x = 2$. We compute $f(-2)$ and $f(2)$ for each answer choice.

	$f(-2)$	$f(2)$
(A)	9	9
(B)	-6	14
(C)	-18	18
(D)	-3	13

Since choices (B), (C), and (D) do not match up, we can eliminate them. The answer is therefore choice (A).

Important note: (A) is **not** the correct answer simply because both computations gave the same answer. It is correct because all 3 of the other choices did **not** work. **You absolutely must check all four choices!**

* Quick solution: We are looking for an even function. Each answer choice is a polynomial. Therefore the answer is the one with only even powers of x. This is choice (A) (remember that $5 = 5x^0$).

Graphical solution: Begin putting each of the four answer choices into your graphing calculator (starting with choice (B) or (C)), and choose the one that is symmetrical with respect to the y-axis. This is choice (A).

Now try to solve each of the following problems. The answers to these problems, followed by full solutions are at the end of this lesson. **Do not** look at the answers until you have attempted these problems yourself. Please remember to mark off any problems you get wrong.

LEVEL 3: ADVANCED MATH

3. The function h is defined by $h(x) = 5x^2 - cx + 3$, where c is a constant. In the xy-plane, the graph of $y = h(x)$ crosses the x-axis where $x = 1$. What is the value of c ?

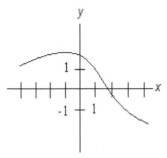

4. The figure above shows the graph of the function f. Which of the following is less than $f(1)$?

   (A) $f(-3)$
   (B) $f(-2)$
   (C) $f(0)$
   (D) $f(3)$

LEVEL 4: ADVANCED MATH

5. If $r^2 s > 10^{200}$, then the value of $\dfrac{rs + \frac{1}{r}}{7rs}$ is closest to which of the following?

   (A) 0.1
   (B) 0.15
   (C) 0.2
   (D) 0.25

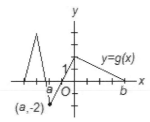

6. The figure above shows the graph of the function g in the xy-plane. Which of the following are true?

    I. $g(b) = 0$
    II. $g(a) + g(b) + g(0) = 0$
    III. $g(a) > g(b)$

    (A) None
    (B) I only
    (C) I and II only
    (D) I, II, and III

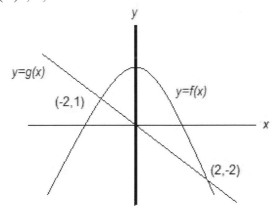

7. In the xy-plane above, the graph of the function f is a parabola, and the graph of the function g is a line. The graphs of f and g intersect at $(-2,1)$ and $(2,-2)$. For which of the following values of x is $f(x) - g(x) < 0$?

    (A) -3
    (B) -1
    (C) $\ \ 0$
    (D) $\ \ 1$

85

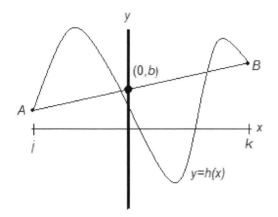

8. The figure above shows the graph of the function h and line segment $\overline{AB}$, which has a y-intercept of $(0, b)$. For how many values of x between j and k does $h(x) = b$?

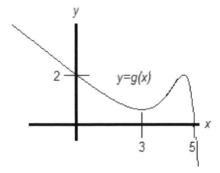

9. A portion of the graph of the function g is shown in the xy-plane above. What is the x-intercept of the graph of the function h defined by $h(x) = g(x - 1)$?

(A) $(1, 0)$
(B) $(2, 0)$
(C) $(3, 0)$
(D) $(6, 0)$

86

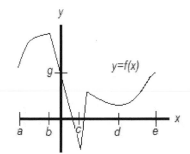

10. The figure above shows the graph of the function f on the interval $a < x < e$. Which of the following expressions represents the difference between the maximum and minimum values of $f(x)$ on this interval?

(A) $f(b - e)$
(B) $f(b - c)$
(C) $f(a) - f(e)$
(D) $f(b) - f(c)$

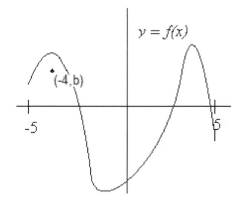

11. The figure above shows the graph of the function f and the point $(-4, b)$. For how many values of x between -5 and 5 does $f(x) = b$?

87

LEVEL 5: ADVANCED MATH

x	3	6	9
$f(x)$	5	a	11

x	6	12	24
$g(x)$	1	b	13

12. The tables above show some values for the functions f and g. If f and g are linear functions, what is the value of $7a - 3b$?

Answers

1. 5	5. B	9. D
2. A	6. C	10. D
3. 8	7. A	11. 4
4. D	8. 3	12. 41

Full Solutions

3.

* A graph crosses the x-axis at a point where $y = 0$. Thus, the point $(1, 0)$ is on the graph of $y = h(x)$. So,

$$0 = h(1) = 5(1)^2 - c + 3 = 5 - c + 3 = 8 - c.$$

So $8 - c = 0$, and therefore $c = \mathbf{8}$.

4.

* Let's draw a horizontal line through the point $(1, f(1))$. To do this start on the x-axis at 1 and go straight up until you hit the curve. This height is $f(1)$. Now draw a horizontal line through this point.

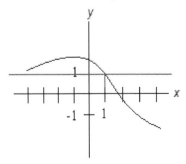

Now, notice that the graph is below this line when $x = 3$. So $f(3)$ is less than $f(1)$. Therefore the answer is choice (D).

5.

Solution by picking a number: Let's let $s = 1$. Then r must be very large. We cannot make r as large as the problem would like (our calculators will give an error), but we can still plug in a large value for r, say $r = 100{,}000$. So we get $\dfrac{(100{,}000)(1) + \frac{1}{100{,}000}}{7(100{,}000)(1)} \approx .14286$. The closest number in the answer choices to this value is 0.15, choice (B).

Algebraic solution: Let's simplify the complex fraction by multiplying the numerator and denominator by r. Then the expression becomes $\dfrac{r\left(rs + \frac{1}{r}\right)}{r(7rs)} = \dfrac{(r^2 s + 1)}{7r^2 s} = \dfrac{r^2 s}{7r^2 s} + \dfrac{1}{7r^2 s} = \dfrac{1}{7} + \dfrac{1}{7r^2 s}$. Since $r^2 s$ is very large, $\dfrac{1}{r^2 s}$ is very small, and $\dfrac{1}{7r^2 s}$ is even smaller. So $\dfrac{1}{7} + 0 = \dfrac{1}{7} \approx .14286$ is a very close approximation to the answer. The closest number in the answer choices to this value is 0.15, choice (B).

* A combination of the two methods: We can begin by plugging in a 1 for s. It follows that r^2 is extremely large. Although r is much smaller than r^2 it is still extremely large so that $\dfrac{1}{r}$ is extremely small. So we can approximate the value of the expression by setting $\dfrac{1}{r} = 0$. So, after setting $s = 1$ and $\dfrac{1}{r} = 0$ we get $\dfrac{r}{7r} = \dfrac{1}{7} \approx .14286$. The closest number in the answer choices to this value is 0.15, choice (B).

6.

* Note that $(a, -2)$, $(0, 2)$, and $(b, 0)$ are on the graph. Equivalently, we have $g(a) = -2$, $g(0) = 2$, and $g(b) = 0$.

Since $g(b) = 0$, I is true. Also $g(a) + g(b) + g(0) = -2 + 0 + 2 = 0$. So II is true. Since $-2 < 0$, we see that III is false. Thus, the answer is choice (C).

7.

Solution by starting with choice (C): Let's add some information to the picture.

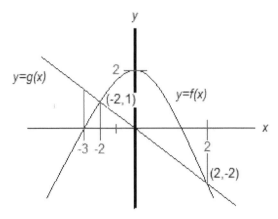

Now let's start with choice (C). Since the point $(0,2)$ is on the graph of f, we have that $f(0) = 2$. Since the point $(0,0)$ is on the graph of g, we have $g(0) = 0$. So $f(0) - g(0) = 2 - 0 = 2 > 0$. So we can eliminate choice (C).

A moment's thought should lead you to suspect that choice (A) might be the answer (if you do not see this it is okay – just keep trying answer choices until you get there). Since the point $(-3,0)$ is on the graph of f, we have $f(-3) = 0$. It looks like $(-3,1.5)$ is on the graph of g, so that $g(-3) = 1.5$. So $f(-3) - g(-3) = 0 - 1.5 = -1.5 < 0$. Thus, the answer is choice (A).

* Geometric solution: $f(x) - g(x) < 0$ is equivalent to $f(x) < g(x)$. Graphically this means that $f(x)$ is lower than $g(x)$. This happens at $x = -3$, choice (A).

Remark: If $-2 < x < 2$, then the graph of f is higher than the graph of g. This means that $f(x) > g(x)$, or equivalently $f(x) - g(x) > 0$. If $x < -2$ or $x > 2$, then the graph of f is lower than the graph of g. This means $f(x) < g(x)$, or equivalently $f(x) - g(x) < 0$.

    8.
* Let's draw a horizontal line through the point $(0, b)$.

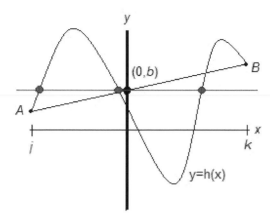

Now, notice that this line hits the graph of h **3** times.

9.

Geometric solution: Since the point $(5,0)$ is on the graph, $g(5) = 0$. It follows that $h(6) = g(6 - 1) = g(5) = 0$. So the point $(6,0)$ is on the graph of h, choice (D).

Remark: Formally, we can solve the equation $x - 1 = 5$ to get $x = 6$.

* Solution using a basic transformation: If we replace x by $x - 1$ in the function g, then the graph of g is shifted to the right 1 unit. So the "new" x-intercept is at $(6,0)$, choice (D).

See Lesson 11 for a review of the basic transformations.

10.

* Let's just point out the maximum and minimum values of $f(x)$ in the figure.

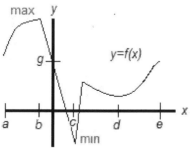

Simply note that the maximum is $f(b)$ and the minimum is $f(c)$. Thus, the difference between the maximum and minimum is $f(b) - f(c)$, choice (D).

91

Note: The maximum and minimum values of a function f are always the y-coordinates of the points. Equivalently, they have the form $f(x)$. We say that the maximum or minimum **occurs** at x.

11.

* We draw a horizontal line through the point $(-4, b)$.

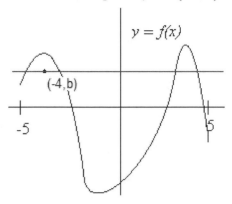

The horizontal line hits the graph 4 times. So $f(x) = b$ for 4 values of x. Thus, the answer is **4**.

Remark: Each point on the horizontal line has the form (x, b), and each point on the curve has the form $(x, f(x))$. So, if a point is simultaneously on the horizontal line **and** the curve, $f(x) = b$.

12.

Clever solution: Since the function f is linear, "**equal jumps in x lead to equal jumps in $f(x)$.**" Note that in the table the jumps in x are equal: x keeps increasing by 3 units. Therefore the jumps in $f(x)$ must be equal. So a must be equal to 8.

Similarly, since the function g is linear, "**equal jumps in x lead to equal jumps in $g(x)$.**" But the jumps in x are **not** equal. We can make them equal however if we just slip in the number 18. The "new" table looks like this.

x	6	12	18	24
$g(x)$	1	b		13

92

Now the jumps in x are equal: x keeps increasing by 6 units. Therefore the jumps in $g(x)$ must be equal. With just a little trial and error it is not hard to see that the jumps in $g(x)$ need to be 4, so that $b = 5$.

Finally, we have $7a - 3b = 7(8) - 3(5) = 56 - 15 = \mathbf{41}$.

Note: By a **jump** in x we mean the difference between two x-values. For example, in the first table, the jump in x when x goes from 3 to 6 is 3. Let us abbreviate this as an "x-jump." For example, in the first table, the x-jump from $x = 6$ to $x = 9$ is $9 - 6 = 3$.

* Quickest solution: We have that $a = \frac{5+11}{2} = \frac{16}{2} = 8$, and we also have $b = \frac{13-1}{3} + 1 = \frac{12}{3} + 1 = 4 + 1 = 5$. So

$$7a - 3b = 7(8) - 3(5) = 56 - 15 = \mathbf{41}.$$

Note about intervals and subintervals: If $a < c$, the length of the interval from a to c is $c - a$. If there are n subintervals between a and c, the length of each subinterval is $\frac{c-a}{n}$. We used this in the quickest solution to find b ($a = 1$, $c = 13$, $n = 3$, and we add the "starting point" 1).

Solution using the slope formula: Let's first compute the slope of the line which is the graph of f. We first need two points. We will use $(3, 5)$ and $(9, 11)$. The slope of the line is then $\frac{11-5}{9-3} = \frac{6}{6} = 1$. We can also use the points $(3, 5)$ and $(6, a)$ to compute the slope. So the slope of the line is $m = \frac{a-5}{6-3} = \frac{a-5}{3}$. So we have $\frac{a-5}{3} = 1$. Therefore $a - 5 = 3$, and so $a = 8$.

Now let's compute the slope of the line which is the graph of g. We will use the points $(6, 1)$ and $(24, 13)$. It then follows that the slope of the line is $\frac{13-1}{24-6} = \frac{12}{18} = \frac{2}{3}$. We can also use the points $(6, 1)$ and $(12, b)$ so that the slope of the line is $m = \frac{b-1}{12-6} = \frac{b-1}{6}$. So we have that $\frac{b-1}{6} = \frac{2}{3}$. Therefore $3(b - 1) = 12$, and so $b - 1 = 4$. Therefore $b = 4 + 1 = 5$.

Finally, we have $7a - 3b = 7(8) - 3(5) = 56 - 15 = \mathbf{41}$.

OPTIONAL MATERIAL

LEVEL 6: ADVANCED MATH

1. The graphs of $y = bx^2$ and $y = k - bx^2$ intersect at points A and B. If the length of $\overline{AB}$ is equal to d, what is the value of $\frac{bd^2}{k}$?

* **Solution:** Let's begin by drawing a picture.

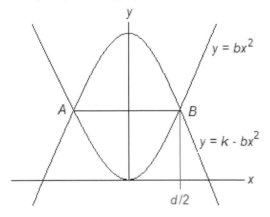

First note that the x-coordinate of point B is $\frac{d}{2}$. Since the two graphs intersect at B, we have $b\left(\frac{d}{2}\right)^2 = k - b\left(\frac{d}{2}\right)^2$. So $2b\left(\frac{d}{2}\right)^2 = k$. Thus, $\frac{2bd^2}{2^2} = k$, so $bd^2 = 2k$, and therefore $\frac{bd^2}{k} = \mathbf{2}$.

Download additional solutions for free here:

www.thesatmathprep.com/28Les800.html

LESSON 8
PROBLEM SOLVING

Reminder: Before beginning this lesson remember to redo the problems from Lesson 4 that you have marked off. Do not "unmark" a question unless you get it correct.

"distance = rate · time charts"

When trying to solve difficult problems involving distance, rate, and time, it helps to set up a little chart, and use the formula when necessary.

Try to answer the following question using a chart. **Do not** check the solution until you have attempted this question yourself.

LEVEL 4: PROBLEM SOLVING

1. Marco drove from home to work at an average speed of 50 miles per hour and returned home along the same route at an average speed of 46 miles per hour. If his total driving time for the trip was 4 hours, how many <u>minutes</u> did it take Marco to drive from work to home?

* **Solution using a chart:** Let's put the given information into the following chart.

	Distance	Rate	Time
home to work	d	50	$\frac{d}{50}$
work to home	d	46	$\frac{d}{46}$
total			4

Note that although we do not know either distance, we do know that they are the same, so we can call them both "d." Also, since

$$\text{distance} = \text{rate} \cdot \text{time},$$

we have that time = $\frac{\text{distance}}{\text{rate}}$. We use this to get the first two entries in the last column. The total time is given in the question. So we have

$$\frac{d}{50} + \frac{d}{46} = 4$$
$$46d + 50d = 4 \cdot 50 \cdot 46$$
$$96d = 4 \cdot 50 \cdot 46$$
$$d = \frac{4 \cdot 50 \cdot 46}{96}$$

We want the time it takes Marco to drive from work to home, that is we want $\frac{d}{46}$. This is equal to $\frac{d}{46} = \frac{4 \cdot 50}{96}$ in hours. To convert to minutes we multiply by 60.

$$\frac{d}{46} = \frac{4 \cdot 50 \cdot 60}{96} = \textbf{125} \text{ minutes.}$$

Xiggi's Formula

The following simple formula can be used to find an average speed when two individual speeds for the same distance are known.

$$\textbf{Average Speed} = \frac{\textbf{2(Speed 1)(Speed 2)}}{\textbf{Speed 1} + \textbf{Speed 2}}$$

*Xiggi's formula is more widely known as the Harmonic Mean formula.

Try to answer the following question using Xiggi's formula. **Do not** check the solution until you have attempted this question yourself.

LEVEL 5: PROBLEM SOLVING

2. An elephant traveled 7 miles at an average rate of 4 miles per hour and then traveled the next 7 miles at an average rate of 1 mile per hour. What was the average speed, in miles per hour, of the elephant for the 14 miles?

* Solution using Xiggi's formula:

$$\text{Average Speed} = \frac{2(4)(1)}{4+1} = \textbf{8/5} \text{ or } \textbf{1.6}$$

Now try to answer this question using a chart.

Solution using a chart:

	Distance	Rate	Time
1st part of trip	7	4	$\frac{7}{4}$
2nd part of trip	7	1	$\frac{7}{1} = 7$
total	14		8.75

Note that we computed the times by using "distance = rate · time" in the form "time $= \frac{\text{distance}}{\text{rate}}$." Finally, we use the formula in the form

$$\text{rate} = \frac{\text{distance}}{\text{time}} = \frac{14}{8.75} = \textbf{1.6}.$$

Note: To get the total distance we add the two distances, and to get the total time we add the two times. Be careful – this doesn't work for rates!

Percent = "Out of 100"

Since the word percent means "out of 100," use the number 100 for totals in percent problems. This is just a specific example of the strategy of picking numbers from Lesson 1.

Try to answer the following question using the number 100. **Do not** check the solution until you have attempted this question yourself.

LEVEL 5: PROBLEM SOLVING

3. * If Ted's weight increased by 36 percent and Jessica's weight decreased by 22 percent during a certain year, the ratio of Ted's weight to Jessica's weight at the end of the year was how many times the ratio at the beginning of the year?

* Solution by picking a number: Since this is a percent problem, let's choose 100 pounds for both Ted's weight and Jessica's weight at the beginning of the year. Ted's weight at the end of the year was then $100 + 36 = 136$ pounds and Jessica's weight at the end of the year was $100 - 22 = 78$ pounds. We then have that the ratio of Ted's weight to Jessica's weight at the beginning of the year was $\frac{100}{100} = 1$, and the ratio of Ted's weight to Jessica's weight at the end of the year was

97

$$\frac{136}{78} \approx 1.7435897.$$

We therefore grid in **1.74**.

Note: The computations are only this simple because we chose both numbers to be 100. Let's choose different numbers so that you can see how the computations become more difficult. Let's choose 150 pounds for Ted's weight at the beginning of the year and 75 pounds for Jessica's weight at the beginning of the year. 36% of 150 is $150(.36) = 54$. So we have that Ted's weight was $150 + 54 = 204$ at the end of the year. Also, 22% of 75 is $75(.22) = 16.5$ pounds. It follows that Jessica's weight at the end of the year was $75 - 16.5 = 58.5$ pounds. The ratio of Ted's weight to Jessica's weight at the beginning of the year was $\frac{150}{75} = 2$, and the ratio of Ted's to Jessica's weight at the end of the year was $\frac{204}{58.5} \approx 3.487179$. Finally, we have to solve the equation

$$2x \approx 3.487179$$
$$x \approx 3.487179/2 \approx 1.74$$

So we do get the same answer, but we put in a lot more effort.

Try to also solve this problem algebraically (without plugging in any numbers).

Algebraic solution: Let Ted's and Jessica's weights at the beginning of the year be x and y, respectively. Then at the end of the year their weights are $1.36x$ and $0.78y$. The ratio of Ted's weight to Jessica's weight at the beginning of the year was $\frac{x}{y}$, and the ratio of Ted's weight to Jessica's weight at the end of the year was $\frac{1.36x}{0.78y} = \frac{68}{39} \cdot \frac{x}{y}$ which is $\frac{68}{39} \approx$ 1.74359 times the ratio at the beginning of the year. We can therefore grid in **1.74**.

Percent Change

Memorize the following simple formula for percent change problems.

$$Percent\ Change = \frac{Change}{Original} \times 100$$

Note that this is the same formula for both a percent increase and a percent decrease problem.

LEVEL 2: PROBLEM SOLVING

4.   In September, Maria was able to type 30 words per minute. In October she was able to type 42 words per minute. By what percent did Jennifer's speed increase from September to October?

    (A) 12%
    (B) 18%
    (C) 30%
    (D) 40%

* This is a percent increase problem. So we will use the formula for percent change. The **original** value is 30. The new value is 42, so that the **change** is 12. Using the percent change formula, we get that the percent increase is $12/30 \cdot 100 = .4 = 40\%$, choice (D).

Warning: Do not accidently use the new value for "change" in the formula. The **change** is the positive difference between the original and new values.

Now try to solve each of the following problems. The answers to these problems, followed by full solutions are at the end of this lesson. **Do not** look at the answers until you have attempted these problems yourself. Please remember to mark off any problems you get wrong.

LEVEL 2: PROBLEM SOLVING

5.   Running at a constant speed, an antelope traveled 150 miles in 6 hours. At this rate, how many miles did the antelope travel in 5 hours?

99

6.   * At Jefferson High School, approximately 3 percent of enrolled freshman, 6 percent of enrolled sophomores, and 8 percent of enrolled juniors scored more than 1300 on their PSAT in October 2015. If there were 412 freshman, 562 sophomores, and 614 juniors at Jefferson High School in 2015, which of the following is closest to the total number of freshmen, sophomores, and juniors at Jefferson High School who scored more than 1300 on their PSAT?

    (A) 72
    (B) 95
    (C) 98
    (D) 126

LEVEL 4: PROBLEM SOLVING

7.   The length of a rectangle was increased by r percent and its width was decreased by 20%. If the area of the rectangle was increased by 4%, what is the value of r ?

    (A) 10
    (B) 20
    (C) 30
    (D) 40

8.   * If $x > 0$, then 4 percent of 7 percent of $5x$ equals what percent of x ? (Disregard the percent symbol when you grid your answer.)

Questions 9 and 10 refer to the following information.

The price of a government issued bond is worth $750 today. A brokerage firm believes that the bond will lose 14% of its value each month for the next four months. The firm uses the equation $A = 750(r)^t$ to model the value, A, of the bond after t months.

9.   What value should be assigned for r ?

10. * To the nearest dollar, what does the firm believe the bond will be worth at the end of four months?

100

LEVEL 5: PROBLEM SOLVING

11. There are m bricks that need to be stacked. After n of them have been stacked, then in terms of m and n, what percent of the bricks have not yet been stacked?

    (A) $\dfrac{m}{100(m-n)}$ %

    (B) $\dfrac{100(m-n)}{m}$ %

    (C) $\dfrac{100m}{n}$ %

    (D) $\dfrac{100n}{m}$ %

12. * Jason ran a race of 1600 meters in two laps of equal distance. His average speeds for the first and second laps were 11 meters per second and 7 meters per second, respectively. What was his average speed for the entire race, in meters per second?

Answers

1. 125	5. 125	9. .86
2. 8/5 or 1.6	6. B	10. 410
3. 1.74	7. C	11. B
4. D	8. 1.4	12. 8.55 or 8.56

Full Solutions

7.

* Solution by starting with choice (C) and picking numbers: Let's start with choice (C) and guess that the length of the rectangle was increased by 30 percent.

If we start with a rectangle with length and width both equal to 10 (yes it's a square), then the original area is 100. We increase the length by 30% to get 13 and we decrease the width by 20% to get 8. So the new area is $13 \cdot 8 = 104$. This is an increase from 100 of 4%. So the answer is choice (C).

8.

Solution by picking a number: Since this is a percent problem let's choose $x = 100$. Then 7 percent of $5x$ is 7 percent of 500 which is $(.07)(500) = 35$. 4 percent of 7 percent of $5x$ is 4 percent of 35 which is $(.04)(35) = 1.4$. Since we began with $x = 100$, the answer is $\mathbf{1.4}$.

* Direct solution: 4% of 7% of $5x$ is $(.04)(.07)(5x) = .014x$ which is 1.4 percent of x. So we grid in $\mathbf{1.4}$.

9.

Solution by picking a number: After 1 month, the bond should lose 14% of its value. So if we let $t = 1$, then $A = 645$ (see notes below if you don't see where this number comes from).

So we have $645 = 750(r)^1 = 750r$. So $r = \frac{645}{750} = \mathbf{.86}$.

Note: (1) To take away 14% is the same as taking 86%. Indeed, $100 - 14 = 86$. So we can find A when $t = 1$ by multiplying $.86$ by 750 to get 645.

(2) We can also take 14% away from 750 by first computing 14% of 750, and then subtracting the result from 750.

$$.14 \cdot 750 = 105$$
$$750 - 105 = 645$$

* Direct solution: $r = 1 - .14 = \mathbf{.86}$.

10.

* $A = 750(.86)^4 = 410.25612$. To the nearest dollar this is $\mathbf{410}$.

11.

Solution by picking numbers: Since this is a percent problem we choose 100 for the total number of bricks. So $m = 100$. For n, let's choose 25, so that 25 bricks have been stacked, and $100 - 25 = 75$ have not been stacked. Since we started with 100 as our total, **75% of the bricks have not been stacked. Remember to put a big, dark circle around 75%.** We make the substitutions $m = 100$ and $n = 25$ into each answer choice.

    (A) $100/7500 \approx 0.0133\%$
    (B) $7500/100 = 75\%$
    (C) $10{,}000/25 = 400\%$
    (D) $2500/100 = 25\%$

We now compare each of these percents to the percent that we put a nice big, dark circle around. Since (A), (C) and (D) are incorrect we can eliminate them. Therefore the answer is choice (B).

Important note: (B) is **not** the correct answer simply because it is equal to 75%. It is correct because all 3 of the other choices are **not** 75%. **You absolutely must check all four choices!**

* Algebraic solution: The total number of bricks is m. Since n bricks have been stacked, it follows that $m - n$ have not been stacked. To get the **fraction** of bricks that have not been stacked we divide the **number** that have not been stacked by the total. This is $\frac{m-n}{m}$. To change this to a **percent** we multiply by 100, to get $\frac{100(m-n)}{m}$ %, choice (B).

Note: The last step in the algebraic solution is equivalent to the usual ratio computation where we are changing the denominator to 100.

$$\begin{array}{ccc} \text{bricks not stacked} & m-n & x \\ \text{total bricks} & m & 100 \end{array}$$

$$\frac{m-n}{m} = \frac{x}{100}$$
$$100(m-n) = mx$$
$$\frac{100(m-n)}{m} = x$$

12.

* Solution using Xiggi's formula:

Average Speed $= \frac{2(11)(7)}{11+7} = \frac{154}{18} \approx 8.555555$. So grid in **8.55** or **8.56**.

Solution using a chart:

	Distance	Rate	Time
lap 1	800	11	$\frac{800}{11} \approx 72.727$
lap 2	800	7	$\frac{800}{7} \approx 114.286$
total	1600	x	187.01

$$x = \text{average rate} = \frac{\text{distance}}{\text{time}} \approx \frac{1600}{187.01} \approx 8.5555$$

So we grid in **8.55** or **8.56**.

OPTIONAL MATERIAL

1. CHALLENGE QUESTION

1.   Use the formula $d = rt$ to derive Xiggi's formula.

Solution

* Recall that Xiggi's formula is used when we are given two rates for the **same** distance. So let d be the common distance, and r_1 and r_2 the two rates. Let's use a chart.

Distance	Rate	Time
d	r_1	$\dfrac{d}{r_1}$
d	r_2	$\dfrac{d}{r_2}$
$2d$		$\dfrac{d}{r_1} + \dfrac{d}{r_2}$

Note that we get the first two entries in the last column by using the formula $d = rt$, and we get the last row by addition (note that the this cannot be done in the middle column). We now apply the formula $d = rt$ to the middle column to get $2d = r(\frac{d}{r_1} + \frac{d}{r_2})$. Multiply each side of this equation by $r_1 r_2$ to get $2dr_1 r_2 = r(dr_2 + dr_1) = rd(r_1 + r_2)$. Finally, we divide each side of this equation by $d(r_1 + r_2)$ to get $r = \dfrac{2r_1 r_2}{r_1 + r_2}$.

Download additional solutions for free here:

www.thesatmathprep.com/28Les800.html

LESSON 9
HEART OF ALGEBRA

Reminder: Before beginning this lesson remember to redo the problems from Lessons 1 and 5 that you have marked off. Do not "unmark" a question unless you get it correct.

Complex Numbers

A **complex number** has the form $a + bi$ where a and b are real numbers and $i = \sqrt{-1}$.

Example: The following are complex numbers:

$$2 + 3i \qquad \frac{3}{2} + (-2i) = \frac{3}{2} - 2i \qquad -\pi + 2.6i \qquad \sqrt{-9} = 3i$$

$0 + 5i = 5i$ This is called a **pure imaginary** number.

$17 + 0i = 17$ This is called a **real number.**

$0 + 0i = 0$ This is **zero**.

Powers of i: Since $i = \sqrt{-1}$, we have the following:

$$i^2 = \sqrt{-1}\,\sqrt{-1} = -1$$

$$i^3 = i^2 i = -1i = -i$$

$$i^4 = i^2 i^2 = (-1)(-1) = 1$$

$$i^5 = i^4 i = 1i = i$$

Notice that the pattern begins to repeat.

Starting with $i^0 = 1$, we have

$i^0 = 1$	$i^1 = i$	$i^2 = -1$	$i^3 = -i$
$i^4 = 1$	$i^5 = i$	$i^6 = -1$	$i^7 = -i$
$i^8 = 1$	$i^9 = i$	$i^{10} = -1$	$i^{11} = -i$

...

105

In other words, when we raise i to a nonnegative integer, there are only four possible answers:

$$1, i, -1, \text{ or } -i$$

To decide which of these values is correct, we can find the remainder upon dividing the exponent by 4.

Example: $i^{73} = i^1 = i$ because when we divide 73 be 4 we get a remainder of 1.

Notes: (1) To get the remainder upon dividing 73 by 4, you **cannot** simply divide 73 by 4 in your calculator. This computation produces the answer 18.75 which does not tell you anything about the remainder.

To find a remainder you must either do the division by hand, or use the Calculator Algorithm below.

(2) This computation can also be done quickly in your calculator, but be careful. Your calculator may sometimes "disguise" the number 0 with a tiny number in scientific notation. For example, when we type i ^ 73 ENTER into our TI-84, we get an output of $-2.3E-12 + i$. The expression $-2.3E-12$ represents a tiny number in scientific notation which is essentially 0. So this should be read as $0 + i = i$.

(3) **Calculator Algorithm for computing a remainder:** Although performing division in your calculator never produces a remainder, there is a simple algorithm you can perform which mimics long division. Let's find the remainder when 73 is divided by 4 using this algorithm.

Step 1: Perform the division in your calculator: 73/4 = 18.75
Step 2: Multiply the integer part of this answer by the divisor: 18*4 = 72
Step 3: Subtract this result from the dividend to get the remainder:

$$73 - 72 = \mathbf{1}.$$

Addition and subtraction: We add two complex numbers simply by adding their real parts, and then adding their imaginary parts.

$$(a + bi) + (c + di) = (a + c) + (b + d)i$$

106

LEVEL 1: HEART OF ALGEBRA

1. For $i = \sqrt{-1}$, the sum $(2 - 3i) + (-5 + 6i)$ is

    (A) $-7 + 3i$
    (B) $-7 + 9i$
    (C) $-3 - 3i$
    (D) $-3 + 3i$

* **Solution:** $(2 - 3i) + (-5 + 6i) = (2 - 5) + (-3 + 6)i = -3 + 3i$, choice (D).

Multiplication: We can multiply two complex numbers by formally taking the product of two binomials and then replacing i^2 by -1.

$$(a + bi)(c + di) = (ac - bd) + (ad + bc)i$$

LEVEL 3: HEART OF ALGEBRA

2. Which of the following complex numbers is equivalent to $(2 - 3i)(-5 + 6i)$? (Note: $i = \sqrt{-1}$)

    (A) $-7 + 3i$
    (B) $-7 + 9i$
    (C) $-3 - 3i$
    (D) $8 + 27i$

* **Solution:** $(2 - 3i)(-5 + 6i) = (-10 + 18) + (12 + 15)i = 8 + 27i$, choice (D).

The **conjugate** of the complex number $a + bi$ is the complex number $a - bi$.

Example: The conjugate of $-5 + 6i$ is $-5 - 6i$.

Note that when we multiply conjugates together we always get a real number. In fact, we have

$$(a + bi)(a - bi) = a^2 + b^2$$

Division: We can put the quotient of two complex numbers into standard form by multiplying both the numerator and denominator by the conjugate of the denominator. This is best understood with an example.

107

LEVEL 4: HEART OF ALGEBRA

$$\frac{1+5i}{2-3i}$$

3.   If the expression above is rewritten in the form $a + bi$, where a and b are real numbers, what is the value of $b - a$?

Solution: We multiply the numerator and denominator of $\frac{1+5i}{2-3i}$ by $(2 + 3i)$ to get

$$\frac{(1+5i)}{(2-3i)} \cdot \frac{(2+3i)}{(2+3i)} = \frac{(2-15)+(3+10)i}{4+9} = \frac{-13+13i}{13} = -\frac{13}{13} + \frac{13}{13}i = -1 + i$$

So $a = -1$, $b = 1$, and $b - a = 1 - (-1) = 1 + 1 = \mathbf{2}$.

Systems of Linear Inequalities

Let's use an example to see how to solve a system of linear inequalities.

LEVEL 5: HEART OF ALGEBRA

$$y \leq 2x + 2$$
$$y \geq -3x - 3$$

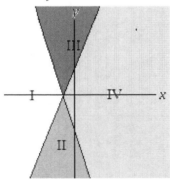

4.   A system of inequalities and a graph are shown above. Which section or sections of the graph could represent all of the solutions to the system?

    (A) Section I
    (B) Section IV
    (C) Sections II and III
    (D) Sections I, II, and IV

* **Quick solution:** The line $y = 2x + 2$ has a slope of $2 > 0$, and therefore the graph is the line that moves upwards as it is drawn from left to right.

The point $(0,0)$ satisfies the inequality $y \leq 2x + 2$ since $0 \leq 2(0) + 2$, or equivalently $0 \leq 2$ is true.

It follows that the graph of $y \leq 2x + 2$ consists of sections II and IV.

The line $y = -3x - 3$ has a slope of $-3 < 0$, and therefore the graph is a line that moves downwards as it is drawn from left to right.

$(0,0)$ satisfies the inequality $y \geq -3x - 3$ since $0 \geq -3(0) - 3$, or equivalently $0 \geq -3$ is true.

It follows that the graph of $y \geq -3x - 3$ consists of sections III and IV.

The intersection of the two solution graphs is section IV, choice (B).

Complete algebraic solution: Let's sketch each inequality, one at a time, starting with $y \leq 2x + 2$. We first sketch the line $y = 2x + 2$. There are several ways to do this. A quick way is to plot the two intercepts. We get the y-intercept by setting $x = 0$. In this case we get $y = 2 \cdot 0 + 2 = 2$. So the point $(0,2)$ is on the line. We get the x-intercept by setting $y = 0$. In this case we get $0 = 2x + 2$, so that $-2 = 2x$, and $x = -\frac{2}{2} = -1$. So the point $(-1,0)$ is on the line. This line is shown in the figure on the left below.

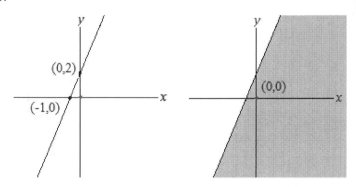

Now we need to figure out which direction to shade. To do this we plug any point *not on the line* into the inequality. For example, we can use $(0,0)$. Substituting this point into $y \leq 2x + 2$ gives $0 \leq 2$. Since this expression is true, we shade the region that includes $(0,0)$ as shown above in the figure on the right.

109

We now do the same thing for the second inequality. The intercepts of $y = -3x - 3$ are $(0,-3)$ and $(-1,0)$. When we test $(0,0)$ we get the true statement $0 \geq -3$.

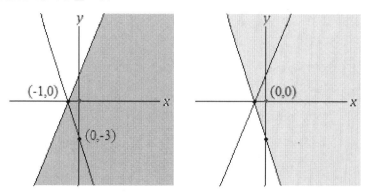

The figure on the above left shows the graph of $y = -3x - 3$ with the intercepts plotted, and the graph on the right shows the solution set of $y \geq -3x - 3$ (the shaded part).

The intersection of the two shaded regions in both figures above is the solution of the system of inequalities. This is region IV, choice (B).

Now try to solve each of the following problems. The answers to these problems, followed by full solutions are at the end of this lesson. **Do not** look at the answers until you have attempted these problems yourself. Please remember to mark off any problems you get wrong.

LEVEL 1: HEART OF ALGEBRA

5. If $-\frac{27}{10} < 2 - 5x < -\frac{13}{5}$, then give one possible value of $20x - 8$.

LEVEL 2: HEART OF ALGEBRA

6. When we subtract $2 - 3i$ from $-5 + 6i$ we get which of the following complex numbers?

    (A) $-7 + 3i$
    (B) $-7 + 9i$
    (C) $-3 - 3i$
    (D) $-3 + 3i$

LEVEL 3: HEART OF ALGEBRA

7. Michael needs a printing job completed. Photoperfect Print Shop charges a fixed fee of $3 for the print job and 5 cents per page. Bargain Printing charges a fixed fee of $2 for the print job and 7 cents per page. If p represents the number of pages being printed, what are all values of p for which Photoperfect Print Shop's total charge is less than Bargain Printing's total charge.

    (A) $p < 20$
    (B) $20 \leq p \leq 35$
    (C) $35 \leq p \leq 50$
    (D) $p > 50$

$$x + k < y$$
$$m - x > y$$

8. In the xy-plane, $(0,0)$ is a solution to the system of inequalities above. Which of the following relationships between k and m must be true?

    (A) $k = -m$
    (B) $k > m$
    (C) $k < m$
    (D) $|k| < |m|$

9. If $5x - 2 < 7$, which inequality represents the possible range of values of $30x - 12$?

    (A) $42 < 30x - 12$
    (B) $42 > 30x - 12$
    (C) $32 < 30x - 12$
    (D) $32 > 30x - 12$

LEVEL 4: HEART OF ALGEBRA

10. * If $i = \sqrt{-1}$, and $\frac{(3+4i)}{(-5-2i)} = a + bi$, where a and b are real numbers, then what is the value of $|b|$ to the nearest tenth?

111

LEVEL 5: HEART OF ALGEBRA

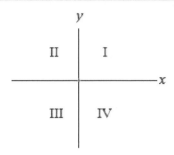

11. If the system of inequalities $y < 4x + 1$ and $y \geq -\frac{1}{2}x - 2$ is graphed in the xy-plane above, which quadrant contains no solutions to the system?

   (A) Quadrant I
   (B) Quadrant II
   (C) Quadrant III
   (D) There are solutions in all four quadrants.

$$y \geq -12x + 600$$
$$y \geq 3x$$

12. In the xy-plane, if a point with coordinates (a, b) lies in the solution set of the system of inequalities above, what is the minimum possible value of b?

Answers

1. D	5. 53/5, 10.5, 10.6, 10.7	9. B
2. D	6. B	10. .5
3. 2	7. D	11. D
4. B	8. C	12.120

Full Solutions

7.

Algebraic solution: Photoperfect Print Shop's total charge for printing p pages is $.05p + 3$ dollars. Bargain Printing's total charge for printing p pages is $.07p + 2$ dollars.

We need to solve the inequality $.05p + 3 < .07p + 2$. Subtracting $.05p$ and subtracting 2 from each side of the inequality gives $1 < .02p$. Dividing by $.02$ yields $\frac{1}{.02} < p$, or $p > \frac{1}{.02} = \frac{100}{2} = 50$, choice (D).

Solution by picking a number: Let's choose a value for p, say $p = 40$ pages. Then Photoperfect Print Shop charges $3 + 40 \cdot .05 = 5$ dollars, and Bargain Printing charges $2 + 40 \cdot .07 = 4$ dollars and 80 cents. So Photoperfect charges *more than* Bargain. Therefore p CANNOT equal 40, and so we can eliminate choice (C).

Let's try $p = 100$ next. Then Photoperfect charges $3 + 100 \cdot .05 = 8$ dollars, and Bargain charges $2 + 100 \cdot .07 = 9$ dollars. So Photoperfect charges *less than* Bargain. Therefore p CAN equal 100, and so we can also eliminate choices (A) and (B).

So the answer is choice (D).

Note: We used the answer choices as a guide here to help pick numbers.

We first looked at choice (C) and chose a value for p between 35 and 50. Since that value of p did not satisfy the conclusion in the problem, we eliminate choice (C) (if it had worked, we would eliminate the other three choices).

We then looked at choice (D) next and chose a value for p greater than 50. This value of p did satisfy the conclusion in the problem allowing us to eliminate choices (A) and (B) (choice (C) is also eliminated here, but we already eliminated it with the last choice of p).

* Solution by logical reasoning: Since Photoperfect Print Shop's price per page is less than Bargain Printing's price per page, if we keep increasing the number of pages, then *eventually* Photoperfect's total cost will be less than Bargain Print Shop's price per page from that point on. So the answer must have the form $p > \square$, where $\square$ is some positive integer. The only answer choice of this form is choice (D).

8.
* Solution by plugging in the point: We replace x and y by 0 in the first equation to get $0 + k < 0$, or equivalently, $k < 0$.

We then replace x and y by 0 in the second equation to get $m - 0 > 0$, or equivalently, $m > 0$.

So we have $k < 0 < m$, so that $k < m$, choice (C).

9.

* Solution by trying a simple operation: We multiply each side of the given inequality by 6 to get

$$6(5x - 2) < 7$$
$$30x - 12 < 42$$

This last inequality is equivalent to $42 > 30x - 12$, choice (B).

10.

$$* \frac{(3+4i)}{(-5-2i)} = \frac{(3+4i)}{(-5-2i)} \cdot \frac{(-5+2i)}{(-5+2i)} = \frac{(-15-8)+(6-20)i}{25+4} = \frac{-23-14i}{29} = -\frac{23}{29} - \frac{14}{29}i$$

So $b = -\frac{14}{29}$.

Therefore $|b| = \frac{14}{29} \approx .4827586207$. To the nearest tenth this is . **5**.

11.

* Complete algebraic solution: Let's sketch each inequality, one at a time, starting with $y < 4x + 1$. We first sketch the line $y = 4x + 1$ by plotting the two intercepts. We get the y-intercept by setting $x = 0$. In this case we get $y = 4 \cdot 0 + 1 = 1$. So the point $(0,1)$ is on the line. We get the x-intercept by setting $y = 0$. In this case we get $0 = 4x + 1$, so that $-1 = 4x$, and $x = -\frac{1}{4}$. So the point $(-\frac{1}{4}, 0)$ is on the line. This line is shown in the figure on the left below. Note that we draw a dotted line because the strict inequality $<$ tells us that points on this line are not actually solutions to the inequality $y < 4x + 1$.

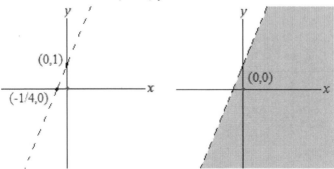

Now we need to figure out which direction to shade. To do this we plug any point *not on the line* into the inequality. For example, we can use $(0,0)$. Substituting this point into $y < 4x + 1$ gives $0 < 1$. Since this expression is true, we shade the region that includes $(0,0)$ as shown above in the figure on the right.

We now do the same thing for the second inequality. The intercepts of $y = -\frac{1}{2}x - 2$ are $(0, -2)$ and $(-4, 0)$. When we test $(0,0)$ we get the true statement $0 \geq -2$.

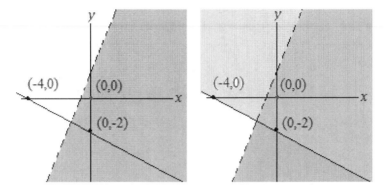

The figure on the above left shows the graph of $y = -\frac{1}{2}x - 2$ with the intercepts plotted, and the graph on the right shows three different shadings. The rightmost shading is the solution set of the given system.

Note that there are solutions in all four quadrants, choice (D).

12.

* Solution by solving the corresponding system of equations: We solve the system of equations

$$y = -12x + 600$$
$$y = 3x$$

In Lesson 5 we learned several ways to solve this system. I will do it here by substitution. We have $3x = -12x + 600$, so that $15x = 600$. Therefore $x = \frac{600}{15} = 40$. It follows that $y = 3 \cdot 40 = \mathbf{120}$.

Notes: (1) It's probably not obvious to you that 120 is actually the answer to the question. But it would certainly be a good guess that if a minimum value for b exists, then it would be given by the y-coordinate of the point of intersection of the two lines.

(2) Although a minimum does not necessarily have to exist, since this is an SAT question, we are expected to give an answer. It follows that a minimum must exist, and Note (1) gives us a quick way to find it.

(3) To be certain that 120 is actually the minimum possible value of b, we should sketch the system of inequalities as was done in problems 4 and 11 from this lesson. I leave this as an exercise for the reader.

115

LESSON 10
TRIGONOMETRY

Reminder: Before beginning this lesson remember to redo the problems from Lessons 2 and 6 that you have marked off. Do not "unmark" a question unless you get it correct.

Right Triangle Trigonometry

Let's consider the following right triangle, and let's focus our attention on angle A.

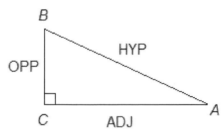

Note that the **hypotenuse** is ALWAYS the side opposite the right angle.

The other two sides of the right triangle, called the **legs**, depend on which angle is chosen. In this picture we chose to focus on angle A. Therefore the opposite side is BC, and the adjacent side is AC.

It's worth memorizing how to compute the six trig functions:

$$\sin A = \frac{\text{OPP}}{\text{HYP}} \qquad \csc A = \frac{\text{HYP}}{\text{OPP}}$$

$$\cos A = \frac{\text{ADJ}}{\text{HYP}} \qquad \sec A = \frac{\text{HYP}}{\text{ADJ}}$$

$$\tan A = \frac{\text{OPP}}{\text{ADJ}} \qquad \cot A = \frac{\text{ADJ}}{\text{OPP}}$$

Here are a couple of tips to help you remember these:

(1) Many students find it helpful to use the word SOHCAHTOA. You can think of the letters here as representing sin, opp, hyp, cos, adj, hyp, tan, opp, adj.

(2) The three trig functions on the right are the reciprocals of the three trig functions on the left. In other words, you get them by interchanging the numerator and denominator. It's pretty easy to remember that the reciprocal of tangent is cotangent. For the other two, just remember that the "s" goes with the "c" and the "c" goes with the "s." In other words, the reciprocal of sine is cosecant, and the reciprocal of cosine is secant.

Example: Compute all six trig functions for each of the angles (except the right angle) in the triangle below.

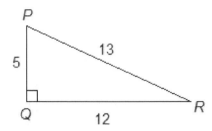

Solution:

$$\sin P = \frac{12}{13} \qquad \csc P = \frac{13}{12} \qquad \sin R = \frac{5}{13} \qquad \csc R = \frac{13}{5}$$

$$\cos P = \frac{5}{13} \qquad \sec P = \frac{13}{5} \qquad \cos R = \frac{12}{13} \qquad \sec R = \frac{13}{12}$$

$$\tan P = \frac{12}{5} \qquad \cot P = \frac{5}{12} \qquad \tan R = \frac{5}{12} \qquad \cot R = \frac{12}{5}$$

LEVEL 2: TRIGONOMETRY

1.   If $0 \leq x \leq 90°$ and $\cos x = \frac{5}{13}$, then $\tan x =$

* **Trigonometric solution:** Let's draw a picture. We begin with a right triangle and label one of the angles x.

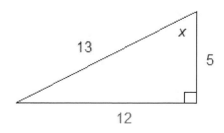

117

Since $\cos x = \dfrac{\text{ADJ}}{\text{HYP}}$, we label the leg adjacent to x with a 5 and the hypotenuse with 13. We can use the Pythagorean triple 5, 12, 13 to see that the other side is 12.

Finally, $\tan x = \dfrac{\text{OPP}}{\text{ADJ}} = \mathbf{12/5}$ or $\mathbf{2.4}$.

Notes: (1) The most common Pythagorean triples are 3, 4, 5 and 5, 12, 13. Two others that may come up are 8, 15, 17 and 7, 24, 25.

(2) If you don't remember the Pythagorean triple 5, 12, 13, you can use the Pythagorean Theorem:

Here we have $5^2 + b^2 = 13^2$. Therefore $25 + b^2 = 169$. Subtracting 25 from each side of this equation gives $b^2 = 169 - 25 = 144$. So $b = 12$.

(3) The equation $b^2 = 144$ would normally have two solutions: $b = 12$ and $b = -12$. But the length of a side of a triangle cannot be negative, so we reject -12.

Special Right Triangles

Recall that the following two special right triangles are given to you on the SAT.

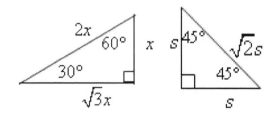

Now try to answer the following question. **Do not** check the solution until you have attempted this question yourself.

LEVEL 4: TRIGONOMETRY

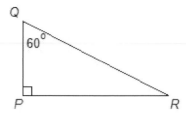

2.   In the triangle above, $QR = 8$. What is the area of ΔPQR?

(A) $32\sqrt{3}$
(B) 32
(C) $16\sqrt{3}$
(D) $8\sqrt{3}$

* Solution using a 30, 60, 90 triangle: Using the special 30, 60, 90 triangle we can label each side with its length as follows.

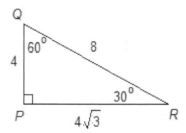

The area is then $A = \frac{1}{2}bh = \frac{1}{2}(4\sqrt{3})(4) = 8\sqrt{3}$, choice (D).

Note: The hypotenuse of a 30, 60, 90 triangle is always twice the length of the side opposite the 30 degree angle.

Also, if we always think of a side as going with its opposite angle, there will never be any confusion, even if our picture is facing a different direction than the triangle on the SAT. This is actually good advice for any triangle problem. Always think of a side in terms of its opposite angle and vice versa.

Trigonometric solution: Let's label the sides of the triangle.

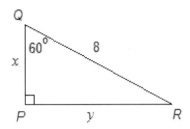

We have $\cos 60° = \dfrac{\text{ADJ}}{\text{HYP}} = \dfrac{x}{8}$. So $x = 8\cos 60°$.

We also have $\sin 60° = \dfrac{\text{OPP}}{\text{HYP}} = \dfrac{y}{8}$. So $y = 8\sin 60°$.

The area of the triangle is

$$\frac{1}{2}xy = \frac{1}{2} \cdot 8\cos 60° \cdot 8\sin 60° = 32 \cdot \frac{1}{2} \cdot \frac{\sqrt{3}}{2} = 8\sqrt{3}$$

This is choice (D).

Notes: (1) If we are allowed to use a calculator for this problem we could do the computation $\frac{1}{2} \cdot 8\cos 60° \cdot 8\sin 60°$ right in our calculator to get approximately 13.8564.

We could then put the answer choices in our calculator to see which choice matches that decimal approximation. We see $8\sqrt{3} \approx 13.8564$. So the answer is choice (D).

(2) We could use the special 30, 60, 90 triangle to get

$$\cos 60° = \frac{\text{ADJ}}{\text{HYP}} = \frac{1}{2} \qquad \text{and} \qquad \sin 60° = \frac{\text{OPP}}{\text{HYP}} = \frac{\sqrt{3}}{2}$$

So we have $\frac{1}{2} \cdot 8\cos 60° \cdot 8\sin 60° = \frac{1}{2} \cdot 8 \cdot \frac{1}{2} \cdot 8 \cdot \frac{\sqrt{3}}{2} = 8\sqrt{3}$, choice (D).

(3) We can actually substitute any value for x in the picture of the 30, 60, 90 triangle that we like, because the x's always cancel when doing any trigonometric computation. For example, with $x = 1$, we have the following picture:

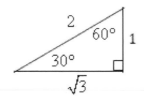

Trigonometric Identities

Here is a list of the trigonometric identities that are useful to know for the SAT:

Quotient Identity:

$$\tan x = \frac{\sin x}{\cos x}$$

Negative Identities:

$$\cos(-x) = \cos x \qquad \sin(-x) = -\sin x \qquad \tan(-x) = -\tan x$$

Cofunction Identities:

$$\sin(90° - x) = \cos x \qquad\qquad \cos(90° - x) = \sin x$$

Pythagorean Identity:

$$\cos^2 x + \sin^2 x = 1$$

LEVEL 3: TRIGONOMETRY

3.   In a right triangle, one angle measures $x°$, where $\cos x° = \frac{2}{3}$. What is $\sin((90 - x)°)$?

* Solution using a cofunction identity: $\sin((90 - x)°) = \cos x° = 2/3$.

If we were to encounter this problem, and we do not remember the cofunction identity, we can also solve this problem with a picture and some basic trigonometry.

Basic trig solution: Let's draw a picture:

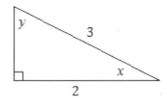

Notice that I labeled one of the angles with x, and used the fact that $\cos x = \frac{\text{ADJ}}{\text{HYP}}$ to label 2 sides of the triangle.

Now observe that $y° = (90 − x)°$, so that

$$\sin((90 − x)°) = \sin y° = \frac{\text{OPP}}{\text{HYP}} = \mathbf{2/3}.$$

Radian Measure

One full rotation of a circle is 360°. All other rotations are in proportion to the full rotation. For example, half of a rotation of a circle is $\frac{360}{2} = 180°$.

In addition to degree measure, another way to measure rotations of a circle is to divide the arc length of the circle by the radius of the circle. This is called **radian** measure. For example, one full rotation of a circle is $\frac{2\pi r}{r} = 2\pi$ radians, and so half of a rotation of a circle is π radians.

So, we just showed that $180° = \pi$ radians.

We can convert between degree measure and radian measure by using the following simple ratio:

$$\frac{\text{degree measure}}{180°} = \frac{\text{radian measure}}{\pi}$$

Example 1: Convert 45° to radians.

Solution: $\frac{45°}{180°} = \frac{x}{\pi} \Rightarrow x = \frac{45\pi}{180} = \frac{\pi}{4}$ radians.

Shortcut: We can convert from degrees to radians by multiplying the given angle by $\frac{\pi}{180}$.

Example 2: Convert $\frac{\pi}{6}$ radians to degrees.

Solution: $\dfrac{x°}{180°} = \dfrac{\pi/6}{\pi} \Rightarrow x = \dfrac{180}{6} = \mathbf{30°}.$

Shortcut: We can convert from radians to degrees by multiplying the given angle by $\dfrac{180}{\pi}$.

If the angle has π in the numerator, we can simply replace π by 180.

LEVEL 4: TRIGONOMETRY

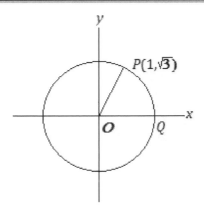

4.   In the xy-plane above, O is the center of the circle, and the measure of $\angle POQ$ is $\dfrac{2\pi}{b}$ radians. What is the value of b ?

* Solution using a 30, 60, 90 triangle: We draw a right triangle inside the picture

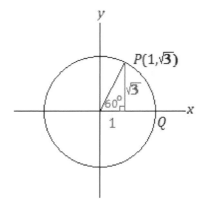

Observe that $\angle POQ$ measures 60°. Converting to radians gives us

123

$$\frac{60\pi}{180} = \frac{\pi}{3}\text{ radians.}$$

So we have $\frac{2\pi}{b} = \frac{\pi}{3}$. Cross multiplying gives us $\pi b = 6\pi$, and so $b = \textbf{6}$.

Note: If we had forgotten that the correct angle in that picture was $60°$, we could also use the TAN^{-1} button (2ND TAN) to get $\tan^{-1}\frac{\sqrt{3}}{1} = 60$.

Of course we can do this only if we are allowed to use a calculator for the problem.

Also, make sure your calculator is in degree mode when doing this computation.

Now try to solve each of the following problems. The answers to these problems, followed by full solutions are at the end of this lesson. **Do not** look at the answers until you have attempted these problems yourself. Please remember to mark off any problems you get wrong.

LEVEL 2: TRIGONOMETRY

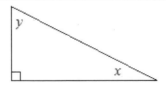

5. In the triangle above, the cosine of $x°$ is 0.7. What is the sine of $y°$?

LEVEL 4: TRIGONOMETRY

6. Which of the following is equal to $\cos\left(\frac{\pi}{5}\right)$?

(A) $-\cos\left(-\frac{\pi}{5}\right)$

(B) $-\sin\left(\frac{\pi}{5}\right)$

(C) $\sin\left(\frac{3\pi}{10}\right)$

(D) $-\cos\left(\frac{3\pi}{10}\right)$

7. If a square has a side of length $x + 5$ and a diagonal of length $x + 10$, what is the value of x ?

(A) 5
(B) 10
(C) 20
(D) $5\sqrt{2}$

8. What is the area of a square whose diagonal has length $5\sqrt{2}$?

LEVEL 5: TRIGONOMETRY

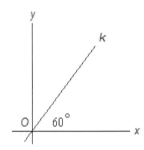

9. In the figure above, what is the equation of line k?

(A) $y = \dfrac{x}{2}$

(B) $y = \dfrac{x}{\sqrt{2}}$

(C) $y = \dfrac{x}{\sqrt{3}}$

(D) $y = \sqrt{3}x$

10. A diagonal of a rectangle forms an angle of measure 30° with each of the two longer sides of the rectangle. If the length of the shorter side of the rectangle is 12, what is the length of the diagonal?

(A) 26
(B) 24
(C) 18
(D) $12\sqrt{3}$

11. A ladder rests against the side of a wall and reaches a point that is h meters above the ground. The angle formed by the ladder and the ground is $\theta°$. A point on the ladder is k meters from the wall. What is the vertical distance, in meters, from this point on the ladder to the ground?

   (A) $(h - k) \tan \theta°$
   (B) $(h - k) \cos \theta°$
   (C) $h - k \sin \theta°$
   (D) $h - k \tan \theta°$

12. It is given that $\cos x = k$, where k is the radian measure of an angle and $\pi < x < \frac{3\pi}{2}$. If $\cos z = -k$, which of the following could <u>not</u> be the value of z ?

   (A) $x - \pi$
   (B) $\pi - x$
   (C) $2\pi - x$
   (D) $3\pi - x$

Answers

1. 12/5 or 2.4	5. .7 or 7/10	9. D
2. D	6. C	10. B
3. 2/3, .666, or .667	7. D	11. D
4. 6	8. 25	12. C

Full Solutions

6.

* Solution using a cofunction identity:

$$\cos\left(\frac{\pi}{5}\right) = \sin\left(\frac{\pi}{2} - \frac{\pi}{5}\right) = \sin\left(\frac{3\pi}{10}\right), \text{ choice (C).}$$

Notes: (1) A function f with the property that $f(-x) = f(x)$ for all x in the domain of f is called an **even** function.

$\cos x$ is an even function. It follows that $\cos(-A) = \cos A$. In particular, $\cos\left(-\frac{\pi}{5}\right) = \cos\left(\frac{\pi}{5}\right)$, and so $-\cos\left(-\frac{\pi}{5}\right) = -\cos\left(\frac{\pi}{5}\right) \neq \cos\left(\frac{\pi}{5}\right)$. This eliminates choice (A).

126

(2) $\cos A$ and $\sin A$ are *not* negatives of each other in general. If $\cos A = -\sin A$, then $\frac{\cos A}{\sin A} = -1$. Taking reciprocals, $\frac{\sin A}{\cos A} = -1$, so that $\tan A = -1$. This happens only when $A = \pm\frac{3\pi}{4}, \pm\frac{7\pi}{4}, \pm\frac{11\pi}{4}, \ldots$

This eliminates choice (B).

(3) Since we know that choice (C) is the answer, we can use the same reasoning as in note (2) to show that $\cos\left(\frac{\pi}{5}\right)$ cannot be equal to $-\cos\left(\frac{3\pi}{10}\right)$.

(4) If a calculator were allowed for this problem, we could simply approximate the given expression and all the answer choices in our calculator to get the answer.

7.

* We begin by drawing a picture

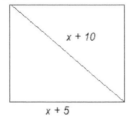

Solution using a 45, 45, 90 triangle: Note that since the sides of a square are congruent, each triangle is an isosceles right triangle. This is the same as a 45, 45, 90 right triangle. So we need $x + 10 = \sqrt{2}(x + 5)$. We can now either solve this algebraically or by starting with choice (C) and using our calculator. We will do the more difficult algebraic method and leave the second method to the reader.

$$x + 10 = \sqrt{2}(x + 5)$$
$$x + 10 = x\sqrt{2} + 5\sqrt{2}$$
$$x\sqrt{2} - x = 10 - 5\sqrt{2}$$
$$x(\sqrt{2} - 1) = 10 - 5\sqrt{2}$$
$$x = \frac{10 - 5\sqrt{2}}{\sqrt{2} - 1} \approx 7.07$$

Putting $5\sqrt{2}$ into your calculator gives the same output. So the answer is choice (D).

127

Solution using the Pythagorean Theorem: We have

$$(x + 5)^2 + (x + 5)^2 = (x + 10)^2$$
$$x^2 + 10x + 25 + x^2 + 10x + 25 = x^2 + 20x + 100$$
$$2x^2 + 20x + 50 = x^2 + 20x + 100$$
$$x^2 = 50$$
$$x = \sqrt{50} = \sqrt{25 \cdot 2} = \sqrt{25} \cdot \sqrt{2} = 5\sqrt{2}, \text{ choice (D)}.$$

Some clarification: $(x + 5)^2 = (x + 5)(x + 5) = x^2 + 5x + 5x + 25$. Therefore $(x + 5)^2 = x^2 + 10x + 25$.

8.

We begin by drawing a picture

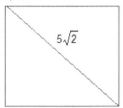

Solution using a 45, 45, 90 triangle: Since all sides of a square have equal length, an isosceles right triangle is formed. An isosceles right triangle is the same as a 45, 45, 90 triangle. So we can get the length of a side of the triangle just by looking at the formula for a 45, 45, 90 right triangle. Here $s = 5$. The area of the square is then $A = s^2 = 5^2 = \mathbf{25}$.

Solution using the Pythagorean Theorem: If we let s be the length of a side of the square, then by the Pythagorean Theorem

$$s^2 + s^2 = \left(5\sqrt{2}\right)^2$$
$$2s^2 = 50$$
$$s^2 = 25$$
$$s = 5$$

Thus, the area of the square is $A = s^2 = 5^2 = \mathbf{25}$.

Remark: We did a bit more work than we had to here. The area of the square is $A = s^2$. We already found that $s^2 = 25$. There was no need to solve this equation for s.

* Using an area formula: The area of a square is $A = \dfrac{d^2}{2}$ where d is the length of a diagonal of the square. Therefore in this problem

$$A = \frac{d^2}{2} = \frac{\left(5\sqrt{2}\right)^2}{2} = \frac{50}{2} = \mathbf{25}.$$

9.

* We begin by forming a 30, 60, 90 triangle. If we let $x = 1$ in the special triangle given to us at the beginning of each math section of the SAT we get the following picture.

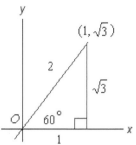

Note that we plotted the point by going right 1, then up $\sqrt{3}$. The slope of the line is $m = \frac{\sqrt{3}}{1} = \sqrt{3}$. Since the line passes through the origin, we have $b = 0$. Thus, the equation of the line in slope-intercept form is

$$y = mx + b = \sqrt{3}x + 0.$$

So $y = \sqrt{3}x$, choice (D).

10.

* **Solution using a 30, 60, 90 triangle:** We begin by drawing a picture.

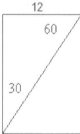

The side opposite the 30 degree angle has length 12. Thus, the hypotenuse has length 24, choice (B).

11.

* Let's draw a picture.

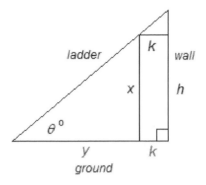

Note that there are two triangles in this picture. We will need to use both of them.

Also recall that for any angle A, $\tan A = \frac{\text{OPP}}{\text{ADJ}}$. Using the smaller triangle we have $\tan \theta° = \frac{x}{y}$ and using the larger triangle we have $\tan \theta° = \frac{h}{y+k}$. The first equation gives us $y \tan \theta° = x$, and the second equation gives $(y + k) \tan \theta° = h$. Distributing this last equation on the left gives $y \tan \theta° + k \tan \theta = h$. Substituting from the first equation yields $x + k \tan \theta = h$. We subtract $k \tan \theta°$ from each side of this last equation to get $x = h - k \tan \theta$, choice (D).

12.

* Solution using coterminal angles and a negative identity:

$$\cos(2\pi - x) = \cos(x - 2\pi) = \cos x = k \neq -k.$$

So $2\pi - x$ could not be the value of z, choice (C).

Notes: (1) For the first equality we used the negative identity

$$\cos(-A) = \cos A,$$

together with the fact that $x - 2\pi = -(2\pi - x)$.

(2) In general we have $a - b = -(b - a)$. To see this simply distribute:

$$-(b - a) = -b + a = a - b.$$

(3) Using notes (1) and (2) together, we have

$$\cos(2\pi - x) = \cos(-(x - 2\pi)) = \cos(x - 2\pi).$$

130

(4) For the second equality we used the fact that x and $x - 2\pi$ are **coterminal angles**.

If a and b are coterminal angles, then $\cos a = \cos b$.

(5) Given an angle x, we get a coterminal angle by adding or subtracting any integer multiple of 2π. So the following are all coterminal with x:

$$... x - 4\pi, x - 2\pi, x, x + 2\pi, x + 4\pi, ...$$

Solution using the cosine difference identity:

$$\cos(A - B) = \cos A \, \cos B + \sin A \, \sin B$$

Let's start with choice (C), and apply the difference identity:

$$\cos(2\pi - x) = \cos 2\pi \, \cos x + \sin 2\pi \, \sin x$$

$$= 1 \cdot \cos x + 0 \cdot \sin x = \cos x = k \neq -k.$$

So $2\pi - x$ could not be the value of z, choice (C).

Notes: (1) Choice (C) is always a good choice to start with when plugging in (See Lesson 1).

(2) Let's apply the difference formula to the other answer choices as well:

$$\cos(x - \pi) = \cos x \, \cos \pi + \sin x \, \sin \pi$$

$$= \cos x \, (-1) + \sin x \, (0) = - \cos x = -k.$$

This shows that z can be $x - \pi$, and so we can eliminate choice (A).

For $\pi - x$, we can use the difference identity again, or we can use the negative identity as we did in the last solution to get

$$\cos(\pi - x) = \cos(x - \pi) = -k$$

This shows that z can also be $\pi - x$, and so we can eliminate choice (B).

$$\cos(3\pi - x) = \cos 3\pi \, \cos x + \sin 3\pi \, \sin x$$

$$= (-1) \cos x + 0 \cdot \sin x = - \cos x = -k.$$

This shows that z can also be $3\pi - x$, and we can eliminate choice (D).

(3) $3\pi = \pi + 2\pi$, and so π and 3π are coterminal angles. It follows that $\cos 3\pi = \cos \pi = -1$ and $\sin 3\pi = \sin \pi = 0$.

Solution using the unit circle: Since $\pi < x < \frac{3\pi}{2}$, when x is placed in standard position, its terminal side falls in the third quadrant, and $\cos x$ will be the x-coordinate of the point where the terminal side intersects the unit circle.

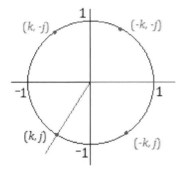

Since x is a third quadrant angle, it's reference angle is the first quadrant angle $x - \pi$, and so from the figure above we see $\cos(x - \pi) = -k$.

The corresponding second quadrant angle is $\pi - (x - \pi) = 2\pi - x$, and so we see from the figure that $\cos(2\pi - x) = k \neq -k$, and so z cannot equal $2\pi - k$, choice (C).

Notes: (1) If θ is a first quadrant angle, then the corresponding angle in the second quadrant is $\pi - \theta$.

The corresponding angle in the third quadrant is $\pi + \theta$.

And the corresponding angle in the fourth quadrant is $2\pi - \theta$.

So in this problem, the first quadrant angle is $x - \pi$, the corresponding second quadrant angle is $\pi - (x - \pi) = \pi - x + \pi = 2\pi - x$, the corresponding third quadrant angle is $(x - \pi) + \pi = x$, and the fourth quadrant angle is $2\pi - (x - \pi) = 2\pi - x + \pi = 3\pi - x$.

(2) From the last note, and the picture above we have $\cos(x - \pi) = -k$, $\cos(2\pi - x) = k$, $\cos x = k$, and $\cos(3\pi - x) = -k$.

132

OPTIONAL MATERIAL

LEVEL 6: TRIGONOMETRY

1. Suppose that quadrilateral $PQRS$ has four congruent sides and satisfies $PQ = PR$. What is the value of $\frac{QS}{PR}$?

Solution

1.

* Note that the quadrilateral is a rhombus. Let's draw a picture.

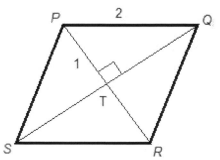

Now, let's choose a value for PQ, say $PQ = 2$. Since $PQ = PR$, $PR = 2$ as well. In a rhombus, the diagonals bisect each other, and are perpendicular to each other. It follows that $PT = 1$ and angle PTQ is a right angle. So triangle PTQ is a 30, 60, 90 triangle, and $QT = \sqrt{3}$. Thus, $QS = 2\sqrt{3}$, and it follows that $\frac{QS}{PR} = \frac{2\sqrt{3}}{2} = \sqrt{3} \approx 1.73205$. If this were an actual grid in question we would grid in **1.73**.

Note: If we let $PT = x$, then $PQ = 2x$, and by a similar argument to the solution above $PR = 2x$ and $QS = 2x\sqrt{3}$. So $\frac{QS}{PR} = \frac{2x\sqrt{3}}{2x} = \sqrt{3}$, as before.

LESSON 11
PASSPORT TO ADVANCED MATH

Reminder: Before beginning this lesson remember to redo the problems from Lessons 3 and 7 that you have marked off. Do not "unmark" a question unless you get it correct.

Standard Form for a Quadratic Function

The standard form for a quadratic function is

$$y - k = a(x - h)^2.$$

The graph is a parabola with **vertex** at (h, k). The parabola opens upwards if $a > 0$ and downwards if $a < 0$.

Example 1: Let the function f be defined by $f(x) = 7(x - 3)^2 + 5$. For what value of x will the function f have its minimum value?

The graph of this function is an upward facing parabola with vertex $(3,5)$. Therefore the answer is $x = \mathbf{3}$.

Remark: Note that in this example $k = 5$ and k is on the right hand side of the equation instead of on the left.

General Form for a Quadratic Function

The general form for a quadratic function is

$$y = ax^2 + bx + c.$$

The graph of this function is a parabola whose vertex has x-coordinate

$$-\frac{b}{2a}$$

The parabola opens upwards if $a > 0$ and downwards if $a < 0$.

Example 2: Let the function f be defined by $f(x) = -3x^2 - 8x + 1$. For what value of x will the function f have its maximum value?

The graph of this function is a downward facing parabola, and we see that $a = -3$, and $b = -8$. Therefore the x-coordinate of the vertex is $x = \frac{8}{-6} = \mathbf{-4/3}$.

134

Sum and Product of Roots of a Quadratic Function

Let r and s be the roots of the quadratic equation $x^2 + bx + c = 0$. Then

$$b = -(r+s) \quad \text{and} \quad c = rs.$$

Try to answer the following question using these formulas. **Do not** check the solution until you have attempted this question yourself.

LEVEL 4: ADVANCED MATH

$$(x-6)(x-2n) = x^2 - 8nx + k$$

1. In the equation above, n and k are constants. If the equation is true for all values of x, what is the value of k?

* Solution: The left hand side is 0 when $x = 6$ and $x = 2n$. The coefficient of x is the negative of the sum of these roots, and so $8n = 2n + 6$, or $6n = 6$. So $n = 1$. The constant term is the product of these roots, so that $k = 6 \cdot 2 = \mathbf{12}$.

Before we go on, try to solve this problem in two other ways.

(1) By plugging in specific values for x (Picking numbers).
(2) By multiplying out the left hand side and equating coefficients.

Solution by picking numbers: Let's plug in some simple values for x.

$x = 0$: $12n = k$
$x = 6$: $0 = 36 - 48n + k$

Substituting $12n$ for k in the second equation yields $0 = 36 - 36n$, so that $36n = 36$, and $n = 1$. Finally, $k = 12n = 12 \cdot 1 = \mathbf{12}$.

Algebraic solution: Multiply out the left hand side (FOIL) to get

$$x^2 - 2nx - 6x + 12n = x^2 - (2n+6)x + 12n$$

Setting the coefficient of x on the left equal to the coefficient of x on the right yields $-(2n+6) = -8n$, or $2n + 6 = 8n$, or $6n = 6$. So $n = 1$. Equating the constant terms on left and right yields $12n = k$. Substituting 1 in for n gives $k = 12 \cdot 1 = \mathbf{12}$.

Special Factoring

Students that are trying for an 800 may want to memorize the following three special factoring formulas.

$$(x + y)^2 = x^2 + y^2 + 2xy$$
$$(x - y)^2 = x^2 + y^2 - 2xy$$
$$(x + y)(x - y) = x^2 - y^2$$

Try to answer the following question using the appropriate formula. **Do not** check the solution until you have attempted this question yourself.

LEVEL 4: ADVANCED MATH

2. If $c > 0$, $s^2 + t^2 = c$, and $st = c + 5$, what is $(s + t)^2$ in terms of c ?

    (A) $c + 5$
    (B) $c + 10$
    (C) $2c + 10$
    (D) $3c + 10$

* Solution:

$(s + t)^2 = s^2 + t^2 + 2st = c + 2(c + 5) = c + 2c + 10 = 3c + 10.$

This is choice (D).

Basic Transformations

Let $y = f(x)$, and $k > 0$. We can move the graph of f around by applying the following basic transformations.

$y = f(x) + k$ shift up k units
$y = f(x) - k$ shift down k units
$y = f(x - k)$ shift right k units
$y = f(x + k)$ shift left k units
$y = -f(x)$ reflect in x-axis
$y = f(-x)$ reflect in y-axis.

Example: Let $f(x) = x^2$. If you move the graph of f right 3 units and down 2 units you get the graph of the function g. What is the definition of g?

We have $g(x) = (x - 3)^2 - 2$. Here is a picture.

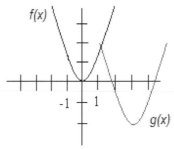

Now try to solve each of the following problems. The answers to these problems, followed by full solutions are at the end of this lesson. **Do not** look at the answers until you have attempted these problems yourself. Please remember to mark off any problems you get wrong.

LEVEL 4: ADVANCED MATH

$$y = -5(x-3)^2 + 2$$

3. In the xy-plane, line ℓ passes through the point $(-1,5)$ and the vertex of the parabola with the equation above. What is the slope of line ℓ?

(A) $-\dfrac{4}{3}$

(B) $-\dfrac{3}{4}$

(C) $\dfrac{3}{4}$

(D) $\dfrac{4}{3}$

4. The function g is defined by $g(x) = 4x^2 - 7$. What are all possible values of $g(x)$ where $-3 < x < 3$?

(A) $4 < g(x) < 36$
(B) $0 < g(x) < 36$
(C) $0 < g(x) < 29$
(D) $-7 \leq g(x) < 29$

$$-2x^2 + bx + 5$$

5. In the xy-plane, the graph of the equation above assumes its maximum value at $x = 2$. What is the value of b?

6. For all real numbers x, let the function g be defined by $g(x) = p(x - h)^2 + k$, where p, h, and k are constants with $p, k > 0$. Which of the following CANNOT be true?

    (A) $g(7) = -h$

    (B) $g(7) = 2$

    (C) $g(0) = -2$

    (D) $g(0) = 2$

LEVEL 5: ADVANCED MATH

7. If $x + y = 2k - 1$, and $x^2 + y^2 = 9 - 4k + 2k^2$, what is xy in terms of k?

    (A) $k - 2$

    (B) $(k - 2)^2$

    (C) $(k + 2)^2$

    (D) $k^2 - 4$

8. If $x^2 = 9$ and $y^2 = 5$, then $(2x + y)^2$ could equal which of the following?

    (A) 41

    (B) 61

    (C) $61 - 12\sqrt{5}$

    (D) $41 + 12\sqrt{5}$

9. Let the function g be defined by $g(x) = a(x - h)^2$, where h is a positive constant, and a is a negative constant. For what value of x will the function g have its maximum value?

    (A) $-h$

    (B) $-a$

    (C) a

    (D) h

10. What is the sum of all values of k that satisfy $3k^2 - 27k + 18 = 0$?

11. If $x^2 - y^2 = 10 - k - 3k^2$, $x - y = 5 - 3k$, and $k \neq \frac{5}{3}$, what is $x + y$ in terms of k?

    (A) $k - 2$
    (B) $(k - 2)^2$
    (C) $k + 2$
    (D) $(k + 2)^2$

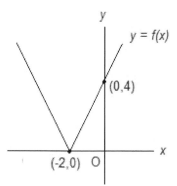 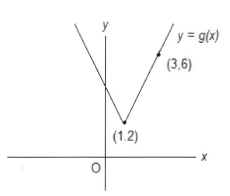

12. The figures above show the graphs of the functions f and g. The function f is defined by $f(x) = 2|x + 2|$ and the function g is defined by $g(x) = f(x + h) + k$, where h and k are constants. What is the value of $|h - k|$?

Answers

1. 12	5. 8	9. D
2. D	6. C	10. 9
3. B	7. D	11. C
4. D	8. D	12. 5

Full Solutions

3.
* Solution using the standard form of a quadratic equation: The vertex of the parabola is (3,2). Therefore the slope of the line is

$$\frac{5 - 2}{-1 - 3} = \frac{3}{-4} = -\frac{3}{4}$$

This is answer choice (B).

4.

Solution by picking a number: Let's try a value for x in the given range, say $x = 0$. Then $g(x) = -7$. So we can eliminate choices (A), (B), and (C). Thus, the answer is choice (D).

* **Quick solution:** g is an **even** function. So we need only check the possible values of $g(x)$ for which $0 \leq x < 3$. We have $g(0) = -7$ and $g(3) = 4(3)^2 - 7 = 4(9) - 7 = 36 - 7 = 29$. So the answer is (D).

Solution using the general form for a quadratic function: Using the formula $x = -\frac{b}{2a}$ we see that the x-coordinate of the vertex of the parabola is $x = 0$ (since $b = 0$). The parabola opens upwards ($a = 4 > 0$). So the minimum value of $g(x)$ is $g(0) = -7$. We substitute $x = 3$ (or $x = -3$) to find the upper bound:

$$g(3) = 4(3)^2 - 7 = 4 \cdot 9 - 7 = 36 - 7 = 29.$$

So we must have $-7 \leq g(x) < 29$, choice (D).

Graphical solution: In your graphing calculator press Y=, and under Y1=, type 4X^2 – 7. Press WINDOW and set Xmin = –3, Xmax = 3, Ymin = –7, and Ymax = 29. Then press GRAPH. The graph is a perfect fit, so the answer is choice (D).

Remark: We chose the window in the last solution by using the smallest and largest values that appear in the answer choices.

5.

Solution using the general form for a quadratic function: Using the formula $x = -\frac{b}{2a}$ we have $-\frac{b}{2(-2)} = 2$. So $b = 8$.

Solution using calculus: The derivative of $y = -2x^2 + bx + 5$ is $y' = -4x + b$. We set the derivative equal to 0 and plug in $x = 2$ to get $-4(2) + b = 0$, or $b = 8$.

6.

Solution by starting with choice (C): Let's start with choice (C) and suppose that $g(0) = -2$. Then $-2 = p(0 - h)^2 + k = ph^2 + k$. Since p and k are greater than 0, $ph^2 + k > 0$. Therefore $ph^2 + k$ CANNOT be -2, and the answer is choice (C).

Eliminating the other answer choices: This isn't necessary to solve the problem, but for completeness let's show that each of the other answer choices CAN be true.

(A) If $g(7) = -h$, then $-h = p(7 - h)^2 + k$. Let $h = -1$. Then $1 = 64p + k$, so $k = 1 - 64p$. Now let $p = \frac{1}{128}$. Then $k = 1 - \frac{1}{2} = \frac{1}{2}$.

(B) If $g(7) = 2$, then $2 = p(7 - h)^2 + k$. Let $h = 0$. So $2 = 49p + k$, and therefore $k = 2 - 49p$. Now let $p = \frac{1}{49}$. Then $k = 2 - 1 = 1$.

(D) If $g(0) = 2$, then $2 = p(0 - h)^2 + k$. Let $h = 0$ and $p = 1$. Then $k = 2$.

7.
Solution by picking numbers: Let $k = 0$. Then $x + y = -1$, and $x^2 + y^2 = 9$.

$$(x + y)^2 = (x + y)(x + y) = x^2 + 2xy + y^2 = x^2 + y^2 + 2xy.$$
$$(-1)^2 = 9 + 2xy$$
$$1 = 9 + 2xy$$
$$-8 = 2xy$$
$$-4 = xy$$

Put a nice big dark circle around the number **−4**. Now substitute $k = 0$ into each answer choice.

(A) −2
(B) 4
(C) 4
(D) −4

Since (A), (B), and (C) came out incorrect we can eliminate them, and the answer is choice (D).

* **Algebraic solution:** We use the first special factoring formula.

$$(x + y)^2 = x^2 + y^2 + 2xy.$$
$$(2k - 1)^2 = 9 - 4k + 2k^2 + 2xy$$
$$4k^2 - 4k + 1 = 9 - 4k + 2k^2 + 2xy$$
$$2k^2 - 8 = 2xy$$
$$2(k^2 - 4) = 2xy$$
$$k^2 - 4 = xy$$

So $xy = k^2 - 4$, choice (D).

8.
* Calculator solution: Taking positive square roots in our calculator gives $x = 3$ and $y \approx 2.236$. Substituting into the given expression we get $(2 \cdot 3 + 2.236)^2 \approx 67.832$. Let's see if choice (D) matches with this. We put the number in choice (D) in our calculator to get approximately 67.832. Thus, the answer is choice (D).

Remark: There is no reason that choice (D) has to be the answer. The values we got for x and y are not the only solutions to the given equations. x can also be -3, and y can also be approximately -2.236. If the answer we got didn't agree with any of the answer choices we would have to try other values for x and y (there are four possibilities all together).

Algebraic solution: There are two possibilities for x: $x = 3$ and $x = -3$
There are two possibilities for y: $y = \sqrt{5}$ and $y = -\sqrt{5}$
So, there are 4 possibilities for $(2x + y)^2$.

$$\left(2 \cdot 3 + \sqrt{5}\right)^2 = \left(6 + \sqrt{5}\right)\left(6 + \sqrt{5}\right)$$

$$= 36 + 6\sqrt{5} + 6\sqrt{5} + 5 = 41 + 12\sqrt{5}$$

Since this is answer choice (D) we can stop. We do not need to do the other three computations. The answer is choice (D).

9.
* Solution using the standard form of a quadratic equation: The function $g(x) = a(x - h)^2$ is in standard form and thus has a graph that is a parabola with $(h, 0)$ for its vertex. Since $a < 0$ the parabola opens downwards. Thus the maximum occurs at $x = h$, choice (D).

Graphical solution: Let's choose values for h and a, say $h = 2$ and $a = -1$. So $g(x) = -(x - 2)^2$. If we put this in our graphing calculator we see that the maximum occurs when $x = 2$. Substituting our chosen values for h and a into each answer choice yields

(A) -2
(B) 1
(C) -1
(D) 2

We can therefore eliminate choices (A), (B), and (C). Thus, the answer is choice (D).

10.
* We divide each side of the equation by 3 to get $k^2 - 9k + 6$. The sum we are looking for is the negative of the coefficient of k in the equation, i.e. the answer is **9**.

11.
Solution by picking numbers: Let $k = 0$. Then $x^2 - y^2 = 10$ and $x - y = 5$. We have

$$x^2 - y^2 = (x-y)(x+y)$$
$$10 = 5(x+y)$$
$$x+y = \frac{10}{5} = 2$$

Put a nice big dark circle around the number **2**. Now let's substitute $k = 0$ into each answer choice.

(A) −2
(B) 4
(C) 2
(D) 4

Since (A), (B), and (D) came out incorrect we can eliminate them, and the answer is choice (C).

* **Algebraic solution:** We use the third special factoring formula.

$$(x+y)(x-y) = x^2 - y^2$$
$$(x+y)(5-3k) = 10 - k - 3k^2$$
$$(x+y)(5-3k) = (5-3k)(2+k)$$
$$(x+y) = 2+k$$

So $x + y = k + 2$, choice (C).

Remark: The question excludes $k = \frac{5}{3}$ because in this case we cannot divide each side of the equation by $5 - 3k$ (we would be dividing by zero).

12.
* Notice that to get the graph of g we shift the graph of f 3 units to the right, and 2 units up. Therefore $g(x) = f(x-3) + 2$. So $h = -3$ and $k = 2$. Therefore $|h - k| = |-3 - 2| = |-5| = $ **5**.

OPTIONAL MATERIAL

CHALLENGE QUESTION

1. Show that $x^2 + y^2 + z^2 \geq xy + yz + zx$ for positive numbers x, y, and z.

Solution

1.

The following inequalities are equivalent.

$$x^2 + y^2 + z^2 \geq xy + yz + zx$$
$$2x^2 + 2y^2 + 2z^2 \geq 2xy + 2yz + 2zx$$
$$(x^2 - 2xy + y^2) + (y^2 - 2yz + z^2) + (z^2 - 2zx + x^2) \geq 0$$
$$(x - y)^2 + (y - z)^2 + (z - x)^2 \geq 0$$

Since the last inequality is obviously true, so is the original inequality.

Download additional solutions for free here:

www.thesatmathprep.com/28Les800.html

LESSON 12
PROBLEM SOLVING

Reminder: Before beginning this lesson remember to redo the problems from Lessons 4 and 8 that you have marked off. Do not "unmark" a question unless you get it correct.

Simple Probability Principle

To compute a simple probability where all outcomes are equally likely, divide the number of "successes" by the total number of outcomes.

Try to answer the following question using the simple probability principle. **Do not** check the solution until you have attempted this question yourself.

LEVEL 3: PROBLEM SOLVING

TEST GRADES OF STUDENTS IN MATH CLASS

Test Grade	75	82	87	93	100
Number of students with that grade	5	7	10	3	1

1. * The test grades of the 26 students in a math class are shown in the chart above. If a student is chosen at random, which of the following is closest to the probability that the student scored more than 82 on the test?

    (A) .80
    (B) .55
    (C) .40
    (D) .15

* **Solution using the simple probability principle:** The total number of outcomes is 26 and the number of successes is 14. So the desired probability is $14/26 \approx .53846154$. The closest answer choice is .55, choice (B).

Conditional Probability

A **conditional probability** measures the probability of an event given that another event has occurred. Let's use an example to illustrate conditional probability.

LEVEL 4: PROBLEM SOLVING

Questions 2 - 3 refer to the following information.

743 children from the United States, aged 6 through 11, were tested to see if they were overweight. The data are shown in the table below.

	Overweight	Not overweight	Total
Ages 6-8	31	286	317
Ages 9-11	163	263	426
Total	194	549	743

2. * According to the table, what is the probability that a randomly selected 9-11 year old is overweight?

* We are being asked to use the table to compute a **conditional probability**. Let's name the **events** as follows: O will stand for "the 6-11 year old child is Overweight," and we will use "9-11" to indicate the child is 9-11 years old.

The requested probability is $P(O|9\text{-}11)$. This is read as "the probability that the 6-11 year old child is overweight *given* that the child is 9-11 years old" (in particular, the vertical line is read "given").

In this case for the total, we use the total column in the "Ages 9-11" row. So the total is 426.

For the successes we use the "Overweight" column and the "Ages 9-11" row. This is 163.

So the answer is $P(O|9\text{-}11) = \frac{163}{426} \approx .382629$. So we grid in .**382** or .**383**.

146

Note: $P(X|Y)$ is the probability of X *given* Y, and can be computed with the formula $P(X|Y) = \frac{P(X \cap Y)}{P(Y)}$. Here $X \cap Y$, read "X intersect Y" is the event consisting of all outcomes common to both X and Y. For example, $O \cap$ 9-11 is the event consisting of overweight children of ages 9-11.

For example, $P(O|9\text{-}11) = \frac{P(O \cap (9-11))}{P(9-11)}$.

For $P(O \cap (9\text{-}11))$, the "successes" can be found in the table by looking at the entry in the "Overweight" column and the "Ages 9-11" row.

$P(O \cap (9\text{-}11)) = \frac{163}{743}$.

We also have $P(9\text{-}11) = \frac{426}{743}$.

It follows that $P(O|9\text{-}11) = \frac{P(O \cap (9-11))}{P(9-11)} = \frac{163}{743} \div \frac{426}{743} = \frac{163}{743} \cdot \frac{743}{426} = \frac{163}{426}$.

In practice, we can "forget" the 743's and just put 163 over 426.

3. * According to the table, what is the probability that a randomly selected overweight child aged 6-11 is less than 9 years old?

* This time we want $P(6\text{-}8|O)$. This is read as "the probability that the child is 6-8 *given* that the child is overweight."

In this case for the total, we use the total row in the "Overweight" column. So the total is 194.

For the successes we use the "Overweight" column and the "Ages 6-8" row. This is 31.

So the answer is $P(6\text{-}8|O) = \frac{31}{194} \approx .1597938$. So we can grid in . **159**.

Now try to solve each of the following problems. The answers to these problems, followed by full solutions are at the end of this lesson. **Do not** look at the answers until you have attempted these problems yourself. Please remember to mark off any problems you get wrong.

LEVEL 3: PROBLEM SOLVING

Questions 4 - 7 refer to the following information.

The data in the table below categorizes the GPAs of the students from two high schools.

	Less than 2.5	Between 2.5 and 3.5	Greater than 3.5	Total
School A	272	117	36	425
School B	146	308	121	575
Total	358	425	217	1000

4. * If a student with a GPA between 2.5 and 3.5 is chosen at random, what is the probability that the student goes to school B?

5. * What proportion of the students are from school A with a GPA greater than 3.5?

6. * Which of the following accounts for approximately 36 percent of the 1000 students?

    (A) Students from either school with GPAs less than 2.5
    (B) Students from school A with GPAs greater than 3.5
    (C) Students from school B with GPAs between 2.5 and 3.5
    (D) Students from school B.

7. * If a student from School A is chosen at random, what is the probability that the student has a GPA of at least 2.5?

LEVEL 4: PROBLEM SOLVING

	At least 6 feet tall	Less than 6 feet tall
Male		
Female		
Total	15	34

8.   * The incomplete table above classifies the number of students by height for the twelfth-grade students at Washington High School. There are twice as many male students that are less than 6 feet tall as there are male students that are at least 6 feet tall, and there are four times as many female students that are less than 6 feet tall as there are female students that are at least 6 feet tall. What is the probability that a randomly selected student that is at least 6 feet tall is female?

LEVEL 5: PROBLEM SOLVING

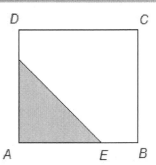

Note: Figure not drawn to scale.

9.   In the figure above, $ABCD$ is a square, the triangle is isosceles, $EB = 10 - 2c$, and $AD = 10$. A point in square $ABCD$ is to be chosen at random. If the probability that the point will be in the shaded triangle is $\frac{2}{25}$, what is the value of c?

Questions 10 - 11 refer to the following information.

743 children from the United States, aged 6 through 11, were tested to see if they were overweight. The data are shown in the table below.

	Overweight	Not overweight	Total
Ages 6-8	31	286	317
Ages 9-11	163	263	426
Total	194	549	743

10. In 2014 the total population of children between 6 and 11 years old, inclusive, in the United Sates was about 74.3 million. If the test results are used to estimate information about children across the country, which of the following is the best estimate of the total number of children between 9 and 11 years old in the United States who were overweight in 2014?

    (A) 3,100,000
    (B) 16,300,000
    (C) 19,400,000
    (D) 42,600,000

11. * According to the table, which of the following statements is most likely to be true about children between 6 and 11 years old, inclusive, in the United Sates?

    (A) The probability that a 6-8 year old is overweight is greater than the probability that an overweight child aged 6-11 is less than 9 years old.
    (B) The probability that a 6-11 year old is overweight is greater than the probability that a 9-11 year old is not overweight.
    (C) The probability that an overweight 6-11 year old is at least 9 years old is greater than the probability that a 6-11 year old is not overweight.
    (D) The probability that a 6-8 year old is overweight is greater than the probability that a 9-11 year old is not overweight.

150

SURVEY RESULTS

12. * The circle graph above shows the distribution of responses to a survey in which a group of men were asked how often they donate to charity. If a man that participated in this survey is selected at random, what is the probability that he donates at least monthly?

Answers

1. B	5. .036	9. 2
2. .382 or .383	6. A	10. B
3. .159	7. 9/25 or .36	11. C
4. .724 or .725	8. 2/15 or .133	12. .33

Full Solutions

4.

* This is a conditional probability. We want the probability the student goes to school B *given* the student has a GPA between 2.5 and 3.5. This is $\frac{308}{425} \approx .724$ or $.725$.

5.

* There are 36 students from school A with a GPA greater than 3.5, and there are a total of 1000 students. So the desired proportion is $\frac{36}{1000} = .036$.

6.

* **Solution by starting with choice (C):** Let's start with choice (C). There are 308 students from school B with GPAs between 2.5 and 3.5. So the percentage is $\frac{308}{1000} \cdot 100 = 30.8\%$.

151

Let's try (B) next: $\frac{36}{1000} \cdot 100 = 3.6\%$.

Let's try (A): $\frac{358}{1000} \cdot 100 = 35.8\%$. This is very close to 36%. So the answer is choice (A).

Note: For completeness let's do choice (D): $\frac{575}{1000} \cdot 100 = 57.5\%$.

7.

* This is a conditional probability. We want the probability the student has a GPA of at least 2.5 *given* the student is from school A. Note that a student has a GPA of at least 2.5 if the student has a GPA between 2.5 and 3.5 **or** the student has a GPA greater than 3.5. So the desired probability is $\frac{117+36}{425} = \mathbf{9/25}$ or $\mathbf{.36}$.

8.

* Let's let x be the number of male students that are at least 6 feet tall, and y the number of female students that are at least 6 feet tall. We can fill in the table as follows:

	At least 6 feet tall	Less than 6 feet tall
Male	x	$2x$
Female	y	$4y$
Total	15	34

We now solve the following system of equations:

$$2x + 4y = 34$$
$$x + y = 15$$

We multiply the second equation by 2 and subtract:

$$2x + 4y = 34$$
$$\underline{2x + 2y = 30}$$
$$2y = 4$$

So $y = \frac{4}{2} = 2$, and the probability that a randomly selected student that is at least 6 feet tall is female is $\mathbf{2/15}$ or $\mathbf{.133}$.

9.
* $AE = 10 - (10 - 2c) = 10 - 10 + 2c = 2c$. So the area of the triangle is

$$\left(\tfrac{1}{2}\right)(2c)(2c) = 2c^2.$$

The area of the square is $(10)(10) = 100$. Thus the probability of choosing a point in the triangle is $\frac{2c^2}{100} = \frac{c^2}{50}$. We are given that this is equal to $\frac{2}{25}$. We cross multiply and divide to get $25c^2 = 100$. So $c^2 = 4$, and thus, $c = \mathbf{2}$.

10.
* 74.3 million $= 74{,}300{,}000 = 743 \times 10^5$. So the best estimate of the total number of children between 9 and 11 years old in the United States who were overweight in 2014 is $163 \times 10^5 = 16{,}300{,}000$, choice (B).

Notes: (1) We are being asked to extrapolate information from a random sample. In this case we want to estimate the number of children between 9 and 11 years old in the United States who were overweight in 2014.

(2) Another way to do this is to set up a ratio.

| Total number of children | 743 | 74,300,000 |
| Overweight children aged 9-11 | 163 | x |

Now draw in the division symbols and equal sign, cross multiply and divide the corresponding ratio to find the unknown quantity x.

$$\frac{743}{163} = \frac{74{,}300{,}000}{x}$$

$$743x = 163 \cdot 74{,}300{,}000$$

$$x = \frac{163 \cdot 74{,}300{,}000}{743} = 16{,}300{,}000$$

11.

* We are being asked to use the table to compute conditional probabilities. Let's name the events we will be referring to as follows: O will stand for "the 6-11 year old child is Overweight," O' will stand for "the 6-11 year old child is Not Overweight," We will use "6-8" and "9-11" to indicate the appropriate age range.

As an example, the probability that "an overweight 6-11 year old is at least 9 years old" will be written $P(9\text{-}11|O)$. The expression $P(9\text{-}11|O)$ is a conditional probability and should be read "the probability the child is 9-11 *given* that the child is 6-11 and overweight," or "the probability an overweight 6-11 year old is at least 9 years old."

Let's start with choice (C) and first compute the probability that an overweight 6-11 year old is at least 9 years old. Note that we are *given* that the child is overweight. So we restrict our attention to the first column (the column labeled "Overweight"), and we see that this probability is $P(9\text{-}11|O) = \frac{163}{194} \approx .84$.

We next compute the probability that a 6-11 year old is not overweight as $P(O') = \frac{549}{743} = .739$.

Since $.84 > .739$, the answer is choice (C).

Note: The reader should check the other answer choices as well for additional practice with conditional probability computations.

12.

* At least monthly means monthly or weekly (think about this carefully). So the desired probability is $\frac{20+13}{100} = \frac{33}{100} = .33$.

LESSON 13
HEART OF ALGEBRA

Reminder: Before beginning this lesson remember to redo the problems from Lessons 1, 5 and 9 that you have marked off. Do not "unmark" a question unless you get it correct.

Laws of Exponents

Law	Example
$x^0 = 1$	$3^0 = 1$
$x^1 = x$	$9^1 = 9$
$x^a x^b = x^{a+b}$	$x^3 x^5 = x^8$
$x^a / x^b = x^{a-b}$	$x^{11}/x^4 = x^7$
$(x^a)^b = x^{ab}$	$(x^5)^3 = x^{15}$
$(xy)^a = x^a y^a$	$(xy)^4 = x^4 y^4$
$(x/y)^a = x^a / y^a$	$(x/y)^6 = x^6 / y^6$
$x^{-1} = 1/x$	$3^{-1} = 1/3$
$x^{-a} = 1/x^a$	$9^{-2} = 1/81$
$x^{1/n} = \sqrt[n]{x}$	$x^{1/3} = \sqrt[3]{x}$
$x^{m/n} = \sqrt[n]{x^m} = \left(\sqrt[n]{x}\right)^m$	$x^{9/2} = \sqrt{x^9} = \left(\sqrt{x}\right)^9$

Now let's practice. Simplify the following expressions using the basic laws of exponents. Get rid of all negative and fractional exponents.

1. $5^2 \cdot 5^3$

2. $\dfrac{5^3}{5^2}$

3. $\dfrac{x^5 \cdot x^3}{x^8}$

4. $(2^3)^4$

5. $\dfrac{(xy)^7 (yz)^2}{y^9}$

6. $\left(\dfrac{2}{3}\right)^3 \left(\dfrac{9}{4}\right)^2$

7. $\dfrac{x^4 + x^2}{x^2}$

8. $\dfrac{(x^{10} + x^9 + x^8)(y^5 + y^4)}{y^4 (x^2 + x + 1)}$

9. 7^{-1}

10. $\dfrac{5^2}{5^5}$

11. $\dfrac{x^{-5} \cdot x^{-3}}{x^{-4}}$

12. $5^{\frac{1}{2}}$

13. $5^{-\frac{1}{2}}$

14. $7^{-\frac{11}{3}}$

15. $\dfrac{x^{-\frac{5}{2}} \cdot x^{-1}}{x^{-\frac{4}{3}}}$

155

Answers

1. $5^5 = 3125$

2. $5^1 = 5$

3. $\dfrac{x^8}{x^8} = 1$

4. $2^{12} = 4096$

5. $\dfrac{x^7 y^7 y^2 z^2}{y^9} = \dfrac{x^7 y^9 z^2}{y^9} = x^7 z^2$

6. $\dfrac{2^3}{3^3} \cdot \dfrac{9^2}{4^2} = \dfrac{2^3}{3^3} \cdot \dfrac{(3^2)^2}{(2^2)^2} = \dfrac{2^3}{3^3} \cdot \dfrac{3^4}{2^4} = \dfrac{3^1}{2^1} = \dfrac{3}{2}$

7. $\dfrac{x^2(x^2+1)}{x^2} = x^2 + 1$

8. $\dfrac{x^8(x^2+x+1)y^4(y+1)}{y^4(x^2+x+1)} = x^8(y+1)$

9. $\dfrac{1}{7}$

10. $5^{-3} = \dfrac{1}{5^3} = \dfrac{1}{125}$

11. $\dfrac{x^{-8}}{x^{-4}} = x^{-4} = \dfrac{1}{x^4}$

12. $\sqrt{5}$

13. $\dfrac{1}{5^{\frac{1}{2}}} = \dfrac{1}{\sqrt{5}}$

14. $\dfrac{1}{7^{\frac{11}{3}}} = \dfrac{1}{\sqrt[3]{7^{11}}}$

15. $\dfrac{x^{-\frac{7}{2}}}{x^{-\frac{4}{3}}} = x^{-\frac{13}{6}} = \dfrac{1}{x^{\frac{13}{6}}} = \dfrac{1}{\sqrt[6]{x^{13}}}$

Now try to solve each of the following problems. The answers to these problems, followed by full solutions are at the end of this lesson. **Do not** look at the answers until you have attempted these problems yourself. Please remember to mark off any problems you get wrong.

LEVEL 1: HEART OF ALGEBRA

1. If $\sqrt[3]{b^2} = b^k$, what is the value of k ?

LEVEL 2: HEART OF ALGEBRA

2. If $8^{x+1} = 4096$, what is the value of x ?

LEVEL 3: HEART OF ALGEBRA

3. If $7^x = 6$, then $7^{3x} =$

4. If $(x^a)^b = \dfrac{x^{c^2}}{x^{d^2}}$, $x > 1$, $ab = c - d$, and $c \neq d$, what is the value of $c + d$?

156

LEVEL 4: HEART OF ALGEBRA

$$2^{9x} = 27z^3$$

5. In the equation above, x is a positive integer and $z > 0$. If $8^x = nz$, what is the value of n?

6. If $y = 7^x$, which of the following expressions is equivalent to $49^x - 7^{x+2}$ for all positive integer values of x ?

   (A) y^2
   (B) $y^2 - y$
   (C) $y^2 - 7y$
   (D) $y^2 - 49y$

x	-3	0	3
$g(x)$	$\dfrac{7}{27}$	7	189

7. The table above shows some values for the function g. If $g(x) = ab^x$ for some positive constants a and b , what is the value of b?

8. If $a^{\frac{2}{5}} = b$, what does a^6 equal in terms of b?

   (A) b^2
   (B) $b^{\frac{12}{5}}$
   (C) b^5
   (D) b^{15}

9. Positive integers a, b, and c satisfy the equations $a^{-b} = \dfrac{1}{64}$ and $b^c = 216$. If $a < b$, what is the value of abc ?

10. If $a \neq 13$ and $\dfrac{a^2 - 169}{a - 13} = b^2$, what does a equal in terms of b ?

    (A) $b^2 - 13$
    (B) $b^2 + 13$
    (C) $\sqrt{b} - \sqrt{13}$
    (D) $b - \sqrt{13}$

11. * If $x = 2\sqrt{3}$ and $5x = \sqrt{27y}$, what is the value of y ?

LEVEL 5: HEART OF ALGEBRA

12. If a and b are positive integers, which of the following is equivalent to $(7a)^{5b} - (7a)^{2b}$?

    (A) $(7a)^{3b}$
    (B) $7^b(a^5 - a^2)$
    (C) $(7a)^{2b}[(7a)^{3b} - 1]$
    (D) $(7a)^{2b}[49a^b - 1]$

Answers

1. 2/3, .666, or .667   5. 3   9. 36
2. 3   6. D   10. A
3. 216   7. 3   11. 11.1
4. 1   8. D   12. C

Full Solutions

3.
* $7^{3x} = (7^x)^3 = 6^3 = \mathbf{216}$.

4.
$(x^a)^b = x^{ab}$ and $\frac{x^{c^2}}{x^{d^2}} = x^{c^2-d^2}$. So $c - d = ab = c^2 - d^2$. We can factor $c^2 - d^2$ as $(c + d)(c - d)$. So we have $c - d = (c + d)(c - d)$. Therefore $c + d = \frac{c-d}{c-d} = \mathbf{1}$.

5.
* $2^{9x} = (2^3)^{3x} = 8^{3x} = (8^x)^3 = (nz)^3 = n^3z^3$. So $n^3 = 27$, and therefore $n = \mathbf{3}$.

158

6.

Solution by picking a number: Let's choose a value for x, say $x = 2$. Then we have $y = 7^2 = 49$, and $49^x - 7^{x+2} = 49^2 - 7^4 = 0$. **Put a nice big dark circle around the number 0.** Now substitute $y = 49$ into each answer choice.

      (A) $49^2 = 2401$
      (B) $49^2 - 49 = 2401 - 49 = 2352$
      (C) $49^2 - 7*49 = 2401 - 343 = 2058$
      (D) $49^2 - 49*49 = 2401 - 2401 = 0$

Since (A), (B) and (C) are incorrect we can eliminate them. Therefore the answer is choice (D)

* Algebraic solution:

$$49^x - 7^{x+2} = (7^2)^x - 7^x 7^2 = (7^x)^2 - 49(7^x) = y^2 - 49y.$$

This is choice (D).

7.

* Let's start with the easiest point $(0,7)$. We have $7 = f(0) = ab^0 = a$.

So the function is now $f(x) = 7b^x$. Let's use the point $(3,189)$ to find b: $189 = f(3) = 7b^3$ so that $b^3 = 27$ and $b = 3$ (since $b > 0$).

Note: Be careful with order of operations here. Exponentiation is always done before multiplication. So ab^x means raise b to the x power, and **then** multiply by a. **Do not** multiply a times b first.

8.

Solution by picking a number: Let's choose a value for a, say $a = 3$. Then using our calculator we have $b = a^{\frac{2}{5}} = 3^{\frac{2}{5}} \approx 1.5518$. Also $a^6 = 729$. **Put a nice big, dark circle around this number so that you can find it easily later.** We now substitute 1.5518 in for b into **all** four answer choices.

(A) 2.408
(B) 2.8708
(C) 8.9987
(D) 728.6789

The answer is choice (D).

Notes: (1) The number in choice (D) didn't come out to exactly 729 because we used a decimal approximation for b, and not b's exact value.

(2) Normally we would have chosen a value for b here (as opposed to a), but in this case choosing a value for a is much simpler. If we were to choose a value for b, then we would have to solve the equation $a^{\frac{2}{5}} = b$, which is precisely what we were trying to avoid.

* **Algebraic solution:** Since $a^{\frac{2}{5}} = b$, we have that $a = b^{\frac{5}{2}}$, and so $a^6 = \left(b^{\frac{5}{2}}\right)^6 = b^{\left(\frac{5}{2}\right)6} = b^{15}$.

This is choice (D).

Remark: To eliminate an exponent we raise to the reciprocal power. The reciprocal of $\frac{2}{5}$ is $\frac{5}{2}$. So in this question we raise each side of the equation $a^{\frac{2}{5}} = b$ to the $\frac{5}{2}$ power. On the left we get $\left(a^{\frac{2}{5}}\right)^{\frac{5}{2}} = a^1 = a$. And as we have seen, on the right we get $b^{\frac{5}{2}}$.

9.

* 64 can be rewritten as 2^6, 4^3, 8^2, or 64^1. Therefore $\frac{1}{64}$ can be written as 2^{-6}, 4^{-3}, 8^{-2} or 64^{-1}. Since $a < b$, $a = 2$ and $b = 6$. When we raise 6 to the 3rd power we get 216. Thus, $c = 3$, and therefore $abc = (2)(6)(3) = \mathbf{36}$.

10.

Solution by picking a number: Let's choose a value for a, say $a = \mathbf{14}$. Then $b^2 = \frac{196 - 169}{14 - 13} \frac{196 - 169}{1} = 27$, and so $b = \sqrt{27}$. We now substitute $b = \sqrt{27}$ into each answer and eliminate any choice that does not come out to 14.

(A) $27 - 13 = 14$

(B) $27 + 13 = 40$

(C) $\sqrt{\sqrt{27}} - \sqrt{13} \approx -1.326$

(D) $\sqrt{27} - \sqrt{13} \approx 1.59$

Since (B), (C) and (D) are incorrect we can eliminate them. Therefore the answer is choice (A).

Remark: Technically it is possible that $b = -\sqrt{27}$. This will lead to a negative value in choice (D), and choice (C) will be undefined.

* Algebraic solution: Recall that $x^2 - y^2$ factors as $(x - y)(x + y)$. Therefore $\frac{a^2 - 169}{a - 13} = \frac{(a - 13)(a + 13)}{a - 13} = a + 13$. So $b^2 = a + 13$, and thus, $a = b^2 - 13$, choice (A).

Remark: The condition $a \neq 13$ guarantees that $a + 13$ is always equal to $\frac{(a - 13)(a + 13)}{a - 13}$. For if a was allowed to be 13, then we would have that $a + 13 = 26$, whereas $\frac{(a - 13)(a + 13)}{a - 13}$ would be undefined.

11.

Squaring each side of the equation $5x = \sqrt{27y}$ gives $25x^2 = 27y$. So we have $y = \frac{25x^2}{27} = \frac{25\left(2\sqrt{3}\right)^2}{27} = \frac{25 \cdot 4 \cdot 3}{27} = \frac{100}{9} \approx 11.11111$. So we can grid in **11.1**.

12.

Solution by picking numbers: Let's pick numbers for a and b, say $a = b = 1$. Then $(7a)^{5b} - (7a)^{2b} = 7^5 - 7^2 = \mathbf{16,758}$. Put a nice big, dark circle around this number. Let's substitute $a = b = 1$ into each answer choice.

(A) $7^3 = 343$

(B) $7(1 - 1) = 0$

(C) $7^2[7^3 - 1] = 16,758$

(D) $7^2[49 - 1] = 2352$

Since (A), (B) and (D) all came out incorrect, the answer is choice (C).

Algebraic solution: Let's consider $7a$ as a **block**, and rename it x. So $(7a)^{5b} - (7a)^{2b} = x^{5b} - x^{2b} = x^{2b}(x^{3b} - 1) = (7a)^{2b}[(7a)^{3b} - 1]$, choice (C).

Remarks: In going from step 2 to step 3 in the sequence of equations above, we factored, and used the following rule of exponents:

$$x^z x^w = x^{z+w}.$$

If you are having trouble seeing this, look at the equation in reverse:

$$x^{2b}\left(x^{3b} - 1\right) = x^{2b} x^{3b} - x^{2b} = x^{2b+3b} - x^{2b} = x^{5b} - x^{2b}$$

Also note that we do not actually need to perform a substitution here. We can solve this problem in one step:

$$(7a)^{5b} - (7a)^{2b} = (7a)^{2b}[(7a)^{3b} - 1]$$

OPTIONAL MATERIAL

LEVEL 6: ADVANCED MATH

1. Let the function h be defined by $h(x) = x^3 + 12$. If c is a positive number such that $h(c^2) = h(3d)$ and $d = \sqrt{c}$, what is the value of $c^{\frac{3}{2}}$?

Solution

1.

* $h(c^2) = (c^2)^3 + 12 = c^6 + 12$, $\quad h(3d) = (3d)^3 + 12 = 27d^3 + 12$.

So we have $c^6 + 12 = 27d^3 + 12$, and so $\dfrac{c^6}{d^3} = 27$. Substituting $c^{\frac{1}{2}}$ for d,

we have $\dfrac{c^6}{c^{\frac{3}{2}}} = 27$. Now $\dfrac{c^6}{c^{\frac{3}{2}}} = c^{6-\frac{3}{2}} = c^{\frac{9}{2}}$. So $c^{\frac{9}{2}} = 27$. Now let's raise each

side of this equation to the $\dfrac{1}{3}$ power. So $\left(c^{\frac{9}{2}}\right)^{\frac{1}{3}} = 27^{\frac{1}{3}}$, and finally $c^{\frac{3}{2}} = \mathbf{3}$.

LESSON 14
GEOMETRY

Reminder: Before beginning this lesson, remember to redo the problems from Lessons 2, 6 and 10 that you have marked off. Do not "unmark" a question unless you get it correct.

Similarity

Two triangles are **similar** if their angles are congruent. Note that similar triangles **do not** have to be the same size. Also note that to show that two triangles are similar we need only show that two pairs of angles are congruent. We get the third pair for free because all triangles have angle measures summing to 180 degrees.

Example:

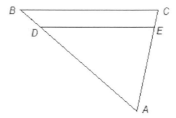

In the figure above, assume that $\overline{BC}$ is parallel to $\overline{DE}$. It then follows that angles ADE and ABC are congruent (corresponding angles). Since triangles ADE and ABC share angle A, the two triangles are similar.

Note that **corresponding sides of similar triangles are in proportion**. So for example, in the figure above $\frac{AD}{AB} = \frac{DE}{BC}$.

Now consider the following figure.

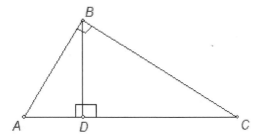

163

We have a right triangle with an **altitude** drawn from the right angle to the hypotenuse. In this figure triangles BDC, ADB and ABC are similar to each other. When solving a problem involving this figure I strongly recommend redrawing all 3 triangles next to each other so that congruent angles match up. The 3 figures will look like this.

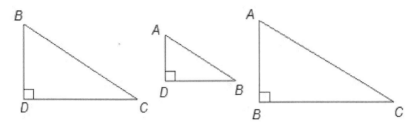

As an example, let's find h in the following figure.

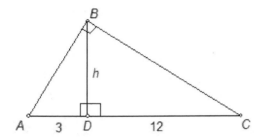

Solution: We redraw the three triangles next to each other so that congruent angles match up.

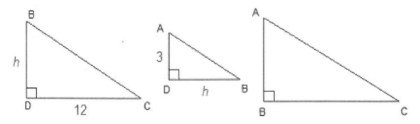

We now set up a ratio, cross multiply, and divide: $\frac{h}{12} = \frac{3}{h}$. So $h^2 = 36$, and therefore $h = \mathbf{6}$.

Remark: Clearly we didn't need to redraw the third triangle, but I suggest drawing all three until you get the hang of this.

164

The Measure of an Exterior Angle of a Triangle is the Sum of the Measures of the Two Opposite Interior Angles of the Triangle

Try to answer the following question using this strategy. **Do not** check the solution until you have attempted this question yourself.

LEVEL 2: GEOMETRY

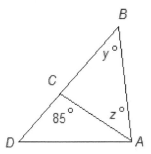

1.　In $\triangle ABD$ above, if $y = 39$, what is the value of z ?

* $85 = 39 + z$, and therefore $z = 85 - 39 = \mathbf{46}$.

Alternate method: Angles ACD and ACB form a **linear pair** and are therefore **supplementary**. It follows that angle ACB measures $180 - 85 = 95$ degrees. Since the angle measures of a triangle add up to 180 degrees, it follows that $z = 180 - 39 - 95 = \mathbf{46}$.

Parallel Lines Cut by a Transversal

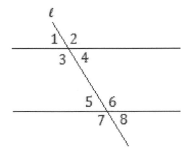

The figure above shows two parallel lines cut by the transversal ℓ.

165

Angles 1, 4, 5, and 8 all have the same measure. Also, angles 2, 3, 6, and 7 all have the same measure. Any two angles that do not have the same measure are supplementary, that is their measures add to 180°.

Let's look at an example.

LEVEL 2: GEOMETRY

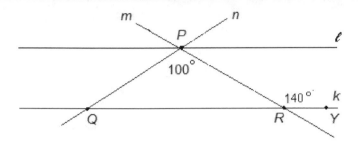

2.   In the figure above, line ℓ is parallel to line k. Transversals m and n intersect at point P on ℓ and intersect k at points R and Q, respectively. Point Y is on k, the measure of $\angle PRY$ is 140°, and the measure of $\angle QPR$ is 100°. How many of the angles formed by rays $\ell, k, m,$ and n have measure 40° ?

    (A) 4
    (B) 6
    (C) 8
    (D) 10

* $\angle QRP$ is supplementary with $\angle PRY$. So $m\angle QRP$ is $180 - 140 = 40°$. We can then use vertical angles to get the remaining angles in the lower right hand corner.

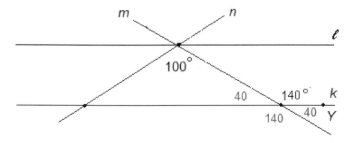

We now use the fact that the sum of the angle measures in a triangle is 180° to get that the measure of the third angle of the triangle is 180 − 100 − 40 = 40°. We then once again use supplementary and vertical angles to get the remaining angles in the lower left hand corner.

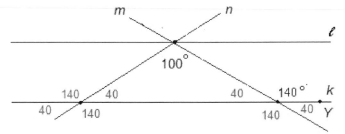

Now notice the following alternate interior angles.

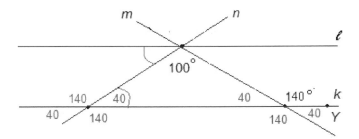

Since ℓ ∥ k, the alternate interior angles are congruent. So the angle marked above has a measure of 40°. We use supplementary and vertical angles to find the remaining angle measures.

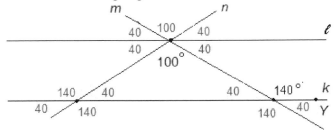

Finally, we see that there are eight angles with measure 40°, choice (C).

Angles of Regular Polygons

A **regular** polygon is a polygon with all sides equal in length, and all angles equal in measure.

167

The total number of degrees in the interior of an n-sided polygon is

$$(n - 2) \cdot 180$$

For example, a six-sided polygon (or hexagon) has

$$(6 - 2) \cdot 180 = 4 \cdot 180 = 720 \text{ degrees}$$

in its interior. Therefore each angle of a **regular** hexagon has

$$\frac{720}{6} = 120 \text{ degrees.}$$

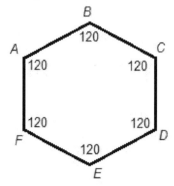

For those of us that do not like to memorize formulas, there is a quick visual way to determine the total number of degrees in the interior of an n-sided polygon. Simply split the polygon up into triangles and quadrilaterals by drawing nonintersecting line segments between vertices. Then add 180 degrees for each triangle and 360 degrees for each quadrilateral. For example, here is one way to do it for a hexagon.

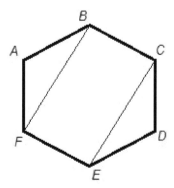

Since the hexagon has been split up into 2 triangles and 1 quadrilateral, the hexagon has $2(180) + 360 = 720$ degrees. This is the same number we got from the formula.

To avoid potential mistakes, let me give a picture that would be incorrect.

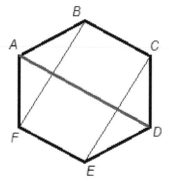

The above figure **cannot** be used to compute the number of interior angles in the hexagon because segment $\overline{AD}$ is "crossing through" segment $\overline{BF}$.

Now let's draw a segment from the center of a regular hexagon to each vertex of the hexagon.

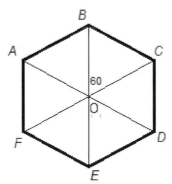

We see that the central angles formed must add up to 360 degrees. Therefore each central angle measures 60 degrees as shown in the figure above.

In general, the number of degrees in a central angle of a regular n-sided polygon is $\frac{360}{n}$.

It is worth looking at a regular hexagon in a bit more detail.

Each of the segments just drawn in the previous figure is a radius of the circumscribed circle of this hexagon, and therefore they are all congruent. This means that each triangle is isosceles, and so the measure of each of the other two angles of any of these triangles is $\frac{180-60}{2} = 60$. Therefore each of these triangles is equilateral. This fact is worth committing to memory.

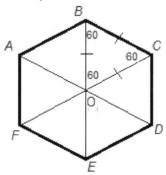

Now try to solve each of the following problems. The answers to these problems, followed by full solutions are at the end of this lesson. **Do not** look at the answers until you have attempted these problems yourself. Please remember to mark off any problems you get wrong.

LEVEL 2: GEOMETRY

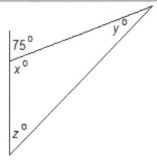

3.   In the figure above, one side of a triangle is extended. Which of the following is true?

(A) $y = 75$
(B) $z = 75$
(C) $z - y = 75$
(D) $y + z = 75$

170

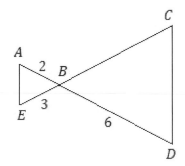

4. In the figure above, $AE \parallel CD$ and segment AD intersects segment CE at B. What is the length of segment CE ?

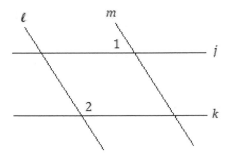

5. In the figure above, lines j and k are parallel and lines l and m are parallel. If the measure of $\angle 2$ is $112°$, what is the measure of $\angle 1$?

    (A) 22°
    (B) 68°
    (C) 82°
    (D) 112°

LEVEL 3: GEOMETRY

6. The measure x, in degrees, of an exterior angle of a regular polygon is related to the number of sides, n, of the polygon by the formula $nx = 360$. If the measure of an exterior angle of a regular polygon is less than $60°$, what is the least number of sides it can have?

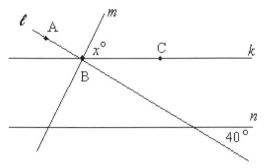

Note: Figure not drawn to scale.

7. In the figure above, line k is parallel to line n. If line m bisects angle ABC, what is the value of x ?

LEVEL 4: GEOMETRY

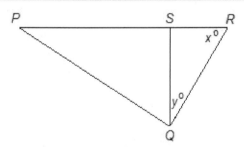

Note: Figure not drawn to scale.

8. In the figure above, if $x = 35$, $PQ \perp QR$, and $PQ = PS$, what is the value of y ?

LEVEL 5: GEOMETRY

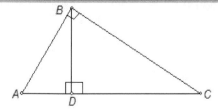

9. In the triangle above, $DC = 3$ and $BC = 6$. What is the value of AC ?

172

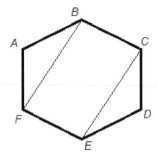

10. * In the figure above, *ABCDEF* is a regular hexagon and $CD =$ 6. What is the perimeter of rectangle *BCEF* to the nearest tenth?

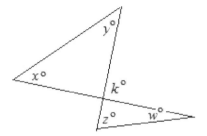

11. In the figure above, what is $xw + xz + yw + yz$ in terms of k?

 (A) $\dfrac{k^2}{4}$

 (B) $\dfrac{k}{2}$

 (C) k

 (D) k^2

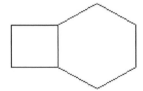

12. The figure above shows a regular hexagon and a square sharing a common side. If the area of the hexagon is $\dfrac{75\sqrt{3}}{2}$ square centimeters, what is the perimeter, in square centimeters, of the square?

173

Answers

1. 46	5. B	9. 12
2. C	6. 7	10. 32.8
3. D	7. 70	11. D
4. 12	8. 27.5	12. 20

Full Solutions

6.

* We are given $x < 60$, so that $\frac{1}{x} > \frac{1}{60}$. It follows that

$$n = \frac{360}{x} = 360\left(\frac{1}{x}\right) > 360\left(\frac{1}{60}\right) = 6.$$

So the least possible value for n is **7.**

7.

* Let's isolate one of the transversals.

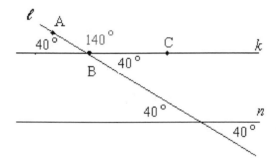

Note that the transversal ℓ creates 8 angles, four of which have measure 40 degrees. The other four are 140 degrees (only one is labeled in the picture). Any two non-congruent angles are supplementary, ie. they add up to 180 degrees. Finally we note that x is half of 140 because line m bisects angle ABC. Thus $x = $ **70**.

8.

* We are given that $\overline{PQ}$ is perpendicular to $\overline{QR}$. It follows that the measure of angle PQR is 90 degrees. Since $x = 35$, the measure of angle QPR is $180 - 90 - 35 = 55$. Now, since $PQ = PS$, the angles opposite these sides are congruent. So angle PQS has measure $\frac{180-55}{2} = $ 62.5. Therefore $y = 90 - 62.5 = $ **27.5**.

Here is a picture of the triangle with some of the angles filled in.

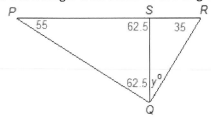

9.
* We redraw the three triangles next to each other so that congruent angles match up.

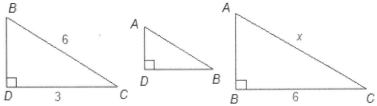

We now set up a ratio, cross multiply, and divide: $\frac{6}{3} = \frac{x}{6}$. So $36 = 3x$, and therefore $x = \mathbf{12}$.

10.
* Since the hexagon is regular, $BC = EF = CD = 6$. Now let's add a bit to the picture.

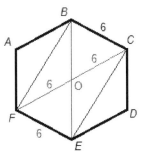

Again, note that the hexagon is regular. So each angle of triangle BOC is 60 degrees. Thus, triangle BOC is equilateral. So $OF = OC = BC = 6$. Since $EF = 6$ and $FC = 12$, triangle CEF is a 30, 60, 90 triangle. It follows that $CE = 6\sqrt{3}$. Since $BCEF$ is a rectangle, $BF = 6\sqrt{3}$ as well. Therefore the perimeter of rectangle is

$$6 + 6 + 6\sqrt{3} + 6\sqrt{3} = 12 + 12\sqrt{3} \approx 32.78.$$

To the nearest tenth the answer is **32.8**.

11.

* First note that

$$xw + xz + yw + yz = x(w + z) + y(w + z) = (x + y)(w + z)$$

Now, $k = x + y$, $k = w + z$, and so $(x + y)(w + z) = k \cdot k = k^2$. So the answer is choice (D).

Remark: Note that the angle labeled k is an exterior angle of both triangles. We have used two exterior angles here, one for each triangle.

Solution by picking numbers: Let's choose values for x, y and z, say $x = 40$, $y = 50$, and $z = 30$. Each unlabeled interior angle is $180 - 40 - 50 = 90$, and so $w = 180 - 90 - 30 = 60$. Now,

$$xw + xz + yw + yz$$
$$= (40)(60) + (40)(30) + (50)(60) + (50)(30)$$
$$= \mathbf{8100}$$

Since the angle labeled with k is supplementary with the unlabeled angle, $k = 180 - 90 = 90$. So let's plug $k = 90$ into each answer choice.

    (A) 2025
    (B) 45
    (C) 90
    (D) 8100

Since (A), (B), and (C), came out incorrect, the answer is choice (D).

12.

* Recall that the hexagon consists of 6 equilateral triangles each of equal area.

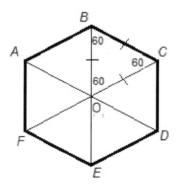

So the area of one of these triangles is $\frac{1}{6} \cdot \frac{75\sqrt{3}}{2} = \frac{25\sqrt{3}}{4}$. The side length of one of these triangles is then 5 (see notes below). Since the square and hexagon share a common side, the length of a side of the square is also 5. It follows that the perimeter of the square is $4 \cdot 5 = \mathbf{20}$.

Notes: (1) The area of an equilateral triangle with side length s is $\boldsymbol{A} = \frac{\sqrt{3}}{4} \boldsymbol{s^2}$ (see note (2) below).

In this problem we found that the area of one equilateral triangle was $\frac{25\sqrt{3}}{4}$. It follows that $\frac{\sqrt{3}}{4} s^2 = \frac{\sqrt{3}}{4} \cdot 25$. So $s^2 = 25$, and therefore $s = 5$.

(2) Most students do not know the formula for the area of an equilateral triangle, so here is a quick derivation.

Let's start by drawing a picture of an equilateral triangle with side length s, and draw an **altitude** from a vertex to the opposite base. Note that an altitude of an equilateral triangle is the same as the **median** and **angle bisector** (this is in fact true for any isosceles triangle).

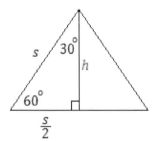

So we get two 30, 60, 90 right triangles with a leg of length $\frac{s}{2}$ and hypotenuse of length s.

We can find h by recalling that the side opposite the 60 degree angle has length $\sqrt{3}$ times the length of the side opposite the 30 degree angle. So $h = \frac{\sqrt{3}s}{2}$.

Alternatively, we can use the Pythagorean Theorem to find h:

$$h^2 = s^2 - \left(\frac{s}{2}\right)^2 = s^2 - \frac{s^2}{4} = \frac{3s^2}{4}. \text{ So } h = \frac{\sqrt{3}s}{2}.$$

It follows that the area of the triangle is

$$A = \frac{1}{2}\left(\frac{s}{2} + \frac{s}{2}\right)\left(\frac{\sqrt{3}s}{2}\right) = \frac{1}{2}s\left(\frac{\sqrt{3}s}{2}\right) = \frac{\sqrt{3}}{4}s^2.$$

OPTIONAL MATERIAL

CHALLENGE QUESTIONS

1. A cube is inscribed in a cone of radius 1 and height 2 so that one face of the cube is contained in the base of the cone. What is the length of a side of the cube?

Solution

1.

Let x be the length of a side of the cube. Slice the cone from the vertex to the base so that it cuts through the diagonal of the square base of the cube. We get the following picture.

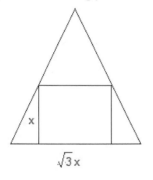
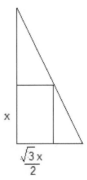

We can now set up the following ratio: $\frac{1}{2} = \frac{1 - \frac{x\sqrt{2}}{2}}{x}$. Cross multiplying gives $x = 2 - x\sqrt{2}$ or $x + x\sqrt{2} = 2$. So we have $x(1 + \sqrt{2}) = 2$, and therefore $x = \frac{2}{1+\sqrt{2}}$. By rationalizing the denominator, this can be simplified to $x = 2\sqrt{2} - 2$.

178

LESSON 15
PASSPORT TO ADVANCED MATH

Reminder: Before beginning this lesson remember to redo the problems from Lessons 3, 7 and 11 that you have marked off. Do not "unmark" a question unless you get it correct.

The Distributive Property

The **distributive property** says that for all real numbers a, b, and c

$$a(b + c) = ab + ac$$

More specifically, this property says that the operation of multiplication distributes over addition. The distributive property is very important as it allows us to multiply and factor algebraic expressions.

Numeric example: Show that $2(3 + 4) = 2 \cdot 3 + 2 \cdot 4$

Solution: $2(3 + 4) = 2 \cdot 7 = 14$ and $2 \cdot 3 + 2 \cdot 4 = 6 + 8 = 14$.

Geometric Justification: The following picture gives a physical representation of the distributive property for this example.

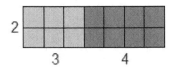

Note that the area of the light grey rectangle is $2 \cdot 3$, the area of the dark grey rectangle is $2 \cdot 4$, and the area of the whole rectangle is $2(3 + 4)$.

Algebraic examples: Use the distributive property to write each algebraic expression in an equivalent form.

$\qquad$ (1) $2(x + 1)$ $\qquad$ (2) $x(y - 3)$ $\qquad$ (3) $-(x - y)$

Solutions: (1) $2(x + 1) = 2x + 2$

(2) $x(y - 3) = xy - 3x$

(3) $-(x - y) = -x + y$

179

Factoring

When we use the distributive property in the opposite direction, we usually call it **factoring**.

Examples: (1) $2x + 4y = 2(x + 2y)$

(2) $3x + 5xy = x(3 + 5y)$

(3) $6xy + 9yz = 3y(2x + 3z)$

Here are some more sophisticated techniques for factoring:

The Difference of Two Squares: $a^2 - b^2 = (a - b)(a + b)$

Examples: (1) $x^2 - 9 = (x - 3)(x + 3)$
(2) $4x^2 - 25y^2 = (2x - 5y)(2x + 5y)$
(3) $36 - 49x^2y^2 = (6 - 7xy)(6 + 7xy)$

Trinomial Factoring: $x^2 - (a + b)x + ab = (x - a)(x - b)$

Examples: (1) $x^2 - 5x + 6 = (x - 2)(x - 3)$

(2) $x^2 - 2x - 35 = (x - 7)(x + 5)$

(3) $x^2 + 14x + 33 = (x + 3)(x + 11)$

Square Root Property

The **square root property** says that if $x^2 = a^2$, then $x = \pm a$.

For example, the equation $x^2 = 9$ has the two solutions $x = 3$ and $x = -3$.

Important note: Using the square root property is different from taking a square root. We apply the square root property to an equation of the form $x^2 = a^2$ to get two solutions, whereas when we take the positive square root of a number we get just one answer.

For example when we take the positive square root of 9 we get 3, i.e. $\sqrt{9} = 3$. But when we apply the square root property to the equation $x^2 = 9$, we have seen that we get the two solutions $x = 3$ and $x = -3$.

Example: Solve the equation $(x - 3)^2 = 2$ using the square root property.

180

Solution: When we apply the square root property we get $x - 3 = \pm\sqrt{2}$. We then add 3 to each side of this last equation to get the two solutions $x = 3 \pm \sqrt{2}$.

Completing the Square

Completing the square is a technique with many useful applications. We complete the square on an expression of the form

$$x^2 + bx$$

To complete the square we simply take half of b, and then square the result. In other words we get $\left(\frac{b}{2}\right)^2$.

The expression $x^2 + bx + \left(\frac{b}{2}\right)^2$ is always a perfect square. In fact,

$$x^2 + bx + \left(\frac{b}{2}\right)^2 = \left(x + \frac{b}{2}\right)^2$$

For example, let's complete the square in the expression $x^2 + 6x$.

Well half of 6 is 3, and when we square 3 we get 9. So the new expression is $x^2 + 6x + 9$ which factors as $(x + 3)^2$.

Important notes: (1) When we complete the square we usually get an expression that is <u>not</u> equal to the original expression. For example, $x^2 + 6x \neq x^2 + 6x + 9$.

(2) The coefficient of x^2 <u>must</u> be 1 before we complete the square. So, for example, we cannot complete the square on the expression $2x^2 + 32x$.

But we can first factor out the 2 to get $2(x^2 + 16x)$, and then complete the square on the expression $x^2 + 16x$ to get $2(x^2 + 16x + 64)$.

Note that we increased the expression by $2 \cdot 64 = 128$.

We will see many applications of completing the square below.

Solving Quadratic Equations

A quadratic equation has the form $\boldsymbol{ax^2 + bx + c = 0}$.

181

Let's use a simple example to illustrate the various methods for solving such an equation

LEVEL 3: ADVANCED MATH

$$x^2 - 2x = 15$$

1. In the quadratic equation above, find the positive solution for x.

Solution by guessing: We plug in guesses for x until we find the answer. For example, if we guess that $x = 3$, then we get $3^2 - 2 \cdot 3 = 9 - 6 = 3$. This is too small.

Let's try $x = 5$ next. We get $5^2 - 2 \cdot 5 = 25 - 10 = 15$. This is correct. So the answer is **5**.

Solution by factoring: We bring everything to the left hand side of the equation to get $x^2 - 2x - 15 = 0$. We then factor the left hand side to get $(x - 5)(x + 3) = 0$. So $x - 5 = 0$ or $x + 3 = 0$. It follows that $x = 5$ or $x = -3$. Since we want the positive solution for x, the answer is **5**.

Solution by using the quadratic formula: As in the last solution we bring everything to the left hand side of the equation to get

$$x^2 - 2x - 15 = 0.$$

We identify $a = 1$, $b = -2$, and $c = -15$.

$$x = \frac{-b \pm \sqrt{b^2 - 4ac}}{2a} = \frac{2 \pm \sqrt{4 + 60}}{2} = \frac{2 \pm \sqrt{64}}{2} = \frac{2 \pm 8}{2} = 1 \pm 4.$$

So we get $x = 1 + 4 = 5$ or $x = 1 - 4 = -3$. Since we want the positive solution for x, the answer is **5**.

Solution by completing the square: For this solution we leave the constant on the right hand side: $x^2 - 2x = 15$.

We take half of -2, which is -1, and square this number to get 1. We then add 1 to each side of the equation to get $x^2 - 2x + 1 = 15 + 1$. This is equivalent to $(x - 1)^2 = 16$. We now apply the square root property to get $x - 1 = \pm 4$. So $x = 1 \pm 4$. This yields the two solutions $1 + 4 = 5$, and $1 - 4 = -3$. Since we want the positive solution for x, the answer is **5**.

Graphical solution: In your graphing calculator press the Y= button, and enter the following.

$$Y1 = X\text{^}2 - 2X - 15$$

Now press ZOOM 6 to graph the parabola in a standard window. Then press 2nd TRACE (which is CALC) 2 (or select ZERO), move the cursor just to the left of the second x-intercept and press ENTER. Now move the cursor just to the right of the second x-intercept and press ENTER again. Press ENTER once more, and you will see that the x-coordinate of the second x-intercept is **5**.

Standard Form for the Equation of a Circle

The standard form for the equation of a circle with center (h, k) and radius r is

$$(x - h)^2 + (y - k)^2 = r^2.$$

Example: Find the center and radius of the circle with equation $(x - 1)^2 + (y + 2)^2 = 3$

We have $h = 1$ and $k = -2$. So the center of the circle is $(1, -2)$. The radius is $r = \sqrt{3}$.

Remark: Note that in this example $(y + 2) = (y - (-2))$. This is why $k = -2$ instead of 2.

General Form for the Equation of a Circle

The general form for the equation of a circle is

$$x^2 + y^2 + ax + by + c = 0.$$

This form for the equation is not very useful since we cannot easily determine the center or radius of the circle. We will want to apply the method of completing the square twice in order to change the equation into standard form. Let's use an example to illustrate this procedure.

183

LEVEL 4: ADVANCED MATH

2. In the standard (x, y) coordinate plane, what are the coordinates of the center of the circle whose equation is

$$x^2 - 8x + y^2 + 10y + 15 = 0 ?$$

(A) $(4,5)$
(B) $(4,-5)$
(C) $(-4,5)$
(D) $(-5,-4)$

* Solution by completing the square:

$x^2 - 8x = x^2 - 8x + 16 - 16 = (x-4)^2 - 16.$

$y^2 + 10y = y^2 + 10y + 25 - 25 = (y+5)^2 - 25.$

So $x^2 - 8x + y^2 + 10y + 15 = (x-4)^2 - 16 + (y+5)^2 - 25 + 15$
$$= (x-4)^2 + (y+5)^2 - 26.$$

So the center of the circle is $(4, -5)$, choice (B).

Notes: (1) To complete the square in the expression $x^2 - 8x$, we first take half of -8 to get -4. We then square this result to get 16. Note that $x^2 - 8x + 16 = (x-4)(x-4) = (x-4)^2$.

But be aware that it is not really okay to add 16 here – this changes the expression. So we have to undo the damage we just did. We undo this damage by subtracting 16.

(2) To complete the square in the expression $y^2 + 10y$, we first take half of 10 to get 5. We then square this result to get 25. Note that we have $y^2 + 10y + 25 = (y+5)(y+5) = (y+5)^2$.

But be aware that it is not really okay to add 25 here – this changes the expression. So we have to undo the damage we just did. We undo this damage by subtracting 25.

(3) Note that we never finished writing the equation of the circle. We didn't need to since the question asked only to find the center of the circle.

For completeness let's write the equation of the circle. We have

$$(x - 4)^2 + (y + 5)^2 - 26 = 0,$$

or equivalently

$$(x - 4)^2 + (y + 5)^2 = 26$$

So we have an equation of a circle with center $(4, -5)$ and radius $\sqrt{26}$.

Now try to solve each of the following problems. The answers to these problems, followed by full solutions are at the end of this lesson. **Do not** look at the answers until you have attempted these problems yourself. Please remember to mark off any problems you get wrong.

LEVEL 2: ADVANCED MATH

$$5(3x - 2)(2x + 1)$$

3. Which of the following is equivalent to the expression above?

    (A) $30x^2 - 10$
    (B) $30x^2 - 5x - 10$
    (C) $25x^2 - 20$
    (D) $15x$

LEVEL 3: ADVANCED MATH

4. In the xy-plane, the parabola with equation $y = (x + 7)^2$ intersects the line with equation $y = 9$ at two points, P and Q. What is the length of $\overline{PQ}$?

LEVEL 4: ADVANCED MATH

$$h(x) = (x - 3)(x + 7)$$

5. Which of the following is an equivalent form of the function h above in which the minimum value of h appears as a coefficient or constant?

    (A) $h(x) = x^2 - 21$
    (B) $h(x) = x^2 + 4x - 21$
    (C) $h(x) = (x - 2)^2 - 21$
    (D) $h(x) = (x + 2)^2 - 25$

185

$$y = cx^2 - k$$
$$y = 5$$

6. In the system of equations above, c and k are constants. For which of the following values of c and k does the system of equations have no real solutions?

   (A) $c = -2, k = -6$
   (B) $c = 2, k = -6$
   (C) $c = 2, k = -4$
   (D) $c = 2, k = 4$

$$g(t) = \frac{1}{(t+1)^2 - 6(t+1) + 9}$$

7. For what value of t is the function g above undefined?

LEVEL 5: ADVANCED MATH

8. What are the solutions to $5x^2 - 30x + 20 = 0$?

   (A) $x = -20 \pm 20\sqrt{5}$
   (B) $x = -20 \pm \sqrt{5}$
   (C) $x = 3 \pm 20\sqrt{5}$
   (D) $x = 3 \pm \sqrt{5}$

$$y = p(x+3)(x-5)$$

9. In the quadratic equation above, p is a nonzero constant. The graph of the equation in the xy-plane is a parabola with vertex (h, k). What is the value of $h - \frac{k}{p}$?

10. If $(2x + m)(kx + n) = 6x^2 + 29x + c$ for all values of x, and $m + n = 13$, what is the value of c ?

    (A) 9
    (B) 13
    (C) 28
    (D) 30

$$x^2 + y^2 - 6x + 2y = -6$$

11. The equation of a circle in the xy-plane is shown above. What is the radius of the circle?

$$x^3 - 3x^2 + 5x - 15 = 0$$

12. For what real value of x is the equation above true?

Answers

1. 5	5. D	9. 17
2. B	6. B	10. D
3. B	7. 2	11. 2
4. 6	8. D	12. 3

Full Solutions

4.

*Solution using the square root property: Replacing y with 9 in the first equation yields $(x + 7)^2 = 9$. We use the square root property to get $x + 7 = \pm 3$. So $x = -7 \pm 3$. So the two solutions are $x = -7 + 3 = -4$ and $x = -7 - 3 = -10$.

Sp $P = (-4,9)$ and $Q = (-10,9)$. The distance between these two points is $|-10 - (-4)| = |-10 + 4| = |-6| = \mathbf{6}$.

Notes: (1) To find the points of intersection of the parabola and the line, we solve the given system of equations. We chose to use the **substitution method** here.

(2) Instead of formally applying the square root property to solve $(x + 7)^2 = 9$, we can simply "guess" the solutions, or solve the equation informally. It's not too hard to see that $x = -4$ and $x = -10$ will make the equation true.

(3) It's not necessary to write down the points P and Q. Since the y-coordinates of the two points are the same, we can simply subtract one from the other (disregarding the minus sign if it appears) to get the desired distance.

(4) We can also plot the two points and observe that the distance between them is 6

5.

*Quick solution The x-intercepts of the graph of this function (which is a parabola) are $(3,0)$ and $(-7,0)$. The x-coordinate of the vertex is midway between 3 and -7. So the vertex has x-coordinate $\frac{3-7}{2} = -2$. The answer must therefore be choice (D).

Notes: (1) The minimum value of h is the y-coordinate of the vertex of the parabola that is the graph of h. In this case, the minimum value is $h(-2) = (-2 - 3)(-2 + 7) = (-5)(5) = -25$.

(2) The question is really just asking us to rewrite the quadratic function in the standard form $y = a(x - h)^2 + k$. In this form, the minimum value appears as the constant k.

(3) The given equation $h(x) = (x - 3)(x + 7)$ is in a form where the x-intercepts 3 and -7 of the parabola are displayed as constants.

(Technically an x-intercept is a point and not a number, but the SAT seems to abuse language a bit here, and so I will do the same.)

Algebraic solution: We first put the function h into general form by expanding the product $(x - 3)(x + 7) = x^2 + 4x - 21$.

We now complete the square on $x^2 + 4x$ to get $x^2 + 4x + 4$.

So $x^2 + 4x - 21 = x^2 + 4x + 4 - 4 - 21 = (x + 2)^2 - 25$, choice (D).

Important note: The function can also be written $h(x) = x^2 + 4x - 21$ as shown in the algebraic solution. This is answer choice (B). This answer is **wrong** because the minimum value of h, which is -25, does **not** appear as a constant or coefficient!

6.

*Solution using the square root property: Replacing y with 5 in the first equation yields $5 = cx^2 - k$. Adding k to each side of this equation give us $5 + k = cx^2$. We now divide by c (assuming $c \neq 0$) to get $x^2 = \frac{5+k}{c}$. We use the square root property to get $x = \pm\sqrt{\frac{5+k}{c}}$.

This will yield no real solutions if the expression under the square root is negative, that is if $5 + k$ and c have opposite signs.

Let's start with choice (C) and guess that $c = 2$ and $k = -4$. Then $5 + k = 1$. Since c and $5 + k$ are both positive, we get 2 real solutions and so we can eliminate choice (C).

Let's try (B) next and guess that $c = 2$ and $k = -6$. Then $5 + k = -1$. So c is positive and $5 + k$ is negative, and the answer is (B).

7.

* g will be undefined when the denominator is zero. So we solve the equation $(t + 1)^2 - 6(t + 1) + 9 = 0$. The left hand side of the equation factors as $(t + 1 - 3)^2 = 0$, or equivalently $(t - 2)^2 = 0$. So $t - 2 = 0$, and therefore $t = \mathbf{2}$.

Note: Many students might find it hard to see how to factor the expression $(t + 1)^2 - 6(t + 1) + 9$. To help see how to do this we can make a formal substitution of $u = t + 1$. The expression then becomes $u^2 - 6u + 9$ which factors as $(u - 3)^2$. The equation $(u - 3)^2 = 0$ has solution $u = 3$. But remember that $u = t + 1$. So we have $t + 1 = 3$, and so $t = 3 - 1 = \mathbf{2}$.

8.

* Let's divide through by 5 first to simplify the equation. We get $x^2 - 6x + 4 = 0$. Let's solve this equation by completing the square.

$$x^2 - 6x = -4$$
$$x^2 - 6x + 9 = -4 + 9$$
$$(x - 3)^2 = 5$$
$$x - 3 = \pm\sqrt{5}$$
$$\mathbf{x = 3 \pm \sqrt{5}}$$

This is choice (D).

Note: This is just one of several ways to solve this problem. See problem 1 in this lesson for several other methods.

9.

* **Solution by completing the square:** Let's put the equation into standard form. We first multiply $(x + 3)(x - 5)$ to get the equation in general form:

$$y = p(x^2 - 2x - 15)$$

We now complete the square as follows:

$$y = p(x^2 - 2x + 1 - 16) = p(x^2 - 2x + 1) - 16p$$
$$= p(x - 1)^2 - 16p$$

So $h = 1$, $k = -16p$, and $h - \dfrac{k}{p} = 1 - \dfrac{-16p}{p} = 1 + 16 = \mathbf{17}$.

10.

* We need $2k = 6$. So $k = 3$. We now have

$$(2x + m)(3x + n) = 6x^2 + 29x + c$$

We need $2n + 3m = 29$.

We can now either use trial and error or formally solve the system of equations

$$3m + 2n = 29$$
$$m + n = 13$$

to get $m = 3$ and $n = 10$

It follows that $c = mn = 3 \cdot 10 = 30$, choice (D).

11.

* Solution by completing the square: We put the equation into standard form by completing the square twice:

$$x^2 - 6x + 9 + y^2 + 2y + 1 = -6 + 9 + 1$$
$$(x - 3)^2 + (y + 1)^2 = 4$$

So the radius of the circle is **2**.

12.

* Solution by factoring: Let's factor the left hand side of the equation by grouping the first two terms together and the last two terms together.

$$(x^3 - 3x^2) + (5x - 15) = x^2(x - 3) + 5(x - 3) = (x - 3)(x^2 + 5)$$

So we have $(x - 3)(x^2 + 5) = 0$. The only real solution is $x = $ **3**.

OPTIONAL MATERIAL

LEVEL 6: ADVANCED MATH

1. Let f and g be functions such that $f(x) = ax^2 + bx + c$ and $g(x) = ax + b$. If $g(1) = 2b - a + 25$ and $g(2) = 2a - 24$, then for what value of x does $f(x) = f(8)$, where $x \neq 8$?

2. CHALLENGE QUESTION

2. Use the method of completing the square to derive the quadratic formula.

Solutions

1.
* $g(1) = a(1) + b = a + b$. So $a + b = 2b - a + 25$, and therefore $2a = b + 25$. $g(2) = a(2) + b = 2a + b$, and so $2a + b = 2a - 24$. Thus, $b = -24$. We also have $2a = b + 25 = -24 + 25 = 1$. Thus $a = \frac{1}{2}$.

Then $f(x) = \frac{x^2}{2} - 24x + c$, and $f(8) = \frac{8^2}{2} - 24(8) + c = -160 + c$. If $f(x) = f(8)$, then we have $\frac{x^2}{2} - 24x + c = -160 + c$, and so $\frac{x^2}{2} - 24x + 160 = 0$. Let's multiply each side of this equation by 2 to eliminate the denominator. We get $x^2 - 48x + 320 = 0$. There are several ways to solve this equation. Here are a few.

Factoring: $(x - 8)(x - 40) = 0$. So $x = \textbf{40}$.

Completing the square: We take half of -48, which is -24, and square this number to get 576. We then add 576 to each side of the equation to get $x^2 - 48x + 576 + 320 = 576$. This is equivalent to $(x - 24)^2 = 256$. We now apply the square root property to get $x - 24 = \pm 16$. So $x = 24 \pm 16$. This yields the two solutions $24 - 16 = 8$, and $24 + 16 = \textbf{40}$.

The quadratic formula:

$$x = \frac{-b \pm \sqrt{b^2 - 4ac}}{2a} = \frac{48 \pm \sqrt{2304 - 1280}}{2} = \frac{48 \pm \sqrt{1024}}{2} = \frac{48 \pm 32}{2} = \textbf{24} \pm \textbf{16}.$$

As in the previous solution we get $x = 8$ or $x = \textbf{40}$.

Graphically: In your graphing calculator press the Y= button, and enter the following.

$$Y1 = X^2 - 48X + 320$$

Now press ZOOM 6 to graph the parabola in a standard window. It needs to be zoomed out, so we will need to extend the viewing window. Press the WINDOW button, and change Xmax to 100, Ymin to -50, and Ymax to 50. Then press 2nd TRACE (which is CALC) 2 (or select ZERO). Then move the cursor just to the left of the second x-intercept and press ENTER. Now move the cursor just to the right of the second x-intercept and press ENTER again. Press ENTER once more, and you will see that the x-coordinate of the second x-intercept is **40**.

Remark: The choices made for Xmax, Ymin and Ymax were just to try to ensure that the second x-intercept would appear in the viewing window. Many other windows would work just as well.

2.

*

$$ax^2 + bx + c = 0$$

$$ax^2 + bx = -c$$

$$x^2 + \frac{b}{a}x = -\frac{c}{a}$$

$$x^2 + \frac{b}{a}x + \left(\frac{b}{2a}\right)^2 = -\frac{c}{a} + \left(\frac{b}{2a}\right)^2$$

$$\left(x + \frac{b}{2a}\right)^2 = -\frac{c}{a} + \frac{b^2}{4a^2}$$

$$\left(x + \frac{b}{2a}\right)^2 = \frac{b^2}{4a^2} - \frac{c}{a}\left(\frac{4a}{4a}\right)$$

$$\left(x + \frac{b}{2a}\right)^2 = \frac{b^2 - 4ac}{4a^2}$$

$$x + \frac{b}{2a} = \pm\frac{\sqrt{b^2 - 4ac}}{2a}$$

$$x = -\frac{b}{2a} \pm \frac{\sqrt{b^2 - 4ac}}{2a}$$

$$x = \frac{-b \pm \sqrt{b^2 - 4ac}}{2a}$$

Download additional solutions for free here:

www.thesatmathprep.com/28Les800.html

LESSON 16
DATA ANALYSIS

Reminder: Before beginning this lesson remember to redo the problems from Lessons 4, 8 and 12 that you have marked off. Do not "unmark" a question unless you get it correct.

Scatterplots

A scatterplot is a graph of plotted points that show the relationship between two sets of data.

LEVEL 3: DATA ANALYSIS

Questions 1 - 3 refer to the following information.

The scatterplot below shows the numbers of incidences of melanoma, per 100,000 people from 1940 to 1970.

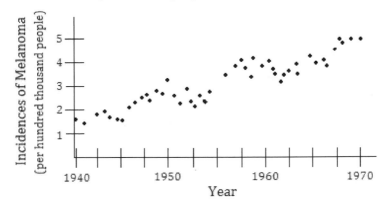

1. Based on the data shown in the figure, in 1969, approximately how many incidences of melanoma were there?

    (A) 5
    (B) 5000
    (C) 400,000
    (D) 500,000

* The following drawing gives the answer:

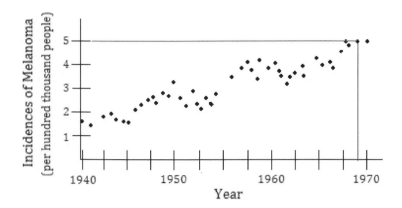

Note that 5 on the vertical axis corresponds to 500,000 people. So the answer is choice (D).

Note: Since the scatterplot is giving incidences of melanoma per hundred thousand people, if we use the labels on the vertical axis to find the range, we need to multiply the result by 100,000.

LEVEL 4: DATA ANALYSIS

2. Based on the data shown in the figure, which of the following values is closest to the range of the number of incidences of melanoma between 1945 and 1950?

   (A) 50,000
   (B) 100,000
   (C) 170,000
   (D) 360,000

* Between 1945 and 1950, the highest data point is at approximately 3.2 and the lowest data point is at approximately 1.5. It follows that the range is approximately

$$(3.2 - 1.5) \times 100,000 = 1.7 \times 100,000 = 170,000 \text{ incidences.}$$

This is choice (C).

Notes: (1) The **range** of a set of data is the difference between the largest data value and the smallest data value.

For example, the range of *all* the data in the scatterplot is approximately $(5 - 1.4) \times 100,000 = 3.6 \times 100,000 = 360,000$ incidences.

194

(2) This question wants the range of data that appears between 1945 and 1950. Here is a picture with the two pieces of data that contribute to the range circled.

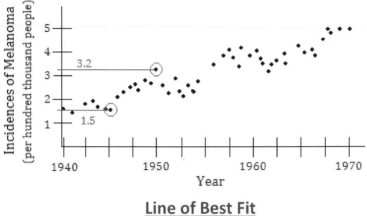

Line of Best Fit

The line of best fit for the scatterplot given above would look something like this.

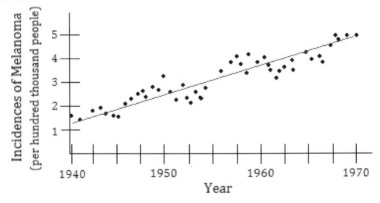

Let's try an SAT problem about the line of best fit that uses this figure.

LEVEL 3: DATA ANALYSIS

3. Based on the line of best fit to the data, as shown in the figure, which of the following values is closest to the average yearly increase in the number of incidences of melanoma?

    (A) 13,000
    (B) 3300
    (C) 0.33
    (D) 0.13

* The average yearly increase in the number of incidences of melanoma is just the slope of the line of best fit. So we get approximately $\frac{500,000-100,000}{1970-1940} = \frac{400,000}{30} \approx 13,333.33$. So the best estimate is 13,000, choice (A).

Notes: (1) Remember that the slope of the line passing through the points (x_1, y_1) and (x_2, y_2) is $m = \frac{y_2-y_1}{x_2-x_1}$.

(2) In this problem we need to be a bit careful about the y-values. As an example, the number 1 on the y-axis actually represents 100,000 people, and not 1 person. So when we compute the slope we are using the points $(1940, 100,000)$ and $(1970, 500,000)$.

If we were to use the points $(1940,1)$ and $(1970,5)$ instead we would get a slope of $\frac{5-1}{1970-1940} = \frac{4}{30} \approx .13$, and we would choose (D), an answer choice which is <u>not</u> correct!

(3) As an alternative, we can use the points $(1940,1)$ and $(1970,5)$ to get a slope of approximately .13, and then multiply by 100,000 to get approximately 13,000, choice (A).

Scatterplot Classification

The following scatterplots show **positive associations**.

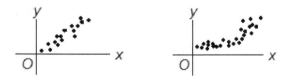

The scatterplot on the left shows a linear positive association, whereas the scatterplot on the right shows a nonlinear positive association. The rightmost scatterplot looks like it might show an exponential positive association.

Here are a few more scatterplots.

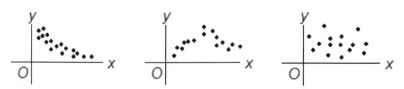

The leftmost scatterplot shows a nonlinear (possibly exponential) **negative association**, whereas the other two show **no association**.

Other Graph Types

Several other types of graphs may appear on the SAT such as bar graphs, line graphs, circle graphs, and histograms. Here is an example of an SAT math problem involving a histogram.

LEVEL 2: PROBLEM SOLVING AND DATA

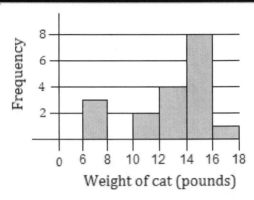

4. The histogram above shows the distribution of the weights, in pounds, of 18 cats in a shelter. Which of the following could be the median weight of the 18 cats represented in the histogram?

   (A) 10 pounds
   (B) 11 pounds
   (C) 13.5 pounds
   (D) 16 pounds

Solution using a specific list: Let's make a possible list of the cats' weights in increasing order, including repetitions. We will always choose the left endpoint of each bar in the histogram.

   6, 6 ,6, 10, 10, 12, 12, 12, 12, 14, 14, 14, 14, 14, 14, 14, 14, 16

Now strike off two numbers at a time simultaneously, one from each end until just two numbers are left.

   ~~6, 6 ,6, 10, 10, 12, 12, 12,~~ 12, 14, ~~14, 14, 14, 14, 14, 14, 14, 16~~

The median of these numbers is the average of 12 and 14, or

$$\frac{12+14}{2} = 13.$$

197

This isn't one of the answer choices, but it should not be too hard to see now that we can get a possible median by taking one number between 12 and 14, and another number between 14 and 16, and then taking their average. For example, we can use 13 and 14 to get $\frac{13+14}{2} = 13.5$, choice (C).

Notes: (1) The **median** of a list of data is the middle number when the data is written in ascending (or descending) order. When the list consists of an even number of data points, the median is the average (arithmetic mean) of the middle two numbers.

(2) Choosing the left endpoint of each bar was arbitrary. We could have started by choosing any numbers between the left and right endpoint of each bar. For example, for the first bar we could have chosen 8, 8, 8, or we could have chosen 6, 7, 8, or even 6.2, 7.1, 7.7.

(3) The important part of the first step is to figure out which bar each of the two middle numbers lies on. This can be done by creating a list as we did in the solution, or visually just by looking at the histogram.

(4) We get a possible median by taking any number on the "12 – 14 bar" and any number on the "14 – 16 bar."

At one extreme we can take 12 and 14 to get a median of $\frac{12+14}{2} = 13$. At the other extreme we can take 14 and 16 to get a median of $\frac{14+16}{2} = 15$.

By choosing the appropriate numbers we can force the median to be any number between 13 and 15.

For example, if we want the median to be 14.2, we can choose 14 and 14.4.

Try to solve each of the following problems. The answers to these problems, followed by full solutions are at the end of this lesson. **Do not** look at the answers until you have attempted these problems yourself. Please remember to mark off any problems you get wrong.

LEVEL 2: DATA ANALYSIS

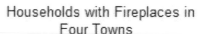

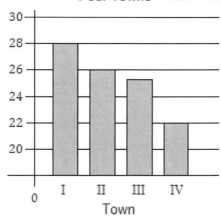

5. * The number of households with fireplaces in 4 towns is shown in the graph above. If the total number of such households is 10,150, what is an appropriate label for the vertical axis of the graph?

   (A) Number of households with fireplaces (in tens)
   (B) Number of households with fireplaces (in hundreds)
   (C) Number of households with fireplaces (in thousands)
   (D) Number of households with fireplaces (in tens of thousands)

199

LEVEL 3: DATA ANALYSIS

6. Which of the following graphs best shows a strong positive association between x and y ?

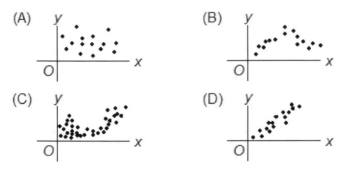

Mean Annual Salary of NBA Players Each Year from 1980 to 1984

7. According to the line graph above, the mean annual salary of an NBA player in 1981 was what fraction of the mean annual salary of an NBA player in 1984 ?

200

Questions 8 - 9 refer to the following information.

The graph below displays the total cost C, in dollars, of renting a car for d days.

8. What does the C-intercept represent in the graph?

    (A) The total number of days the cars is rented
    (B) The total number of cars rented
    (C) The initial cost of renting the car
    (D) The increase in cost to rent the car for each additional day

9. Which of the following represents the relationship between C and d ?

    (A) $d = 50C$
    (B) $C = 50d$
    (C) $C = 100d + 50$
    (D) $C = 50d + 50$

201

LEVEL 4: DATA ANALYSIS

10. Which scatterplot shows a relationship that is modeled with the equation $y = ab^x$, where $a > 0$ and $0 < b < 1$?

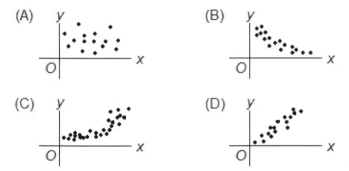

LEVEL 5: DATA ANALYSIS

Questions 11 - 12 refer to the following information.

A biologist places a colony consisting of 5000 bacteria into a petri dish. After the initial placement of the bacteria at time $t = 0$, the biologist measures and estimates the number of bacteria present every half hour. This data was then fitted by an exponential curve of the form $y = c \cdot 2^{kt}$ where c and k are constants, t is measured in hours, and y is measured in thousands of bacteria. The scatterplot together with the exponential curve are shown below.

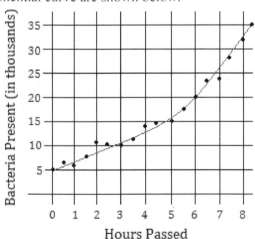

202

11. According to the scatterplot, the biologist's measurements indicate that the number of bacteria present quadrupled in 6 hours, and the exponential curve passes through the corresponding data point at time $t = 6$. The exponential function also agrees with the initial number of bacteria. Compute ck.

12. Suppose that the data was fitted with a quadratic function of the form $t^2 + bt + c$ instead of an exponential function. Assume that the quadratic function agrees with the scatterplot at times $t = 0$ and $t = 6$. What is the t-coordinate of the vertex of the graph of the quadratic function?

Answers

1. D	5. B	9. D
2. C	6. D	10. B
3. A	7. 4/7 or .571	11. 5/3, 1.66 or 1.67
4. C	8. C	12. 7/4 or 1.75

Full Solutions

6.
* Only the scatterplot in choice (D) is continually moving upward from left to right. So the answer is choice (D).

7.
* According to the graph the mean annual salary of an NBA player in 1981 was $200,000 and the mean annual salary of an NBA player in 1984 was $350,000. So the answer is $\frac{200,000}{350,000} = $ **4/7** or **.571**.

8.
* The C-intercept of the graph is the point $(0,50)$. Notice that 50 is a cost. This observation eliminates choices (A) and (B). Since d is 0, the number 50 represents the cost for renting the car for 0 days. That is, it is the initial cost of renting the car, choice (C).

9.
* The slope of the line is 50, and the y-intercept is the point $(0,50)$. It follows that the equation of the line in slope-intercept form is $C = 50d + 50$, choice (D).

203

10.

* Choices (B) and (C) have the basic shape of exponential graphs. Choice (B) has a base between 0 and 1, whereas choice (C) has a base greater than 1. So the answer is choice (B).

11.

* Since there are 5000 bacteria present at time $t = 0$, we have $c = 5$. So $y = 5 \cdot 2^{kt}$.

We are given that $y = 4 \cdot 5 = 20$ when $t = 6$, so that $20 = 5 \cdot 2^{6k}$. Dividing each side of this equation by 5 yields $4 = 2^{6k}$. So we have $2^2 = 2^{6k}$, and therefore $2 = 6k$. So $k = \frac{2}{6} = \frac{1}{3}$, and $ck = 5 \cdot \frac{1}{3} = \mathbf{5/3.}$

Notes: (1) We can also grid in the decimals **1.66** or **1.67**.

(2) Since there are 5000 bacteria present at time $t = 0$, we see that the point $(0,5)$ is a data point. Since the exponential function agrees with the initial number of bacteria, we have that the point $(0,5)$ is also on the exponential curve. So $5 = c \cdot 2^{k \cdot 0} = c$. So $c = 5$.

This computation is not really necessary, because c is always the initial amount in the exponential function $y = c \cdot 2^{kt}$.

(3) After 6 hours, the biologist measured that 20,000 bacteria were present. Since the exponential curve matches the data point at 6 hours, we see that the point $(6,20)$ is both a data point and a point on the exponential curve.

In particular, $20 = 5 \cdot 2^{k \cdot 6} = 5 \cdot 2^{6k}$.

(4) A common mistake is to write $5 \cdot 2^{6k} = 10^{6k}$. The 5 CANNOT be combined in any way with the 2 as this would violate the usual order of operations.

To eliminate the 5, we divide each side of the equation by 5:

$$\frac{20}{5} = \frac{5 \cdot 2^{6k}}{5}$$

$$4 = 2^{6k}$$

(5) The expressions 4 and 2^{6k} both have a common base of 2. Indeed, $4 = 2^2$. So we have $2^2 = 2^{6k}$.

(6) When two expressions have the same base, the exponents must be equal. In this case, since $2^2 = 2^{6k}$, we must have $2 = 6k$.

12.

* Since there are 5000 bacteria present at time $t = 0$, we have $c = 5$. So $y = t^2 + bt + 5$.

According to the scatterplot, $y = 20$ when $t = 6$, so that we have $20 = 6^2 + 6b + 5 = 36 + 6b + 5 = 41 + 6b$. It follows that $6b = 20 - 41 = -21$, and therefore $b = -\frac{21}{6} = -\frac{7}{2}$.

The t-coordinate of the vertex of the graph of the quadratic function is $\frac{-\left(-\frac{7}{2}\right)}{2 \cdot 1} = \frac{7}{2} \div 2 = \frac{7}{2} \cdot \frac{1}{2} = \frac{7}{4}$ or **1.75**.

Notes: (1) Since the quadratic function agrees with the initial number of bacteria, we have that the point $(0,5)$ is on the quadratic curve. So $5 = 0^2 + b(0) + c = c$. Therefore $c = 5$.

This computation is not really necessary, because c is always the y-coordinate of the y-intercept of the graph of the quadratic equation. $y = at^2 + bt + c$.

(3) Recall that the general form for a quadratic function is

$$y = ax^2 + bx + c.$$

The graph of this function is a parabola whose vertex has x-coordinate

$$-\frac{b}{2a}$$

The parabola opens upwards if $a > 0$ and downwards if $a < 0$.

It follows that the graph of $y = t^2 - \frac{7}{2}t + 5$ has a vertex with t-coordinate $-\frac{\left(-\frac{7}{2}\right)}{2(1)} = \frac{7}{4}$.

(4) We can also find the vertex by putting the quadratic function into standard form by completing the square. See Lesson 15 for more details.

LESSON 17
HEART OF ALGEBRA

Reminder: Before beginning this lesson remember to redo the problems from Lessons 1, 5, 9 and 13 that you have marked off. Do not "unmark" a question unless you get it correct.

Absolute Value

Here are a few basic things you might want to know about absolute value for the SAT.

The **absolute value** of x, written $|x|$ is simply x if x is nonnegative, and $-x$ if x is negative. Put simply, $|x|$ just removes the minus sign if one is there.

Examples: $|3| = 3$, and $|-3| = 3$. Also, $|0| = 0$.

Geometrically, $|x - y|$ is the distance between x and y. In particular, $|x - y| = |y - x|$.

Examples: $|5 - 3| = |3 - 5| = 2$ because the distance between 3 and 5 is 2.

If $|x - 3| = 7$, then the distance between x and 3 is 7. So there are two possible values for x. They are $3 + 7 = 10$, and $3 - 7 = -4$. See the figure below for clarification.

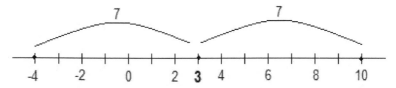

If $|x - 3| < 7$, then the distance between x and 3 is less than 7. If you look at the above figure you should be able to see that this is all x satisfying $-4 < x < 10$.

If $|x - 3| > 7$, then the distance between x and 3 is greater than 7. If you look at the above figure you should be able to see that this is all x satisfying $x < -4$ or $x > 10$.

Algebraically, we have the following. For $c > 0$,

$$|x| = c \text{ is equivalent to } x = c \text{ or } x = -c$$

$$|x| < c \text{ is equivalent to } -c < x < c$$

$$|x| > c \text{ is equivalent to } x < -c \text{ or } x > c.$$

Let's look at the same examples as before algebraically.

Examples: If $|x - 3| = 7$, then $x - 3 = 7$ or $x - 3 = -7$. So $x = 10$ or $x = -4$.

If $|x - 3| < 7$, then $-7 < x - 3 < 7$. So $-4 < x < 10$.

If $|x - 3| > 7$, then $x - 3 < -7$ or $x - 3 > 7$. So $x < -4$ or $x > 10$.

Try to answer the following question involving absolute value by "Starting with choice (C)." **Do not** check the solution until you have attempted this question yourself.

LEVEL 3: HEART OF ALGEBRA

1. If the exact weight of an item is X pounds and the estimated weight of the item is Y pounds, then the error, in pounds, is given by $|X - Y|$. Which of the following could be the exact weight, in pounds, of an object with an estimated weight of 6.2 pounds and with an error of less than 0.02 pounds?

   (A) 6.215
   (B) 6.221
   (C) 6.23
   (D) 6.3

Solution by starting with choice (C): Begin by looking at choice (C). So we are assuming that the exact weight of the object is $X = 6.23$. It follows that $|X - Y| = |6.23 - 6.2| = .03$ which is too large. So we want X to be **closer** in value to Y.

Let's try choice (B) next. In this case $|X - Y| = |6.221 - 6.2| = .021$. This is still a bit too large.

Let's try choice (A). So $|X - Y| = |6.215 - 6.2| = .015$. This is less than .02. Therefore the answer is choice (A).

Before we go on, try to solve this problem in two other ways.

(1) Algebraically
(2) Geometrically

* Algebraic solution: We are given $Y = 6.2$, so we have

$$|X - 6.2| < .02$$
$$-.02 < X - 6.2 < .02$$
$$6.18 < X < 6.22$$

The only answer choice with a number that satisfies this inequality is choice (A).

Geometric solution: We are given that the distance between X and 6.2 is less than $.02$. Let's draw a figure.

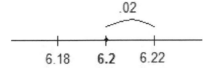

From this picture we see that 6.215 is in the given range, choice (A).

Try to solve each of the following problems. The answers to these problems, followed by full solutions are at the end of this lesson. **Do not** look at the answers until you have attempted these problems yourself. Please remember to mark off any problems you get wrong.

LEVEL 1: HEART OF ALGEBRA

2.   If $3c + 2 < 11$, which of the following cannot be equal to c?

   (A) -1
   (B) 0
   (C) 1
   (D) 3

3.   For which of the following values of k will the value of $11k - 12$ be greater than 21?

   (A) 1
   (B) 2
   (C) 3
   (D) 4

LEVEL 3: HEART OF ALGEBRA

4. Let h be a function such that $h(x) = |5x| + c$ where c is a constant. If $h(4) = -2$, what is the value of $h(-9)$?

5. If $|-2x + 3| < 1$, what is one possible value of x?

6. If $rs = 3$ and $r - s = 6$, what is the value of $r^2 s - r s^2$?

LEVEL 4: HEART OF ALGEBRA

7. If r and s are positive numbers, then the inequality $r\sqrt{7} < s\sqrt{2}$ is equivalent to which of the following?

   (A) $r^2 > \frac{2}{7} s^2$

   (B) $r^2 < \frac{2}{7} s^2$

   (C) $r > \frac{2}{7} s$

   (D) $r < \frac{2}{7} s$

8. If $15 < |b - 11| < 16$ and $b < 0$, what is one possible value of $|b|$?

9. In a certain game a player can attain a score that is a real number between 0 and 100. The player is said to be in scoring range D if his or her score is between 65 and 83. If John has a score of x, and John is in scoring range D, which of the following represents all possible values of x?

   (A) $|x + 74| < 9$

   (B) $|x - 74| < 9$

   (C) $|x + 74| = 9$

   (D) $|x - 74| > 9$

LEVEL 5: HEART OF ALGEBRA

10. On the number line, the distance between the point whose coordinate is s and the point whose coordinate is t is greater than 500. Which of the following must be true?

$$\text{I. } |s| \cdot |t| > 500$$
$$\text{II. } |s - t| > 500$$
$$\text{III. } t - s > 500$$

(A) I only
(B) II only
(C) III only
(D) I, II, and III

11. If $|-3a + 9| = 6$ and $|-2b + 10| = 20,$ what is the greatest possible value of ab?

12. If $f(x) = x^2 - 5,$ which of the following is <u>not</u> true?

(A) $f(-3) = |f(-3)|$

(B) $f(-2) = -|f(2)|$

(C) $f(1) < |f(-1)|$

(D) $f(0) = |f(0)|$

Answers

1. A	5. $1 < x < 2$	9. B
2. D	6. 18	10. B
3. D	7. B	11. 75
4. 23	8. $4 < |b| < 5$	12. D

Full Solutions

4.

* $h(4) = |5(4)| + c = |20| + c = 20 + c.$ But it is given that $h(4) = -2.$ Thus, $20 + c = -2,$ and so $c = -22.$ So $h(x) = |5x| - 22.$ Finally,

$$h(-9) = |5(-9)| - 22 = |-45| - 22 = 45 - 22 = \mathbf{23.}$$

210

Calculator remark: You can take absolute values in your graphing calculator by pressing MATH, scrolling right to NUM and pressing ENTER (or 1). The display will say abs(. For example, in this problem to compute $h(-9)$ you can simply type abs(5*-9) – 22, and the output will read **23**.

5.
Solution by guessing: Let's try to guess a value for x, say $x = 1$. Then we have that $|-2(1) + 3| = |1| = 1$. Almost! Let's try $x = 1.5$. Then we have $|-2(1.5) + 3| = |-3 + 3| = |0| = 0$. This works. So we can grid in **1.5**.

Remark: The number 1.5 is a really nice guess because it makes the expression under the absolute value 0, and certainly $|0| = 0 < 1$.

* **Quick solution:** Just solve the equation $-2x + 3 = 0$. So $2x = 3$, and therefore $x = 3/2$ or **1.5**.

Algebraic solution: Remember that $|-2x + 3| < 1$ is equivalent to the inequality $-1 < -2x + 3 < 1$. Let's solve this.

$$-1 < -2x + 3 < 1$$
$$-4 < -2x < -2$$
$$2 > x > 1$$
$$1 < x < 2$$

So we can grid in any number between 1 and 2 (but be careful! The numbers 1 or 2 will be marked wrong!).

Caution: Note that in going from the second to the third step above we divided by -2. Dividing by a negative number reverses the inequality.

6.
* $r^2s - rs^2 = rs(r - s) = (3)(6) = $ **18**.

7.
* Since r and s are positive, each side of the given inequality is positive. Therefore if we square each side of the inequality, the order is maintained. Now $\left(r\sqrt{7}\right)^2 = r^2 \cdot 7$, and $\left(s\sqrt{2}\right)^2 = s^2 \cdot 2$. So we have $7r^2 < 2s^2$. We divide each side of this inequality by 7 to get $r^2 < \left(\frac{2}{7}\right)s^2$, choice (B).

8.

Solution by guessing: A bit of guessing and checking should lead you to something close to $b = -4.5$. Indeed, $|-4.5 - 11| = |-15.5| = 15.5$. So we see that $b = -4.5$ satisfies both conditions, and therefore we can grid in $|b| = \mathbf{4.5}$.

* **Quick solution:** Just solve the equation $b - 11 = -15.5$, to get $b = -4.5$. So we have $|b| = \mathbf{4.5}$.

Algebraic solution: This is a bit tricky. Since b must be negative we want to solve the inequality $-16 < b - 11 < -15$. Adding 11 to each part gives us $-5 < b < -4$. So $4 < |b| < 5$. Therefore we can grid in any number between 4 and 5 (but 4 or 5 will be marked wrong!).

9.

Solution by picking a number: Let's pick a value for x that is in scoring range D and try to eliminate answer choices. A good choice is a number close to one of the extremes. So let's try $x = 66$, and substitute this value into each answer choice.

(A) $|66 + 74| = |140| = 140$ and $140 < 9$ is False
(B) $|66 - 74| = |-8| = 8$ and $8 < 9$ is True
(C) $|66 + 74| = |140| = 140$ and $140 = 9$ is False
(D) $|66 - 74| = |-8| = 8$ and $8 > 9$ is False

Since choices (A), (C), and (D) came out false we can eliminate them, and the answer is choice (B).

* **Algebraic solution:** We are given that x is between 65 and 83. That is, $65 < x < 83$. Using the answer choices as a guide, let us subtract 74 from each part of this inequality. We have that $65 - 74 = -9$ and $83 - 74 = 9$. Therefore we have $-9 < x - 74 < 9$. This is equivalent to $|x - 74| < 9$, choice (B).

10.

* The first sentence is precisely the statement of II. Letting $s = 1000$ and $t = 0$ gives a counterexample for both I and III. The answer is choice (B).

11.

* The first equation is equivalent to $-3a + 9 = 6$ or $-3a + 9 = -6$. These two equations have solutions $a = 1$ and $a = 5$, respectively.

Similarly, the second equation is equivalent to $-2b + 10 = 20$ or $-2b + 10 = -20$. These two equations have solutions $b = -5$ and $b = 15$, respectively. Finally, we get the greatest value of ab by multiplying the greatest value of a with the greatest value of b. So $ab = (5)(15) = $ **75**.

12.

* Solution by starting with choice (C): Let's start with choice (C). Then $f(1) = 12 - 5 = -4$, $\quad |f(-1)| = |(-1)^2 - 5| = |1 - 5| = |-4| = 4$. Since $-4 < 4$, the inequality in choice (C) is true.

Let's try choice (D) next. Then we have $f(0) = 0^2 - 5 = -5$ and $|f(0)| = |-5| = 5$. Since $f(0)$ is different from $|f(0)|$, the equation in choice (D) is false. Therefore the answer is choice (D).

Remark: The other two computations are similar. If you struggled with the computations in choices (C) and (D), you may want to do the other computations for practice.

OPTIONAL MATERIAL

CHALLENGE QUESTION

10. If 2 real numbers are randomly chosen from a line segment of length 10, what is the probability that the distance between them is at least 7?

Solution

We may assume that the two real numbers, a and b are chosen to be between 0 and 10. Consider the picture below:

Note that we are trying to compute the probability that $|a - b| \geq 7$.

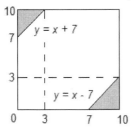

This is equivalent to the two inequalities $a - b \leq -7$ and $a - b \geq 7$. Solving each of these inequalities for b gives $b \geq a + 7$ and $b \leq a - 7$. These inequalities correspond to the two shaded triangles in the figure. The area of the shaded region is $2(\frac{1}{2})(3)(3) = 9$ and the area of the whole square is $10^2 = 100$. Therefore the probability we are looking for is $\frac{9}{100} = .09$.

213

LESSON 18
GEOMETRY

Reminder: Before beginning this lesson remember to redo the problems from Lessons 2, 6, 10 and 14 that you have marked off. Do not "unmark" a question unless you get it correct.

Advanced Relationships in Circles

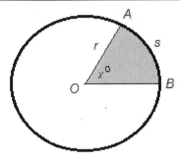

Consider the circle in the figure above. Notice that $\overline{OA}$ and $\overline{OB}$ are both radii of the circle. Therefore $OA = OB = r$. If we know the radius r, then we can find the diameter d of the circle, the circumference C of the circle, and the area A of the circle. Indeed, $d = 2r$, $C = 2\pi r$, and $A = \pi r^2$. In fact, if we know any one of the four quantities we can find the other three. For example, if we know that the area of a circle is $A = 9\pi$, then it follows that $r = 3$, $d = 6$, and $C = 6\pi$.

Now, suppose that in addition to the radius r, we know the angle x. We can then use the following ratio to find the length s of arc AB.

$$\frac{x}{360} = \frac{s}{C}$$

For example, if we are given that $r = 5$ and $x = 45$, then we have

$$\frac{45}{360} = \frac{s}{10\pi}$$

So $360s = 450\pi$, and therefore $s = \frac{450\pi}{360} = \frac{5\pi}{4}$.

214

In this particular example we can use a little shortcut. Just note that a 45 degree angle gives $\frac{1}{8}$ of the total degree measure of the circle, and therefore the arc length is $\frac{1}{8}$ of the circumference. So $s = \frac{10\pi}{8} = \frac{5\pi}{4}$.

We can also use the following ratio to find the area a of sector AOB.

$$\frac{x}{360} = \frac{a}{A}$$

For example, if again we are given that $r = 5$ and $x = 45$, then we have

$$\frac{45}{360} = \frac{a}{25\pi}$$

So $360a = 1125\pi$, and therefore $a = \frac{1125\pi}{360} = \frac{25\pi}{8}$.

Again, we can take a shortcut in this example and just divide the area of the circle by 8 to get $a = \frac{25\pi}{8}$.

A very difficult problem might give you the angle x and the area of sector AOB and ask you to find the length of arc AB, or vice versa.

Example: Suppose that A and B are points on a circle with center O, the measure of angle AOB is 35 degrees and minor arc AB has length π. What is the area of sector AOB?

We begin by setting up a ratio to find the circumference of the circle.

$$\frac{35}{360} = \frac{\pi}{C}$$

We cross multiply to get $35C = 360\pi$. So $C = \frac{360\pi}{35} = \frac{72\pi}{7}$.

Next we find the radius of the circle using the formula $C = 2\pi r$. So we have $2\pi r = \frac{72\pi}{7}$, and so $r = \frac{36}{7}$.

Now, the area of the circle is $\pi \left(\frac{36}{7}\right)^2 = \frac{1296\pi}{49}$.

Finally, we set up another ratio to find the area a of the sector.

$$\frac{35}{360} = \frac{a}{\left(\frac{1296\pi}{49}\right)}$$

We cross multiply to get $\frac{6480\pi}{7} = 360a$. Therefore $a = \frac{6480\pi}{7 \cdot 360} = \frac{18\pi}{7}$.

Now try to solve each of the following problems. The answers to these problems, followed by full solutions are at the end of this lesson. **Do not** look at the answers until you have attempted these problems yourself. Please remember to mark off any problems you get wrong.

LEVEL 2: GEOMETRY

1. In the xy-plane, the point $(0,2)$ is the center of a circle that has radius 2. Which of the following is NOT a point on the circle?

    (A) $(0,4)$
    (B) $(-2,4)$
    (C) $(2,2)$
    (D) $(-2,2)$

LEVEL 3: GEOMETRY

2. In a circle with center O, central angle POQ has a measure of $\frac{2\pi}{3}$ radians. The area of the sector formed by central angle POQ is what fraction of the area of the circle?

LEVEL 4: GEOMETRY

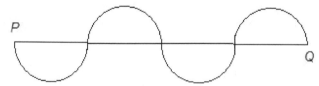

3. In the figure above, the diameters of the four semicircles are equal and lie on line segment $\overline{PQ}$. If the length of line segment $\overline{PQ}$ is $\frac{96}{\pi}$, what is the length of the curve from P to Q?

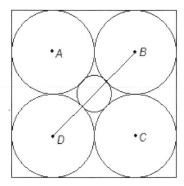

4.   In the figure above, each of the points A, B, C, and D is the center of a circle of diameter 6. Each of the four large circles is tangent to two of the other large circles, the small circle, and two sides of the square. What is the length of segment $\overline{BD}$?

    (A) $6\sqrt{3}$
    (B) $6\sqrt{2}$
    (C) $3\sqrt{2}$
    (D) 9

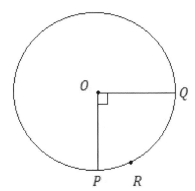

5.   In the circle above with center O, $\angle POQ$ is a right angle. If the length of arc $\overset{\frown}{PRQ}$ is 10π, what is the length of a <u>diameter</u> of the circle?

217

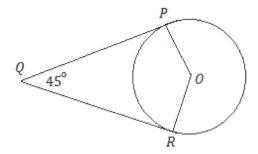

6.   In the figure above, O is the center of the circle, line segments PQ and RQ are tangent to the circle at points P and R, respectively. The two segments intersect at point Q as shown. If the length of minor arc $\overset{\frown}{PR}$ is 9, what is the circumference of the circle?

LEVEL 5: GEOMETRY

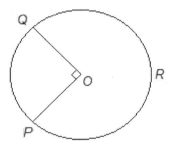

7.   In the figure above, the circle has center O and radius 8. What is the length of arc PRQ?

   (A) 12π
   (B) $24\sqrt{2}$
   (C) 6π
   (D) $12\sqrt{2}$

8.   When the area of a certain circle is divided by 4π, the result is the cube of an integer. Which of the following could be the circumference of the circle?

   (A) 2π
   (B) 8π
   (C) 16π
   (D) 32π

9. If the diameter of a circle is doubled, by what percent is the area of the circle increased? (Disregard the percent symbol when you grid your answer.)

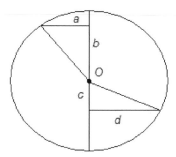

10. In the figure above, O is the center of the circle, the two triangles have legs of lengths a, b, c, and d, as shown, $a^2 + b^2 + c^2 + d^2 = 15$, and the area of the circle is $k\pi$. What is the value of k ?

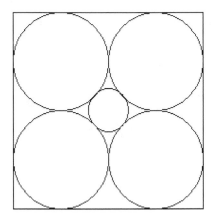

11. In the figure above, each of the four large circles is tangent to two of the other large circles, the small circle, and two sides of the square. If the radius of each of the large circles is 4, what is the diameter of the small circle?

(A) $\sqrt{2}$ (approximately 1.414)
(B) 1
(C) $8\sqrt{2} - 8$ (approximately 3.314)
(D) $4\sqrt{2} - 4$ (approximately 1.657)

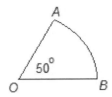

12. * In the figure above, AB is the arc of a circle with center O. If the length of arc AB is 4π, what is the area of region OAB to the nearest tenth?

Answers

1. B	5. 40	9. 300
2. 1/3 or .333	6. 24	10. 15/2 or 7.5
3. 48	7. A	11. C
4. B	8. D	12. 90.5

Full Solutions

2.

* One full rotation is 2π radians, and $\frac{2\pi}{3} \div 2\pi = \frac{2\pi}{3} \cdot \frac{1}{2\pi} = \mathbf{1/3}$ or $.\mathbf{333}$.

Note: We can also change $\frac{2\pi}{3}$ to degrees first: $\frac{2\pi}{3} = \frac{2(180)}{3} = 120°$.

We then have $\frac{120}{360} = \mathbf{1/3}$.

3.

* The diameter of each semicircle is $\frac{96}{\pi} \div 4 = \frac{24}{\pi}$. Thus the circumference of each semicircle is $\frac{1}{2}(\pi)(\frac{24}{\pi}) = 12$. Since we are adding up the lengths of four such semicircles, the answer is $(4)(12) = \mathbf{48}$.

Remark: Since a semicircle is half of a circle, the circumference of a semicircle with radius r is $C = \pi r$ (or $C = \frac{\pi d}{2}$).

4.

* We form a right triangle and observe that segments BC and CD each have length 6.

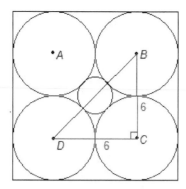

Note that a 45, 45, 90 triangle is formed (or use the Pythagorean Theorem) to get that $BD = 6\sqrt{2}$, choice (B).

5.

* $\overarc{PRQ}$ is $\frac{1}{4}$ of the circumference of the circle. So the circumference of the circle is $4 \cdot 10\pi = 40\pi$. It follows that the length of a diameter of the circle is **40**.

6.

* Since PQ is tangent to the circle and OP is a radius of the circle, $QP \perp OP$. Therefore $m\angle P = 90°$. Similarly $m\angle R = 90°$. It follows that $m\angle O = 360 - 90 - 90 - 45 = 135°$. Since a central angle has the same measure as the arc it intercepts, minor arc $\overarc{PR}$ measures $135°$ as well. We can now find the circumference of the circle by setting up a ratio:

$$\frac{135}{360} = \frac{9}{C}$$

We cross multiply to get $135C = 3240$. Finally we divide by 135 to get $C = \frac{3240}{135} = \textbf{24}$.

7.

Solution using a ratio: Note that there are 270 degrees in arc PRQ and the circumference of the circle is $C = 2\pi r = 16\pi$. So we solve for s in the following ratio.

$$\frac{270}{360} = \frac{s}{16\pi}$$

Cross multiplying gives $360s = 4320\pi$, and so $s = \frac{4320\pi}{360} = 12\pi$, choice (A).

221

* Quick solution: Note that arc PQR is $\frac{3}{4}$ of the circumference of the circle and therefore PQR has length $s = (\frac{3}{4})(16\pi) = 12\pi$, choice (A).

8.
* Solution by starting with choice (C): Let's begin with choice (C) and suppose that the circumference is $C = 2\pi r = 16\pi$. Then $r = 8$ and $A = 64\pi$. When we divide 64π by 4π we get 16 which is **not** the cube of an integer.

Let's try choice (D) next. Then $C = 2\pi r = 32\pi$, so that $r = 16$ and $A = 256\pi$. When we divide 256π by 4π we get 64. Since $64 = 4^3$, the answer is choice (D).

9.
Solution by picking a number: Let's start with $d = 2$. Then $r = 1$ and $A = \pi$. Now let's double the diameter to $d = 4$. Then $r = 2$ and $A = 4\pi$. We now use the percent change formula.

$$Percent\ Change = \frac{Change}{Original} \times 100$$

The **original** value is π and the **change** is $4\pi - \pi = 3\pi$. So the area of the circle is increased by $(\frac{3\pi}{\pi}) \cdot 100 = \mathbf{300}$ percent.

* Algebraic solution: Note that if the diameter is doubled, then so is the radius. So, if the area of the original circle is πr^2, then the area of the new circle is $\pi(2r)^2 = 4\pi r^2$. Thus, the **change** is $4\pi r^2 - \pi r^2 = 3\pi r^2$. So the area of the circle is increased by $(\frac{3\pi r^2}{\pi r^2}) \cdot 100 = \mathbf{300}$ percent.

10.
*** Notice that the hypotenuse of each triangle is a radius of the circle. By the Pythagorean Theorem, $a^2 + b^2 = r^2$ and $c^2 + d^2 = r^2$. So,

$$a^2 + b^2 + c^2 + d^2 = 2r^2$$

Since the left hand side of the above equation is also equal to 15, we have that $2r^2 = 15$, and therefore $r^2 = \frac{15}{2}$.

Since the area of a circle is $A = \pi r^2$, we see that $k = \mathbf{15/2}$ or $\mathbf{7.5}$.

222

11.

* We draw an isosceles right triangle.

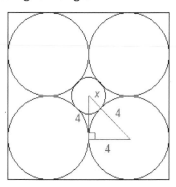

Note that each length labeled with a 4 is equal to the radius of one of the larger circles (the radius is half the diameter). The length labeled x is the radius of the smaller circle. An isosceles right triangle is the same as a 45, 45, 90 right triangle. By looking at the formula for a 45, 45, 90 triangle we see that $x + 4 = 4\sqrt{2}$ and so $x = 4\sqrt{2} - 4$. The diameter is then $2x = 2(4\sqrt{2} - 4) = 8\sqrt{2} - 8$, choice (C).

Remark: We can also use the Pythagorean Theorem to find x. We have $(x + 4)^2 = 4^2 + 4^2 = 16 + 16 = 32$. So $x + 4 = \sqrt{32} = 4\sqrt{2}$ and so $x = 4\sqrt{2} - 4$.

Also, if you are uncomfortable simplifying square roots, and a calculator is allowed, you can simply perform the computations in your calculator and compare with the numbers next to "approximately" in the answer choices.

12.

* We first find the circumference of the circle using the ratio $\frac{50}{360} = \frac{4\pi}{C}$.

Cross multiplying gives $50C = 1440\pi$, so $C = \frac{1440\pi}{50} = \frac{144\pi}{5}$. Since $C = 2\pi r$, we have $2\pi r = \frac{144\pi}{5}$, so $r = \frac{72}{5}$. The area of the circle is $A = \pi r^2 = \frac{5184\pi}{25}$. Now we find the area of the sector using the ratio $\frac{50}{360} = \frac{a}{(5184\pi)/25}$.

Cross multiplying gives us $360a = 10,368\pi$. So $a = \frac{10,368\pi}{360} \approx 90.478$. To the nearest tenth this is **90.5**.

OPTIONAL MATERIAL

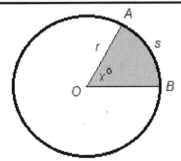

If we solve for s and a in the ratios $\frac{x}{360} = \frac{s}{C}$ and $\frac{x}{360} = \frac{a}{A}$, we get

$$s = \frac{\pi r x}{180} \qquad \text{and} \qquad a = \frac{\pi r^2 x}{360}$$

If you like you can memorize these formulas. I prefer to just set up the ratios.

We can also do these computations in radians. We have the ratios

$$\frac{x}{2\pi} = \frac{s}{C} \qquad \text{and} \qquad \frac{x}{2\pi} = \frac{a}{A}$$

Solving for s and a in these ratios gives us the simpler formulas

$$s = rx \qquad \text{and} \qquad a = \frac{1}{2}r^2x$$

LESSON 19
PASSPORT TO ADVANCED MATH

Reminder: Before beginning this lesson remember to redo the problems from Lessons 3, 7, 11 and 15 that you have marked off. Do not "unmark" a question unless you get it correct.

Addition and Subtraction of Polynomials

We add polynomials by simply combining like terms. We can change any subtraction problem to an addition problem by first distributing the minus sign. Let's look at an example.

LEVEL 2: ADVANCED MATH

$$(a^3 - 3a^2b + 2ab^2 - b^3) - (-a^3 - 3a^2b - 2ab^2 - b^3)$$

1. Which of the following is equivalent to the expression above?

   (A) 0
   (B) $a^3 + b^3$
   (C) $-6a^2b - 2b^3$
   (D) $2a^3 + 4ab^2$

* Algebraic solution:

$$(a^3 - 3a^2b + 2ab^2 - b^3) - (-a^3 - 3a^2b - 2ab^2 - b^3)$$
$$= a^3 - 3a^2b + 2ab^2 - b^3 + a^3 + 3a^2b + 2ab^2 + b^3$$
$$= (a^3 + a^3) + (-3a^2b + 3a^2b) + (2ab^2 + 2ab^2) + (-b^3 + b^3)$$
$$= 2a^3 + 0 + 4ab^2 + 0 = 2a^3 + 4ab^2, \text{choice (D)}.$$

Multiplication of Polynomials

Most students are familiar with the mnemonic FOIL to help them multiply two binomials (polynomials with 2 terms) together. As a simple example, we have

$$(x + 1)(x - 2) = x^2 - 2x + x - 2 = x^2 - x - 2$$

225

Unfortunately this method works ONLY for binomials. It does not extend to polynomials with more than 2 terms. Let's demonstrate another way to multiply polynomials with the same example.

We begin by lining up the polynomials vertically:

$$x + 1$$
$$\underline{x - 2}$$

We multiply the -2 on the bottom by each term on top, moving from right to left. First note that -2 times 1 is -2:

$$x + 1$$
$$\underline{x - 2}$$
$$-2$$

Next note that -2 times x is $-2x$:

$$x + 1$$
$$\underline{x - 2}$$
$$-2x - 2$$

Now we multiply the x on the bottom by each term on top, moving from right to left. This time as we write the answers we leave one blank space on the right:

$$x + 1$$
$$\underline{x - 2}$$
$$-2x - 2$$
$$\underline{x^2 + x}$$

Finally, we add:

$$x + 1$$
$$\underline{x - 2}$$
$$-2x - 2$$
$$\underline{x^2 + x}$$
$$x^2 - x - 2$$

Now try this SAT problem involving multiplication of polynomials.

LEVEL 5: ADVANCED MATH

$$x^2 + 2x - 1$$
$$2x^2 - x + 3$$

2. The product of the two polynomials shown above can be written in the form $ax^4 + bx^3 + cx^2 + dx + e$. What is the value of $\frac{b}{d}$?

* We use the algorithm we just went over:

$$\begin{array}{r}
x^2 + 2x - 1 \\
2x^2 - x + 3 \\
\hline
3x^2 + 6x - 3 \\
-x^3 - 2x^2 + x \\
2x^4 + 4x^3 - 2x^2 \\
\hline
2x^4 + 3x^3 - x^2 + 7x - 3
\end{array}$$

So $b = 3$, $d = 7$, and therefore $\dfrac{b}{d} = 3/7$, $.428$, or $.429$.

The Factor Theorem

Recall that a number r is a **root** (or **zero**, or **solution**) of a function f if $f(r) = 0$.

The **factor theorem** says that r is a root of the polynomial $p(x)$ if and only if $x - r$ is a factor of the polynomial.

LEVEL 4: ADVANCED MATH

x	$p(x)$
-2	2
0	1
2	0
4	-2

3.   The function p is defined by a polynomial. Some values of x and $p(x)$ are shown in the table above. Which of the following must be a factor of $p(x)$?

   (A) $x - 4$
   (B) $x - 2$
   (C) $x - 1$
   (D) $x + 2$

* **Solution using the factor theorem:** According to the chart, we have $p(2) = 0$. By the factor theorem $x - 2$ is a factor of $p(x)$, choice (B).

The Remainder Theorem

The **remainder theorem** says that $p(r) = a$ if and only if the remainder when $p(x)$ is divided by $x - r$ is a.

Note: The factor theorem is the special case of the remainder theorem when $a = 0$.

LEVEL 5: ADVANCED MATH

4. For a polynomial $p(x)$, the value of $p(-3)$ is 5. Which of the following must be true about $p(x)$?

    (A) $x - 8$ is a factor of $p(x)$.
    (B) $x + 5$ is a factor of $p(x)$.
    (C) $x - 5$ is a factor of $p(x)$.
    (D) The remainder when $p(x)$ is divided by $x + 3$ is 5.

* **Solution using the remainder theorem:** Since $p(-3) = 5$, by the remainder theorem , the remainder when $p(x)$ is divided by $x + 3$ is 5, choice (D).

Now try to solve each of the following problems. The answers to these problems, followed by full solutions are at the end of this lesson. **Do not** look at the answers until you have attempted these problems yourself. Please remember to mark off any problems you get wrong.

LEVEL 2: ADVANCED MATH

$$3(-2x^3 + 5x^2 - x + 1) - 3(x^3 - 2x^2 - 5x - 2)$$

5. If we write the above expression in the form $ax^3 + bx^2 + cx + d$, where a, b, c, and d are constants, what is the value of c ?

228

$$6x^2 - 3x - 5$$
$$7x^2 + 4x + 1$$

6. Which of the following is the sum of the two polynomials shown above?

    (A) $13x^2 - x - 4$
    (B) $13x^2 + x - 4$
    (C) $13x^4 - x^2 - 4$
    (D) $13x^4 + x^2 - 4$

LEVEL 3: ADVANCED MATH

7. If -2 and 8 are both zeros of the polynomial $q(x)$, then a factor of $q(x)$ is

    (A) $x^2 - 16$
    (B) $x^2 + 16$
    (C) $x^2 - 6x - 16$
    (D) $x^2 - 6x + 16$

$$h(x) = -2(x^2 - 5x + 3) + 7(c - x)$$

8. In the polynomial $h(x)$ defined above, c is a constant. If $h(x)$ is divisible by x, what is the value of c ?

    (A) $-\dfrac{6}{7}$

    (B) 0

    (C) $\dfrac{6}{7}$

    (D) 6

9. For all x, $(x^2 - 3x + 1)(x + 2) = $?

    (A) $x^3 - x^2 - 5x + 2$
    (B) $x^3 - x^2 - 5x - 2$
    (C) $x^3 - x^2 + 5x + 2$
    (D) $x^3 + x^2 - 5x + 2$

LEVEL 4: ADVANCED MATH

$$3x^2 + 19x = 14$$

10. If a and b are distinct solutions of the equation above, what is the value of $-3ab$?

LEVEL 5: ADVANCED MATH

$$g(x) = x^2 + 2x + 1$$
$$h(x) = 2x^3 + 3x^2 + 2x$$

11. The polynomials g and h are defined above. Which of the following polynomials is divisible by $2x + 1$?

   (A) $k(x) = g(x) + h(x)$
   (B) $k(x) = g(x) + 3h(x)$
   (C) $k(x) = 2g(x) + h(x)$
   (D) $k(x) = 2g(x) + 3h(x)$

12. If $x - 3$ is a factor of $ax^2 - a^2x + 12$, where a is a positive constant, what is the value of a ?

Answers

1. D	5. 12	9. A
2. 3/7, .428, or .429	6. B	10. 14
3. B	7. C	11. C
4. D	8. C	12. 4

Full Solutions

7.

* **Algebraic solution:** By the factor theorem $(x + 2)$ and $(x - 8)$ are both factors of $q(x)$. Therefore so is $(x + 2)(x - 8) = x^2 - 6x - 16$, choice (C).

Note: To multiply $(x + 2)(x - 8)$ we can either FOIL or use the algorithm described in this lesson. Here is the computation using the latter method.

230

$$\begin{array}{r} x+2 \\ x-8 \\ \hline -8x-16 \\ x^2+2x+0 \\ \hline x^2-6x-16 \end{array}$$

Solution by plugging in answer choices: We are looking for the expression that gives 0 when we substitute in -2 and 8 for x.

Starting with choice (C) we have $(-2)^2 - 6(-2) - 16 = 0$ and $8^2 - 6(8) - 16 = 0$. So the answer is choice (C).

8.
Algebraic solution: We begin by distributing the -2 and 7 to get $h(x) = -2x^2 + 10x - 6 + 7c - 7x = -2x^2 + 3x + 7c - 6$.

In order for $h(x)$ to be divisible by x, we must have $7c - 6 = 0$, or equivalently, $7c = 6$. Dividing by 7 gives $c = \frac{6}{7}$, choice (C).

Notes: (1) Make sure you are using the distributive property correctly here.

For example $-2(x^2 - 5x + 3) = -2x^2 + 10x - 6$. A common mistake would be to write $-2(x^2 - 5x + 3) = -2x^2 - 5x + 3$

Also, $7(c - x) = 7c - 7x$. A common mistake would be to write $7(c - x) = 7c - x$.

(2) A polynomial is divisible by x precisely when the constant term is 0.

In this problem we can just set $-2 \cdot 3 + 7c = 0$ right away (without multiplying everything out).

* **Computational solution:** $0 = h(0) = -6 + 7c$. So $7c = 6$, and therefore $c = \frac{6}{7}$, choice (C).

Note: $p(c) = 0$ if and only if $x - c$ is a factor of the polynomial $p(x)$.

In this problem we are given that $x = x - 0$ is a factor of h. It follows that $h(0) = 0$.

9.
Solution by picking a number: Let's choose a value for x, say $x = 1$. Then

$$(x^2 - 3x + 1)(x + 2) = (1^2 - 3(1) + 1)(1 + 2) = (1 - 3 + 1)(3) =$$
$$(-1)(3) = -3.$$

Put a nice big dark circle around **−3** so you can find it easier later. We now substitute 1 for x into each answer choice:

(A) −3
(B) −7
(C) 7
(D) −1

Since B, C, and D each came out incorrect, the answer is choice (A).

Important note: (A) is **not** the correct answer simply because it is equal to −3. It is correct because all three of the other choices are **not** −3. **You absolutely must check all four choices!**

* Algebraic solution: We multiply the two polynomials.

$$
\begin{array}{r}
x^2 - 3x + 1 \\
x + 2 \\
\hline
2x^2 - 6x + 2 \\
x^3 - 3x^2 + x + 0 \\
\hline
x^3 - x^2 - 5x + 2
\end{array}
$$

This is choice (A).

10.

* We divide each side of the equation by 3 to get $x^2 + \frac{19}{3}x = \frac{14}{3}$. We then subtract $\frac{14}{3}$ from each side of this last equation to get $x^2 + \frac{19}{3}x - \frac{14}{3} = 0$. We then see that $ab = -\frac{14}{3}$, and therefore $-3ab = (-3)\left(-\frac{14}{3}\right) = \mathbf{14}$.

Solution by factoring: We subtract 14 from each side of the equation to get $3x^2 + 19x - 14 = 0$. We factor the left hand side of this equation to get $(3x - 2)(x + 7) = 0$. This equation has solutions $a = \frac{2}{3}$ and $b = -7$. So $-3ab = -3 \cdot \frac{2}{3} \cdot (-7) = \mathbf{14}$.

Notes: (1) To solve a quadratic equation by factoring, we must first bring all the terms to one side of the equation (so that the other side is just 0).

Here we subtracted 14 from each side of the original equation to put it in this form.

(2) Let's break down how we factored $3x^2 + 19x - 14$.

(i) The product of the first terms of each factor must be $3x^2$. So these terms must be $3x$ and x:

$$3x^2 + 19x - 14 = (3x + \_)(x - \_), \text{ or } (3x - \_)(x + \_)$$

Note that there is no symmetry here, so that the two possible placements of minus signs leads to different possibilities.

(ii) The product of the last terms of each factor must be 14 (with a minus sign before one of the factors). There are four choices: 1 and 14, 2 and 7, 7 and 2, or 14 and 1.

Again, there is no symmetry. For example 2 and 7 is genuinely different from 7 and 2.

$$(3x - 7)(x + 2) = 3x^2 + 6x - 7x - 14 = 3x^2 - x - 14$$

$$(3x - 2)(x + 7) = 3x^2 + 21x - 2x - 14 = 3x^2 + 19x - 14$$

(iii) Note that 2 and 7 is the correct choice.

(3) The **zero property** of the real numbers says that when you have a product equal to zero, one of the factors must be zero.

In this problem, since $(3x - 2)(x + 7) = 0$, we must have $3x - 2 = 0$ or $x + 7 = 0$. So $x = \frac{2}{3}$ or $x = -7$.

Solution by the "payback" method: We can turn the equation into a more straightforward factoring problem by first multiplying each term by 3. We get $3 \cdot 3x^2 + 3 \cdot 19x - 3 \cdot 14 = 0$. We rewrite this as

$$(3x)^2 + 19(3x) - 42 = 0.$$

We factor the left hand side to get $(3x - 2)(3x + 21) = 0$. This equation has solutions $a = \frac{2}{3}$ and $b = -\frac{21}{3} = -7$.

So $-3ab = -3 \cdot \frac{2}{3} \cdot (-7) = \mathbf{14}$.

Notes: (1) $3 \cdot 3x^2 = 3^2 x^2 = (3x)^2$.

233

(2) We multiplied by 3 to turn the original equation into a quadratic equation in $3x$.

(3) We can formally make the substitution $u = 3x$. The equation $(3x)^2 + 19(3x) - 42 = 0$ then becomes $u^2 + 19u - 42 = 0$ which is equivalent to $(u - 2)(u + 21) = 0$.

This last equation has solutions $u = 2$ and $u = -21$.

We now recall that $u = 3x$, so that these last two equations are equivalent to $3x = 2$ and $3x = -21$. Once again we see that the two solutions are $a = \frac{2}{3}$ and $b = -\frac{21}{3} = -7$.

(4) Many students are taught to perform the payback method as follows:

(i) Move the 3 from the first term of the equation to the last term:

$$3x^2 + 19x - 3 \cdot 14 = 0$$
$$x^2 + 19x - 42 = 0$$

(ii) Solve this new equation: $(x - 2)(x + 21) = 0 \Rightarrow x = 2, -21$.

(iii) Divide each of these "solutions" by 3 to get the "real solutions":

$$a = \frac{2}{3}, b = -\frac{21}{3} = -7$$

(5) This problem can also be solved by completing the square or by using the quadratic formula. Since these are not the most efficient methods for this problem, I leave them as exercises.

11.

* $g\left(-\frac{1}{2}\right) = \left(-\frac{1}{2}\right)^2 + 2\left(-\frac{1}{2}\right) + 1 = \frac{1}{4} - 1 + 1 = \frac{1}{4}$

$h\left(-\frac{1}{2}\right) = 2\left(-\frac{1}{2}\right)^3 + 3\left(-\frac{1}{2}\right)^2 + 2\left(-\frac{1}{2}\right) = 2\left(-\frac{1}{8}\right) + 3\left(\frac{1}{4}\right) - 1$

$$= -\frac{1}{4} + \frac{3}{4} - \frac{4}{4} = -\frac{2}{4} = -\frac{1}{2}$$

Since $2\left(\frac{1}{4}\right) + \left(-\frac{1}{2}\right) = \frac{1}{2} - \frac{1}{2} = 0$, we see that if $k(x) = 2g(x) + h(x)$, then $k\left(-\frac{1}{2}\right) = 0$, and it follows that $2x + 1$ is a factor of k. So the answer is choice (C).

12.
* Solution using the Factor Theorem: Since $x - 3$ is a factor of the expression, 3 is a zero of the expression. So $a \cdot 3^2 - a^2 \cdot 3 + 12 = 0$, or equivalently $-3a^2 + 9a + 12 = 0$. Dividing this expression through by -3 gives $a^2 - 3a - 4 = 0$. The left hand side factors as $(a - 4)(a + 1)$, so that the two solutions are $a = 4$ and $a = -1$. Since the question says that a is a positive constant, $a = \mathbf{4}$.

Note: The **zero property** of the real numbers says that when you have a product equal to zero, one of the factors must be zero.

In this problem, since $(a - 4)(a + 1) = 0$, we must have $a - 4 = 0$ or $a + 1 = 0$. So $a = 4$ or $a = -1$.

Solution by factoring: Since $x - 3$ is a factor of $ax^2 - a^2x + 12$, we have $ax^2 - a^2x + 12 = (x - 3)(ax - 4) = ax^2 + (-4 - 3a)x + 12$. Equating the coefficients of x gives $-a^2 = -4 - 3a$. Adding a^2 to each side of this equation gives $a^2 - 3a - 4 = 0$. As in the previous solution, the left hand side factors as $(a - 4)(a + 1)$, so that the two solutions are $a = 4$ and $a = -1$. Since the question says that a is a positive constant, $a = \mathbf{4}$.

Note: Two polynomials are equal precisely when all the corresponding coefficients are equal. For example, if

$$ax^2 + bx + c = 3x^2 + 2x - 5,$$

then $a = 3$, $b = 2$, and $c = -5$.

Download additional solutions for free here:

www.thesatmathprep.com/28Les800.html

LESSON 20
STATISTICS

Reminder: Before beginning this lesson remember to redo the problems from Lessons 4, 8, 12 and 16 that you have marked off. Do not "unmark" a question unless you get it correct.

Fence-Post Formula

The number of integers from a to b, inclusive, is $b - a + 1$.

For example, let's count the number of integers from 5 to 12, inclusive. They are 5, 6, 7, 8, 9, 10, 11, 12, and we see that there are 8 of them. Now 12 − 5 = 7 which is not the correct amount, but 12 − 5 + 1 = 8 which is the correct amount.

If you ever happen to forget this little formula test it out on a small list of numbers as I just did. But it's nice to have this one committed to memory so that it is there for you when you need it.

Remark: If you put up a fence that is 10 feet long, and put up fence-posts every foot, then there are 10 − 0 + 1 = 11 fence-posts.

The Median of a Set of Consecutive Integers

If x is the least integer in a list of $n + 1$ consecutive integers, then the median of the set is $x + \frac{n}{2}$.

Example: Compute the median of 5, 6, 7,…, 127.

By the fence-post formula there are 127 − 5 + 1 = 123 integers in this list. Therefore the median is 5 + 122/2 = **66**.

Remarks: (1) Note that if the number of integers in the list is odd, the median will be an integer. If the number of integers in the list is even, the median will not be an integer.

(2) If the number of integers in the list is even, then there are two middle numbers, and the median is the average of these two numbers.

Try to solve each of the following problems. The answers to these problems, followed by full solutions are at the end of this lesson. **Do not** look at the answers until you have attempted these problems yourself. Please remember to mark off any problems you get wrong.

LEVEL 1: STATISTICS

1. A biologist was interested in the number of times a field cricket chirps each minute on a sunny day. He randomly selected 100 field crickets from a garden, and found that the mean number of chirps per minute was 112, and the margin of error for this estimate was 6 chirps. The biologist would like to repeat the procedure and attempt to reduce the margin of error. Which of the following samples would most likely result in a smaller margin of error for the estimated mean number of times a field cricket chirps each minute on a sunny day?

   (A) 50 randomly selected crickets from the same garden.
   (B) 50 randomly selected field crickets from the same garden.
   (C) 200 randomly selected crickets from the same garden.
   (D) 200 randomly selected field crickets from the same garden.

LEVEL 2: STATISTICS

2. A psychologist wanted to determine if there is an association between diet and stress levels for the population of middle aged women in New York. He surveyed a random sample of 1500 middle aged female New Yorkers and found substantial evidence of a positive association between diet and stress levels. Which of the following conclusions is well supported by the data?

   (A) A dietary change causes an increase in stress levels for middle aged women from New York.
   (B) An increase in stress levels causes middle aged women from New York to change their diets.
   (C) There is a positive association between diet and stress levels for middle aged women in New York.
   (D) There is a positive association between diet and stress levels for middle aged women in the world.

237

LEVEL 3: STATISTICS

3. Set *X* contains only the integers 0 through 180 inclusive. If a number is selected at random from *X*, what is the probability that the number selected will be greater than the median of the numbers in *X*?

TEST GRADES OF STUDENTS IN MATH CLASS

Test Grade	60	65	75	95	100
Number of students with that grade	3	12	4	5	1

4. The test grades of the 25 students in a math class are shown in the chart above. What is the median test grade for the class?

5. The tables below give the distribution of the grades received by a class of 35 students on a math exam and a chemistry exam.

Math Exam			Chemistry Exam	
Grade	Frequency		Grade	Frequency
100	7		100	1
95	5		95	4
90	5		90	26
85	4		85	2
80	6		80	1
75	8		75	1

Which of the following is true about the data shown for these 35 students?

(A) The standard deviation of grades on the math exam is larger.

(B) The standard deviation of grades on the chemistry exam is larger.

(C) The standard deviation of grades on the math exam is the same as that of the chemistry exam.

(D) The standard deviation of grades on these two exams cannot be calculated with the data provided.

LEVEL 4: STATISTICS

6. If the average (arithmetic mean) of a, b, and 37 is 42, what is the average of a and b?

7. A farmer purchased several animals from a neighboring farmer: 6 animals costing \$100 each, 10 animals costing \$200 each, and k animals costing \$400 each, where k is a positive odd integer. If the median price for all the animals was \$200, what is the greatest possible value of k?

8. If the average (arithmetic mean) of k and $k + 7$ is b and if the average of k and $k - 11$ is c, what is the sum of b and c?

   (A) $2k - 2$
   (B) $2k - 1$
   (C) $2k$
   (D) $2k + \frac{1}{2}$

9. Twenty six people were playing a game. 1 person scored 50 points, 3 people scored 60 points, 4 people scored 70 points, 5 people scored 80 points, 6 people scored 90 points, and 7 people scored 100 points. Which of the following correctly shows the order of the median, mode and average (arithmetic mean) of the 26 scores?

   (A) average < median< mode
   (B) average < mode < median
   (C) median < mode < average
   (D) median < average < mode

10. If the average (arithmetic mean) of the measures of two noncongruent angles of an isosceles triangle is 75°, which of the following is the measure of one of the angles of the triangle?

    (A) 110°
    (B) 120°
    (C) 130°
    (D) 140°

LEVEL 5: STATISTICS

11. Let a, b and c be numbers with $a < b < c$ such that the average of a and b is 7, the average of b and c is 11, and the average of a and c is 10. What is the average of a, b and c?

$$\frac{1}{x^3}, \frac{1}{x^2}, \frac{1}{x}, x^2, x^3$$

12. * If $-1 < x < 0$, what is the median of the five numbers in the list above?

(A) $\frac{1}{x^3}$

(B) $\frac{1}{x^2}$

(C) $\frac{1}{x}$

(D) x^3

Answers

1. D	5. A	9. A
2. C	6. 89/2 or 44.5	10. B
3. .497	7. 15	11. 28/3 or 9.33
4. 65	8. A	12. D

Full Solutions

3.
* There are a total of 181 integers and 90 of them are greater than the median. So the desired probability is $\frac{90}{181} \approx .4972375691$. So we grid in .**497**.

Remark: By the fence-post formula there are $180 - 0 + 1 = 181$ integers in the list. Thus, the median of the numbers in set X is $0 + \frac{180}{2} = 90$.

Again, by the fence-post formula, there are $180 - 91 + 1 = 90$ integers greater than the median.

4.

Solution by listing: Let's list the test grades in increasing order, including repetitions.

60, 60 ,60, 65, 65, 65, 65, 65, 65, 65, 65, 65, 65, 65, 65, 75, 75, 75, 75, 95, 95, 95, 95, 95, 100

Now strike off two numbers at a time simultaneously, one from each end until just one number is left.

~~60, 60 ,60, 65, 65, 65, 65, 65, 65, 65, 65, 65,~~ 65, ~~65, 65, 75, 75, 75, 75,~~ ~~95, 95, 95, 95, 95, 100~~

We see that the answer is **65**.

* Doing it in your head: You can do this problem very quickly without writing anything down. If we "strike off" the 100, the 5 95's and the 4 75's (for a total of 10 numbers), then we should "strike off" the 3 60's, and 7 of the 65's. Since there are more 65's, the median is **65**.

Remark: If n numbers are listed in increasing (or decreasing) order, with n odd, then the median of these numbers is the kth number where $k = \frac{n+1}{2}$. In this example, $n = 25$. So $k = \frac{26}{2} = 13$, and the 13th test grade is 65.

5.

* The scores on the math exam are more "spread out" than the scores on the chemistry exam. It follows that the standard deviation of grades on the math exam is larger, choice (A).

Notes: (1) **Standard deviation** measures how far the data values are from the mean. If the data values are close to the mean, the standard deviation is small. If the data is far from the mean, the standard deviation is large.

For example, if all the data values were the same, then the mean would be that common value and the standard deviation would be 0.

(2) On the SAT it is not necessary to be able to compute the standard deviation. We need only understand what it measures.

(3) The mean of the chemistry grades is approximately 90. Notice that most of the data are near this value (between 85 and 95). So the standard deviation is small.

(4) The mean of the math grades is 87, but the grades are spread out with many values at the extremes 75 and 100. So the standard deviation is large.

6.

* Solution by changing averages to sums: The Sum of the 3 numbers is $42 \cdot 3 = 126$. Thus, $a + b + 37 = 126$, and it follows that $a + b = 89$. So the Average of a and b is $\mathbf{89/2 = 44.5}$.

Solution by picking numbers: Let's let $a = 42$ and $b = 47$. We make this choice because 37 and 47 are both 5 units from 42. Then the average of a and b is $\frac{a+b}{2} = \frac{42+47}{2} = \mathbf{89/2 = 44.5}$.

7.

* Solution by listing: Let's list the prices in increasing order, including repetitions.

100, 100, 100, 100, 100, 100, 200, 200, 200, 200, 200, 200, 200, 200, 200, **200**, 400,…

In order for k to be as large as possible we need the 200 in bold to be the median. Since there are 15 numbers **before** the bold 200, we need 15 numbers **after** the bold 200 as well. So $k = \mathbf{15}$.

8.

* Solution by changing averages to sums: Note that the sum of k and $k + 7$ is $k + (k + 7) = 2k + 7$, so that $2k + 7 = 2b$. Similarly, the sum of k and $k - 11$ is $k + (k - 11) = 2k - 11$ so that $2k - 11 = 2c$. So,

$$2b + 2c = 4k - 4$$
$$2(b + c) = 4k - 4$$
$$b + c = \frac{4k-4}{2} = \frac{4k}{2} - \frac{4}{2} = 2k - 2$$

Thus, the answer is choice (A).

Solution by picking a number: Let us choose a value for k, say $k = 5$. It follows that $k + 7 = 5 + 7 = 12$ and $k - 11 = 5 - 11 = -6$. So,

$$b = \frac{5+12}{2} = \frac{17}{2} = 8.5$$
$$c = \frac{5-6}{2} = -\frac{1}{2} = -0.5$$

and the sum of b and c is $b + c = 8.5 - 0.5 = 8$. **Put a nice big, dark circle around this number so that you can find it easily later.** We now substitute $k = 5$ into each answer choice.

    (A) 8
    (B) 9
    (C) 10
    (D) 10.5

Compare each of these numbers to the number that we put a nice big, dark circle around. Since (B), (C), and (D) are incorrect we can eliminate them. Therefore the answer is choice (A).

Important note: (A) is **not** the correct answer simply because it is equal to 8. It is correct because all three of the other choices are **not** 8. **You absolutely must check all four choices!**

    9.

* The median of 26 numbers is the average of the 13th and 14th numbers when the numbers are listed in increasing order (see remark below).

$$50, 60, 60, 60, 70, 70, 70, 70, 80, 80, 80, 80, \mathbf{80}, \mathbf{90}$$

So we see that the median is $\dfrac{80 + 90}{2} = 85$.

The mode is the number that appears most frequently. This is **100**.

Finally, we compute the average.

$$\frac{1 \cdot 50 + 3 \cdot 60 + 4 \cdot 70 + 5 \cdot 80 + 6 \cdot 90 + 7 \cdot 100}{26} = \frac{2150}{26} \approx 82.69.$$

Thus, we see that average < median < mode. This is choice (A).

Remark: If n numbers are listed in increasing (or decreasing) order, with n even, then the median of these numbers is the average of the kth and $(k + 1)$st numbers where $k = \dfrac{n}{2}$. In this example, $n = 26$. So $k = 13$, and the 13th and 14th numbers are 80 and 90. (Compare this with the remark at the end of the solution to problem 4.)

    10.

* **Solution by changing averages to sums:** The Sum of the measures of the two noncongruent angles of the isosceles triangle is $(75)(2) = 150°$.

Thus, the third angle is $180 - 150 = 30°$. Since the triangle is isosceles, one of the original angles must also be $30°$. It follows that the other original angle was $180 - 30 - 30 = 120°$, choice (B).

11.

* Solution by changing averages to sums: We change the averages to sums.

$$a + b = 14$$
$$b + c = 22$$
$$a + c = 20$$

Adding these 3 equations gives us $2a + 2b + 2c = 56$. So we have $a + b + c = 28$. Finally, we divide by 3 to get that the average of a, b and c is **28/3**.

Remark: We can also grid in the decimal **9.33**.

12.

* Solution by picking a number: Let's choose $x = -0.5$.

We use our calculator to compute the given expressions.

$$\frac{1}{x^3} = -8 \quad \frac{1}{x^2} = 4 \quad \frac{1}{x} = -2 \quad x^2 = 0.25 \quad x^3 = -0.125$$

Now let's place them in increasing order.

$$-8, -2, -0.125, 0.25, 4$$

The median is -0.125 which is x^3, choice (D).

OPTIONAL MATERIAL

CHALLENGE QUESTIONS: STATISTICS

1. Show that if x is the least integer in a set of $n + 1$ consecutive integers, then the median of the set is $x + \frac{n}{2}$.

2. Show that in a set of consecutive integers, the average (arithmetic mean) and median are equal.

Solutions

1.

Assume that the integers are written in increasing order. If n is even, then $n + 1$ is odd, and the median is in position $\frac{n+2}{2} = \frac{n}{2} + 1$. Note that $x = x + 0$ is in the 1st position, $x + 1$ is in the 2nd position, etc. Thus, $x + \frac{n}{2}$ is in position $\frac{n}{2} + 1$.

If n is odd, then $n + 1$ is even, and the median is the average of the integers in positions $\frac{n+1}{2}$ and $\frac{n+1}{2} + 1$. These integers are $x + \frac{n+1}{2} - 1$ and $x + \frac{n+1}{2}$. So their average is

$$(\tfrac{1}{2})(2x + (n+1) - 1) = (\tfrac{1}{2})(2x + n) = x + \tfrac{n}{2}.$$

2.

Let $\{x, x + 1, x + 2,..., x + n\}$ be a set of $n + 1$ consecutive integers. The average is equal to

$$\frac{(n+1)x + (1 + 2 + \cdots + n)}{n+1} = \frac{(n+1)x}{n+1} + \frac{n(n+1)}{2(n+1)} = x + \frac{n}{2}.$$

Remark: $1 + 2 + \cdots + n = \frac{n(n+1)}{2}$.

To see that this we can formally write out the sum of the numbers from 1 through n forwards and backwards, and then add term by term.

$$1 \ + \ 2 \ + \ 3 \ + \cdots + (n-1) + \ n$$
$$n \ + (n-1) + (n-2) + \cdots + \ 2 \ + \ 1$$
$$(n+1) + (n+1) + (n+1) + \cdots + (n+1) + (n+1)$$

We are adding $n + 1$ to itself n times, so that $2(1 + \cdots + n) = n(n + 1)$. So $1 + \cdots + n = \frac{n(n+1)}{2}$.

245

Lesson 21
Heart of Algebra

Reminder: Before beginning this lesson remember to redo the problems from Lessons 1, 5, 9, 13 and 17 that you have marked off. Do not "unmark" a question unless you get it correct.

Setting Up Algebraic Expressions

On the SAT you will need to be able to change "real world" situations into algebraic expressions. Sometimes you will need to recognize the correct setup, and sometimes you will need to solve equations. Here is an example where you simply need to recognize how to set up the expression.

LEVEL 1: HEART OF ALGEBRA

1. James solved k math problems per hour for 3 hours and Paul solved t math problems per hour for 2 hours. Which of the following represents the total number of math problems solved by James and Paul?

    (A) $2k + 3t$
    (B) $3k + 2t$
    (C) $6kt$
    (D) $5kt$

* **Algebraic solution:** James solved a total of $3k$ math problems and Paul solved a total of $2t$ math problems. So together James and Paul solved a total of $3k + 2t$ math problems, choice (B).

Notes: This problem can also be solved by picking numbers. I leave this solution as an exercise for the reader.

Interpreting Algebraic Expressions

You will also need to be able to interpret what the coefficients and constants represent in algebraic expressions. Here is a straightforward example of this.

LEVEL 3: HEART OF ALGEBRA

2. The number of stuffed animals, q, that a toy company can sell per week at a price of p dollars is given by $q = 500 - 23p$. What is the meaning of the value 500 in this equation?

   (A) 500 dollars is the maximum that someone would pay for a stuffed animal.
   (B) 500 people per week would take a stuffed animal for free.
   (C) If the price of a stuffed animal is decreased by 1 dollar, then 500 more people will make a purchase.
   (D) If the price of a stuffed animal is decreased by 100 dollars, then 500 more people will make a purchase.

* $q = 500$ when $p = 0$. This means that the toy company can sell 500 stuffed animals per week at a price of 0 dollars. In other words, 500 people per week would take a stuffed animal for free, choice (B).

Notes: (1) In the equation $q = 500 - 23p$, we are thinking of p as the **independent variable**, and q as the **dependent variable**. In other words, we input a value for p, and we get a q value as an output.

For example, if the input is a price of $p = 0$ dollars, then the output is a quantity of $q = 500 - 23(0) = 500$ stuffed animals.

(2) What if the question instead asked for the meaning of the number 23 in the equation?

First recall that the slope of a line is

$$\text{Slope} = m = \frac{\text{change in the dependent variable}}{\text{change in the independent variable}} = \frac{\text{change in } q}{\text{change in } p}$$

The **slope-intercept form of an equation of a line** is $y = mx + b$ where m is the slope of the line.

The given equation can be written $q = -23p + 500$, and we see that the slope is $m = -23 = -\frac{23}{1}$.

So we see that a change in p by 1 unit corresponds to a change in q by 23 units.

Since the sign of -23 is negative, there is a **negative association** between p and q. It follows that an increase in p corresponds to a decrease in q.

So if the price p of a stuffed animal is increased by 1 dollar, then 23 less people will make a purchase per week.

Isolating a Variable in an Equation

In addition to solving an equation or equations, sometimes you will be asked to solve for one variable in terms of others. Here is a simple example.

LEVEL 2: HEART OF ALGEBRA

$$A = P\frac{r(1+r)^n}{(1+r)^n - 1}$$

3.   The formula above gives the payment amount per period P needed to pay off an amortized loan of P dollars at r percent annual interest with a total of n payments. Which of the following gives P in terms of A, r, and n.

(A) $P = rA$

(B) $P = (1+r)^n A$

(C) $P = A\frac{(1+r)^n - 1}{r(1+r)^n}$

(D) $P = A\frac{r(1+r)^n}{(1+r)^n - 1}$

* **Algebraic solution:** To get P by itself we multiply each side of the equation by the reciprocal of $\frac{r(1+r)^n}{(1+r)^n - 1}$ which is $\frac{(1+r)^n - 1}{r(1+r)^n}$.

$$A\frac{(1+r)^n - 1}{r(1+r)^n} = P\frac{r(1+r)^n}{(1+r)^n - 1} \cdot \frac{(1+r)^n - 1}{r(1+r)^n}$$

$$A\frac{(1+r)^n - 1}{r(1+r)^n} = P$$

This is choice (C).

248

Try to solve each of the following problems. The answers to these problems, followed by full solutions are at the end of this lesson. **Do not** look at the answers until you have attempted these problems yourself. Please remember to mark off any problems you get wrong.

LEVEL 1: HEART OF ALGEBRA

4. Last month Josephine worked 7 less hours than Maria. If they worked a combined total of 137 hours, how many hours did Maria work that month?

LEVEL 2: HEART OF ALGEBRA

5. David and John each ordered an entrée at a diner. The price of David's entrée was d dollars, and the price of John's entrée was $3 more than the price of David's entrée. If David and John split the cost of the entrees evenly and each paid an 18% tip, which of the following expressions represents the amount, in dollars, each of them paid? (Assume there is no sales tax.)

   (A) $2.36d + 3.54$
   (B) $1.18d + 1.77$
   (C) $1.50d + 0.18$
   (D) $.18d + 0.2$

LEVEL 3: HEART OF ALGEBRA

6. Tickets for a concert cost $4.00 for children and $6.00 for adults. 850 concert tickets were sold for a total cost of $3820. How many children's tickets were sold?

7. 28 male lions and 172 female lions are living in a 500 acre conservation enclosure. If 35 more male lions are introduced into the enclosure, how many more female lions must be introduced so that $\frac{6}{7}$ of the total number of lions in the enclosure are female?

LEVEL 4: HEART OF ALGEBRA

8.   A small hotel has 15 rooms which are all occupied. If each room is occupied by either one or two guests and there are 27 guests in total, how many rooms are occupied by two guests?

9.   The cost of internet access on a resort is $0.30 per minute. Which of the following equations represents the total cost, C, in dollars, for x <u>hours</u> of internet access?

   (A) $C = \frac{0.30x}{60}$
   (B) $C = \frac{60x}{0.30}$
   (C) $C = 0.30x + 60$
   (D) $C = 0.30(60x)$

$$T = 3(c + \frac{25}{3})$$

10.   The equation above is used to model the number of chirps, c, made by a certain species of cricket in one minute, and the temperature, T, in degrees Fahrenheit. Based on the equation, which of the following must be true?

   I. An increase of 1 chirp per minute is equivalent to a temperature increase of 3 degrees Fahrenheit.
   II. A temperature increase of 1 degree Fahrenheit is equivalent to an increase of 1 chirp every 3 minutes.
   III. An increase of 3 chirps per minute is equivalent to a temperature increase of 1 degree Fahrenheit.

   (A) I only
   (B) II only
   (C) III only
   (D) I and II only

LEVEL 5: HEART OF ALGEBRA

Questions 11 and 12 refer to the following information.

The quantity of a product supplied (called the *supply*) and the quantity of the product demanded (called the *demand*) in an economic market are functions of the price of the product. The market is said to be in *equilibrium* when the supply and demand are equal. The price at equilibrium is called the *equilibrium price*, and the quantity at equilibrium is called the *equilibrium demand*. Consider the following supply and demand functions where p is the price, in dollars, s is the supply function, and d is the demand function.

$$s = \frac{2}{3}p + 15$$
$$d = -\frac{1}{3}p + 99$$

11. What is the equilibrium price? (Disregard the dollar sign when gridding your answer.)

12. What is the equilibrium demand?

Answers

1. B	5. B	9. D
2. B	6. 640	10. D
3. C	7. 206	11. 84
4. 72	8. 12	12. 71

Full Solutions

6.

Algebraic solution: Let c be the number of children that bought concert tickets, and let a be the number of adults that bought concert tickets. We have the system of equations

$$c + a = 850$$
$$4c + 6a = 3820$$

We multiply each side of the first equation by 6 and subtract.

251

$$6c + 6a = 5100$$
$$\underline{4c + 6a = 3820}$$
$$2c = 1280$$

We divide each side of this last equation by 2 to get $c = \frac{1280}{2} = \mathbf{640}$.

Notes: (1) c is the number of tickets sold to children, a is the number of tickets sold to adults, and 850 is the total number of tickets sold.

It follows that $c + a = 850$.

(2) Since each children's ticket costs \$4.00, it follows that $4c$ is the total cost for children's tickets.

Since each adult's ticket costs \$6, it follows that $6a$ is the total cost for adult's tickets.

So $4c + 6a$ is the total ticket cost, and so $4c + 6a = 1280$.

* Alternate algebraic solution: If we let c be the number of children that bought concert tickets, then $850 - c$ is the number of adults that bought concert tickets, and we have $4c + 6(850 - c) = 3820$.

So we have
$$4c + 5100 - 6c = 3820$$
$$-2c + 5100 = 3820$$
$$-2c = -1280$$
$$c = \mathbf{640}$$

Solution by guessing: We keep taking guesses for c until we zero in on the correct answer. Let's start with $c = 500$.

$$c = 500 \Rightarrow a = 350 \Rightarrow 4c + 6a = 2000 + 2100 = 4100.$$

This is a too big. So let's try $c = 700$.

$$c = 700 \Rightarrow a = 150 \Rightarrow 4c + 6a = 2800 + 900 = 3700.$$

This is too small. Let's try $c = 600$.

$$c = 600 \Rightarrow a = 250 \Rightarrow 4c + 6a = 2400 + 1500 = 3900.$$

Still a bit too big. Let's try $c = 640$.

$$c = 640 \Rightarrow a = 210 \Rightarrow 4c + 6a = 2560 + 1260 = 3820.$$

That's correct! So the answer is **640**.

7.

Algebraic solution: Let x be the number of female lions that must be introduced. The number of female lions will then be $172 + x$ and the total number of lions will be $28 + 35 + 172 + x = 235 + x$. So we must have

$$\frac{172 + x}{235 + x} = \frac{6}{7}$$

We cross multiply to get $7(172 + x) = 6(235 + x)$. Distributing on each side gives $1204 + 7x = 1410 + 6x$. Finally we subtract $6x$ and subtract 1204 from each side of this last equation to get $x = \textbf{206}$.

Note: This problem can also be solved by taking guesses for x. I leave this solution as an exercise for the reader.

8.

Solution by guessing: Let's guess that 10 rooms are occupied by 2 guests. Then there are 5 rooms that are occupied by one guest. So the total number of guests is $10 \cdot 2 + 5 \cdot 1 = 25$. This is too few guests, so there must be **more** rooms with two guests.

Let's guess that 12 rooms are occupied by 2 guests. Then there are 3 rooms that are occupied by one guest. So the total number of guests is $12 \cdot 2 + 3 \cdot 1 = 27$. This is correct, so that the answer is **12**.

* A quick solution: Put one guest into each room. This takes care of 15 guests. There are now $27 - 15 = 12$ guests left. Therefore **12** rooms must have two guests.

An algebraic solution: Let x be the number of rooms occupied by one guest, and let y be the number of rooms occupied by two guests. Since there are 15 rooms in total, we must have that $x + y = 15$. We also have $x + 2y = 27$ because there are 27 guests in total. So we have the following system of equations.

$$x + 2y = 27$$
$$x + y = 15$$

We subtract the second equation from the first to get

$$y = 27 - 15 = \textbf{12}.$$

253

9.

Solution by picking a number: Let's let $x = 2$. Since 2 hours is the same as $60 \cdot 2 = 120$ minutes, the cost C is $0.30 \cdot 120 = \mathbf{36}$ dollars. **Put a nice big, dark circle around this number so that you can find it easily later.** We now substitute 2 in for x into **all** four answer choices (we use our calculator if we're allowed to).

(A) 0.01
(B) 400
(C) 60.6
(D) 36

Since (D) is the only choice that has become 36, we conclude that (D) is the answer.

Important note: (D) is **not** the correct answer simply because it is equal to 36. It is correct because all 3 of the other choices are **not** 36.

*Algebraic solution: x hours is equal to $60x$ minutes. To get the total cost C we multiply the number of minutes, $60x$, by the cost per minute, 0.30. So we get $(60x) \cdot 0.30 = 0.30(60x)$, choice (D).

10.

Solution by picking numbers: Let's see what happens when we increase by 1 chirp per minute. When $c = 0$ chirps per minute, we have $T = 3 \cdot \frac{25}{3} = 25$. When $c = 1$ chirp per minute, we have $T = 3\left(1 + \frac{25}{3}\right) = 3 + 25 = 28$. So T increases from 25 to 28. This is an increase by 3 degrees Fahrenheit. Since the equation is linear, I must be true. We can therefore eliminate choices (B) and (C).

Now let's see what happens when we increase the temperature by 1 degree Fahrenheit. When $T = 0$ degrees Fahrenheit, we have $0 = c + \frac{25}{3}$. So $c = -\frac{25}{3}$. When $T = 1$ degree Fahrenheit, we have $1 = 3\left(c + \frac{25}{3}\right)$. So $\frac{1}{3} = c + \frac{25}{3}$, and therefore $c = \frac{1}{3} - \frac{25}{3} = -\frac{24}{3}$. So c increases from $-\frac{25}{3}$ to $-\frac{24}{3}$. This is an increase by $\frac{1}{3}$ chirps per minute, or equivalently 1 chirp every 3 minutes. Since the equation is linear, II must be true. The answer is therefore choice (D).

Note: To verify that III can be false, note that when $c = 3$, we have $T = 3\left(3 + \frac{25}{3}\right) = 9 + 25 = 34$. So as c increases from 0 to 3, T increases from 25 to 34. This is an increase of 9 degrees, and <u>not</u> 1 degree.

* Algebraic solution: The equation is linear with a slope of $3 = \frac{3}{1}$. This can be read several ways.

One way is that an increase in c by 1 unit is equivalent to an increase in T by 3 units. This is precisely what I says.

Dividing each number in the previous paragraph by 3 gives that an increase in c by $\frac{1}{3}$ unit is equivalent to an increase in T by 1 unit. An increase in c by $\frac{1}{3}$ unit means that the number of chirps is increasing by $\frac{1}{3}$ chirp per minute. This is equivalent to the number of chirps increasing by 1 chirp every 3 minutes. So II works as well.

Therefore the answer is choice (D).

    11.

* Algebraic solution: We set s equal to d to get $\frac{2}{3}p + 15 = -\frac{1}{3}p + 99$. We now add $\frac{1}{3}p$ to each side of the equation and subtract 15 from each side of the equation to get $p = \mathbf{84}$.

    12.

* Algebraic solution: We substitute $p = 84$ into *either* the supply or demand function. If we use the supply function we get

$$s = \frac{2}{3}(84) + 15 = \mathbf{71}.$$

Note: We would get the same answer if we were to use the demand function: $d = -\frac{1}{3}(84) + 99 = \mathbf{71}$.

LESSON 22
GEOMETRY

Reminder: Before beginning this lesson remember to redo the problems from Lessons 2, 6, 10, 14 and 18 that you have marked off. Do not "unmark" a question unless you get it correct.

Move the Sides of a Figure Around

Try to answer the following question using this strategy. **Do not** check the solution until you have attempted this question yourself.

LEVEL 4: GEOMETRY

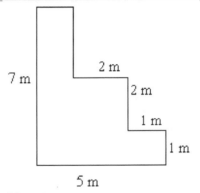

Note: Figure not drawn to scale.

1.   Let P be the perimeter of the figure above in meters, and let A be the area of the figure above in square meters. What is the value of $P + A$?

* Recall that to compute the **perimeter** of the figure we need to add up the lengths of all 8 line segments in the figure. We "move" the two smaller horizontal segments up and the two smaller vertical segments to the right as shown below.

256

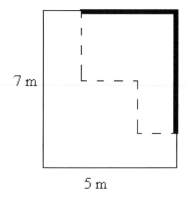

Note that the "bold" length is equal to the "dashed" length. Thus, the perimeter is

$$P = (2)(7) + (2)(5) = 14 + 10 = \textbf{24} \text{ m}.$$

To compute the **area** of the figure we break the figure up into 3 rectangles and compute the length and width of each rectangle.

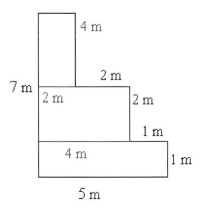

The length and width of the bottom rectangle are 5 and 1 making the area $5 \cdot 1 = 5$ m². The length of the middle rectangle is $5 - 1 = 4$, and the width is given as 2. So the area is $4 \cdot 2 = 8$ m². The length of the top rectangle is $4 - 2 = 2$, and its width is $7 - 1 - 2 = 4$. Thus, the area is $2 \cdot 4 = 8$ m². We then get the total area by adding up the areas of the three rectangles: $A = 5 + 8 + 8 = \textbf{21}$ m².

Finally, $P + A = 24 + 21 = \textbf{45}$.

Remark: Notice that if we have the full length of a line segment, and one partial length of the same line segment, then we get the other partial length by subtracting the two given lengths.

Areas of Shaded Regions

Finding the area of a shaded region often involves subtracting two areas. The area formulas that you need are either formulas that are given to you in the front of the section or are given in the problem itself.

Try to answer the following question using this strategy. **Do not** check the solution until you have attempted this question yourself.

LEVEL 4: GEOMETRY

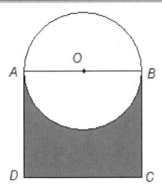

2.   In the figure above, *AB* is a diameter of the circle with center *O* and *ABCD* is a square. What is the area of the shaded region if the radius of the circle is 5?

(A) $25(4 - \frac{\pi}{2})$

(B) $25(2 - \frac{\pi}{2})$

(C) $\pi(4 - \pi)$

(D) $\pi(2 - \pi)$

* A side of the square has length $s = 2r = 2 \cdot 5 = 10$. The area of the square is then $s^2 = 10^2 = 100$.

The area of the circle is $\pi r^2 = \pi(5)^2 = 25\pi$. The area of the semicircle is then $\frac{25\pi}{2}$. The area of the shaded region is

258

Area of Square − Area of Semicircle
$$= 100 - \frac{25\pi}{2}$$
$$= 25(4 - \frac{\pi}{2})$$

Thus, the answer is choice (A).

Note: If a calculator is allowed we can use it to get that $100 - \frac{25\pi}{2}$ is approximately **60.73009183**. We then do the same with the answer choices until we get one that matches up. We would then see that choice (A) gives the same answer. Of course, this would be more time consuming, but it is better to be safe if you are not good at factoring, or you simply do not see that you need to factor.

Fitting Geometric Objects Inside Another Object

To see how many two-dimensional objects fit inside another two-dimensional object we divide areas. To see how many three-dimensional objects fit inside another three-dimensional object we divide volumes.

Try to answer the following question using this strategy. **Do not** check the solution until you have attempted this question yourself.

LEVEL 4: GEOMETRY

3. * Rectangular bricks measuring $\frac{1}{2}$ meter by $\frac{1}{3}$ meter are sold in boxes containing 8 bricks each. What is the least number of boxes of bricks needed to cover a rectangular area that has dimensions 9 meters by 11 meters?

* The area of a face of one rectangular brick is $(\frac{1}{2})(\frac{1}{3}) = \frac{1}{6}$. The area of the rectangular region we want to cover is $(9)(11) = 99$. We can see how many bricks we need to cover this area by dividing the two areas.

$$99 \div (\frac{1}{6}) = 99 \cdot 6 = 594.$$

Now, $\frac{594}{8} = 74.25$. So the number of boxes needed is **75**.

Remark: A common error would be to round 74.25 to 74. This is incorrect because 74 boxes will not contain enough bricks to cover the entire area. Indeed, $8(74) = 592 < 594$.

Open Up a Cylinder to Get a Rectangle

When we cut a cylinder down the height and open it up we get a rectangle. One side of the rectangle has the height of the cylinder as its length. The other side has the circumference of a base of the cylinder as its length.

You may want to take a flat rectangular object such as a piece of paper or paper towel and put two sides together to form a cylinder. Open and close your cylinder and note how one of the sides of the rectangle corresponds to the circumference of the cylinder.

Try to answer the following question using this strategy. **Do not** check the solution until you have attempted this question yourself.

LEVEL 5: GEOMETRY

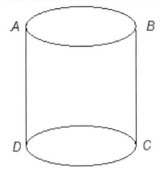

4.   * The figure shown above is a right circular cylinder. The circumference of each circular base is 20, the length of *AD* is 14, and *AB* and *CD* are diameters of each base respectively. If the cylinder is cut along *AD*, opened, and flattened, what is the length of *AC* to the nearest tenth?

* When we cut and unfold the cylinder as described we get the following rectangle.

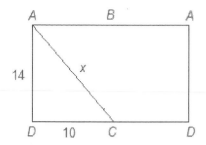

Notice that C is right in the middle of the rectangle. A common error would be to put C as one of the vertices. Note also that the length of the rectangle is 20 so that DC is 10. We can now use the Pythagorean Theorem to find AC.

$$x^2 = 10^2 + 14^2 = 100 + 196 = 296$$
$$x = \sqrt{296} \approx 17.20465$$

Since the question asks for the answer to the nearest tenth, we grid in **17.2**.

Surface Area of a Rectangular Solid

The **surface area of a rectangular solid** is just the sum of the areas of all 6 faces. The formula is

$$A = 2lw + 2lh + 2wh$$

where l, w and h are the length, width and height of the rectangular solid, respectively.

In particular, the **surface area of a cube** is

$$A = 6s^2$$

where s is the length of a side of the cube.

Try to answer the following question about the surface area of a cube. **Do not** check the solution until you have attempted this question yourself.

261

LEVEL 4: GEOMETRY

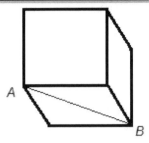

5.   In the figure above, segment $\overline{AB}$ joins two vertices of the cube. If the length of $\overline{AB}$ is $3\sqrt{2}$, what is the surface area of the cube?

* The area of one of the faces is $s^2 = 9$ (see below for several methods of computing this). Thus, the surface area is $A = 6s^2 = 6 \cdot 9 = \mathbf{54}$.

Methods for computing the area of a face:

(1) Since all sides of a square have equal length, an isosceles right triangle is formed. An isosceles right triangle is the same as a 45, 45, 90 triangle. So we can get the length of a side of the triangle just by looking at the formula for a 45, 45, 90 right triangle. Here s is 3. The area of the square is then $(3)(3) = 9$.

(2) If we let s be the length of a side of the square, then by the Pythagorean Theorem

$$s^2 + s^2 = \left(3\sqrt{2}\right)^2$$
$$2s^2 = 18$$
$$s^2 = 9$$

(3) The area of a square is $A = \dfrac{d^2}{2}$ where d is the length of a diagonal of the square. Therefore in this problem

$$A = \frac{d^2}{2} = \frac{\left(3\sqrt{2}\right)^2}{2} = \frac{18}{2} = 9.$$

You're doing great! Let's just practice a bit more. Try to solve each of the following problems. The answers to these problems, followed by full solutions are at the end of this lesson. **Do not** look at the answers until you have attempted these problems yourself. Please remember to mark off any problems you get wrong.

LEVEL 3: GEOMETRY

6. How many spherical snowballs with a radius of 4 centimeters can be made with the amount of snow in a spherical snowball of radius 8 centimeters? (the volume V of a sphere with radius r is given by $\frac{4}{3}\pi r^3$.)

LEVEL 4: GEOMETRY

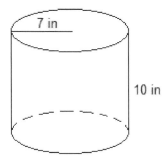

7. * The figure above is a right circular cylinder with a height of 10 inches and a base radius of 7 inches. What is the surface area, in square inches, of the cylinder to the nearest integer?

8. Cube X has surface area A. The edges of cube Y are 4 times as long as the edges of cube X. What is the surface area of cube Y in terms of A?

    (A) $2A$
    (B) $4A$
    (C) $8A$
    (D) $16A$

9. If a 2-centimeter cube were cut in half in all three directions, then in square centimeters, the total surface area of the separated smaller cubes would be how much greater than the surface area of the original 2-centimeter cube?

263

LEVEL 5: GEOMETRY

10. For any cube, if the volume is V cubic centimeters and the surface area is S square centimeters, then S is directly proportional to V^n for $n =$

11. * How many solid wood cubes, each with a total surface area of 294 square centimeters, can be cut from a solid wood cube with a total surface area of 2,646 square centimeters if no wood is lost in the cutting?

    (A) 3
    (B) 9
    (C) 27
    (D) 81

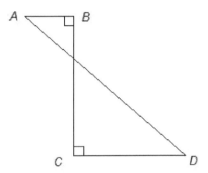

Note: Figure not drawn to scale.

12. In the figure above, $AB = 4$, $BC = 24$, and $AD = 26$. What is the length of line segment $\overline{CD}$?

Answers

1. 45	5. 54	9. 24
2. A	6. 8	10. 2/3, .666 or .667
3. 75	7. 748	11. C
4. 17.2	8. D	12. 6

Full Solutions

6.
* We divide the volumes.

264

$$\frac{\frac{4}{3}\pi \cdot 8^3}{\frac{4}{3}\pi \cdot 4^3} = \frac{8^3}{4^3} = \frac{512}{64} = \mathbf{8}.$$

7.

*: When we cut and unfold the cylinder we get the following rectangle.

$C \approx 43.9823$

Notice that the width of the rectangle is the circumference of the base of the cylinder. Thus the width is $C = 2\pi r = 2\pi(7) = 14\pi$ inches.

The **lateral** surface area of the cylinder is the area of this rectangle.

$$L = 10(14\pi) = 140\pi \text{ inches.}$$

We also need the area of the two bases. Each of these is a circle with area $A = \pi r^2 = \pi(7)^2 = 49\pi$ inches. Therefore the total surface area is

$$S = L + 2A = 140\pi + 2(49\pi) = 238\pi \approx 747.699 \text{ inches.}$$

To the nearest integer this is **748** inches.

8.

Solution by picking numbers: Let's choose a value for the length of an edge of cube X, say $s = 1$. Then the surface area of X is $A = 6s^2 = 6(1)^2 = 6$. The length of an edge of cube Y is $4(1) = 4$, and so the surface area of Y is $6(4)^2 = 6 \cdot 16 = \mathbf{96}$. Now we plug in $A = 6$ into each answer choice and eliminate any choice that does not come out to 96.

    (A) 12
    (B) 24
    (C) 48
    (D) 96

Since (A), (B) and (C) all came out incorrect we can eliminate them. Therefore the answer is choice (D).

265

* Algebraic solution: Let s be the length of an edge of cube X. Then we have $A = 6s^2$. Since an edge of cube Y is 4 times the length of an edge of cube X, the length of an edge of cube Y is $4s$, so that the surface area of cube Y is $6(4s)^2 = 6 \cdot 16s^2 = 16(6s^2) = 16A$, choice (D).

9.

* The surface area of the 2-centimeter cube is $6(2)^2 = 6(4) = 24$. The surface area of each 1-centimeter cube is $6(1)^2 = 6(1) = 6$. Now, there are 8 of these smaller cubes so that the total surface area of the smaller cubes is $8(6) = 48$. So the answer is $48 - 24 = $ 24.

10.

Solution by picking numbers: Let's choose a value for the length of a cube, say $s = 1$. Then $S = 6(1)^2 = 6$ and $V = 1^3 = 1$. Now let's try $s = 2$. Then we have $S = 6(2)^2 = 6(4) = 24$ and $V = 2^3 = 8$. We need

$$\frac{6}{1^n} = \frac{24}{8^n}$$

Cross multiplying gives us $6 \cdot 8^n = 24 \cdot 1^n = 24$, or equivalently $8^n = 4$. To solve this equation let's write $8 = 2^3$ and $4 = 2^2$. So we have $(2^3)^n = 2^2$, or equivalently $2^{3n} = 2^2$, Since the bases are the same we can set the exponents equal to each other. So $3n = 2$, and $n = $ **2/3**, .**666** or .**667**)

* Algebraic solution: If s is the length of a side of the cube, then we have $S = 6s^2$ and $V = s^3$. Solving the second equation for s, we have $s = V^{\frac{1}{3}}$. Therefore $S = 6\left(V^{\frac{1}{3}}\right)^2 = 6V^{\frac{2}{3}}$. So S is directly proportional to $V^{\frac{2}{3}}$ (with constant of proportionality 6). So $n = $ **2/3**.

11.

* We first find the length of a side of each cube.

$$6s^2 = 294 \quad \text{and} \quad 6s^2 = 2646$$
$$s^2 = 49 \qquad\qquad s^2 = 441$$
$$s = 7 \qquad\qquad\quad s = 21$$

Thus the volume of each cube is $7^3 = 343$ and $21^3 = 9261$, respectively. We can see how many smaller cubes can be cut from the larger cube by dividing the two volumes: $\frac{9261}{343} = 27$, choice (C).

12.

* The problem becomes much simpler if we "move" $\overline{BC}$ to the left and $\overline{AB}$ to the bottom as shown below.

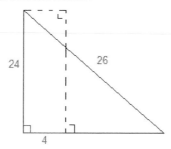

We now have a single right triangle and we can either use the Pythagorean Theorem, or better yet notice that $26 = (13)(2)$ and $24 = (12)(2)$. Thus the other leg of the triangle is $(5)(2) = 10$. So we see that $\overline{CD}$ must have length $10 - 4 = \mathbf{6}$.

Remark: If we didn't notice that this was a multiple of a 5, 12, 13 triangle, then we would use the Pythagorean Theorem as follows.

$$(x + 4)^2 + 24^2 = 26^2$$
$$(x + 4)^2 + 576 = 676$$
$$(x + 4)^2 = 100$$
$$x + 4 = 10$$
$$x = \mathbf{6}$$

Download additional solutions for free here:

www.thesatmathprep.com/28Les800.html

LESSON 23
PASSPORT TO ADVANCED MATH

Reminder: Before beginning this lesson remember to redo the problems from Lessons 3, 7, 11, 15 and 19 that you have marked off. Do not "unmark" a question unless you get it correct.

Nonlinear Systems of Equations

When solving a system of equations where at least one of the equations is not linear, it is usually best to use the substitution method. Let's look at an example.

LEVEL 4: ADVANCED MATH

$$3x^2 + 2y^2 = 550$$
$$2x + 12y = 0$$

1. If (x, y) is a solution to the system of equations above, what is the value of y^2 ?

* Solution by substitution: We solve the second equation for x by first subtracting $12y$ from each side to get $2x = -12y$. We then divide each side of this last equation by 2 to get $x = -6y$.

Now we replace x by $-6y$ in the left hand side of the first equation to get

$$3x^2 + 2y^2 = 3(-6y)^2 + 2y^2 = 3(36y^2) + 2y^2$$

$$= 108y^2 + 2y^2 = 110y^2 .$$

So we have $110y^2 = 550$, and so $y^2 = \dfrac{550}{110} = \textbf{5}$.

Exponential Growth and Decay

A general exponential function has the form $f(t) = a \cdot (1 + r)^{ct}$, where $a = f(0)$ is the *initial amount* and r is the *growth rate*. If $r > 0$, then we have **exponential growth** and if $r < 0$ we have **exponential decay**.

268

Examples: (1) The exponential function $f(t) = 300(2)^t$ can be used to model a population with a growth rate of $1 = 100\%$ each year that begins with 300 specimens. The growth rate of 100% tells us that the population doubles each year.

(2) The exponential function $f(t) = 50(3)^{2t}$ can be used to model a population with a growth rate of $2 = 200\%$ every 6 months that begins with 50 specimens. The growth rate of 200% tells us that the population triples. Since $c = 2$, the tripling occurs every $\frac{1}{2}$ year or 6 months.

(3) The exponential function $f(t) = 120(.75)^{\frac{t}{3}}$ can be used to model a substance which is decaying at a rate of $1 - .75 = .25 = 25\%$ every 3 years. The initial amount of the substance might be 120 grams. Since $c = \frac{1}{3}$, the 25% decay occurs every 3 years.

(4) A quantity that continually doubles over a fixed time period can be modeled by the exponential function $f(t) = c(2)^{\frac{t}{d}}$ where c is the quantity at time $t = 0$, and d is the doubling time in years.

LEVEL 4: ADVANCED MATH

2. On January 1, 2015, a family living on an island releases their two pet rabbits into the wild. Due to the short gestation period of rabbits, and the fact that the rabbits have no natural predators on this island, the rabbit population doubles each month. If P represents the rabbit population t years after January 1, 2015, then which of the following equations best models the rabbit population on this island over time?

   (A) $P = 2^{\frac{t+12}{12}}$
   (B) $P = 2^{t+1}$
   (C) $P = 2^{12t}$
   (D) $P = 2^{12t+1}$

* Solution using the exponential growth model formula: As seen in example (4) above, a quantity that continually doubles over a fixed time period can be modeled by the exponential function $P = c(2)^{\frac{t}{d}}$ where c is the quantity at time $t = 0$, and d is the doubling time in years. In this case, there are initially 2 rabbits, so that $c = 2$, and the doubling time is every month, or every $\frac{1}{12}$ year.

269

It follows that $P = 2(2)^{t \div \frac{1}{12}} = 2(2)^{12t} = 2^1 2^{12t} = 2^{1+12t} = 2^{12t+1}$, choice (D).

Note: See Lesson 13 for a review of the laws of exponents used here.

Solution using a general exponential function: As discussed above, a general exponential function has the form $P(t) = a \cdot (1 + r)^{ct}$, where $a = P(0)$ is the initial amount and r is the growth rate.

In this problem, $a = P(0) = 2$, and since the population is doubling (or increasing by 100%), the exponential rate is $r = 1$. So we have $P(t) = 2 \cdot 2^{ct}$.

We are also given that the population doubles each month, so that $P\left(\frac{1}{12}\right) = 4$. So we have $4 = 2 \cdot 2^{\frac{c}{12}} = 2^{1+\frac{c}{12}}$. So $2^2 = 2^{1+\frac{c}{12}}$, and therefore $1 + \frac{c}{12} = 2$. Subtracting 1 from each side of this equation yields $\frac{c}{12} = 2 - 1 = 1$, and so $c = 1 \cdot 12 = 12$.

So $P(t) = 2 \cdot 2^{12t} = 2^1 \cdot 2^{12t} = 2^{1+12t} = 2^{12t+1}$, choice (D).

Solution by picking a number: Let's choose a value for t, say $t = \frac{1}{2}$. Note that $\frac{1}{2}$ year is equal to 6 months.

Since there are initially 2 rabbits, after 1 month there are $2 \cdot 2 = 4$ rabbits, after 2 months there are $2 \cdot 4 = 8$ rabbits, after 3 months there are $2 \cdot 8 = 16$ rabbits, after 4 months there are $2 \cdot 16 = 32$ rabbits, after 5 months there are $2 \cdot 32 = 64$ rabbits, and after 6 months there are $2 \cdot 64 = \mathbf{128}$ rabbits.

Put a nice big, dark circle around the number **128** so you can find it easily later.

We now substitute $t = \frac{1}{2}$ into each answer choice:

(A) $2^{\frac{\frac{1}{2}+12}{12}} = 2^{\frac{\frac{1}{2}+\frac{24}{2}}{12}} = 2^{\frac{25}{2} \div 12} = 2^{\frac{25}{2} \cdot \frac{1}{12}} = 2^{\frac{25}{24}}$

(B) $2^{\frac{1}{2}+1} = 2^{\frac{1}{2}+\frac{2}{2}} = 2^{\frac{3}{2}} = 8^{\frac{1}{2}} = \sqrt{8} = \sqrt{4}\sqrt{2} = 2\sqrt{2}$

(C) $2^{12 \cdot \frac{1}{2}} = 2^6 = 64$

(D) $2^{12 \cdot \frac{1}{2}+1} = 2^{6+1} = 2^7 = 128$

Since choices (A), (B), and (C) did not come out correct, the answer is choice (D).

Notes: (1) Note that we picked the number $\frac{1}{2}$ as opposed to an integer like 2. This is because an integer like 2 will force us to do 24 computations or recognize a pattern. The fraction minimizes the amount of computation and the amount of critical reasoning needed. An even smaller fraction like $\frac{1}{3}$ or $\frac{1}{4}$ would have saved even more time.

(2) Instead of multiplying by 2 repeatedly we could save time by finding a pattern as follows:

After 0 months there are $2 = 2^1$ rabbits.

After 1 month there are $2 \cdot 2 = 2^2$ rabbits.

After 2 months there are $2 \cdot 2^2 = 2^{1+2} = 2^3$ rabbits.

This should be enough to see the pattern. Can you see that After n months there are 2^{n+1} rabbits? In particular, after 6 months there are $2^7 = 128$ rabbits.

(3) There is no reason to continue evaluating answer choices once it is clear that the choice will not yield the correct answer. For example, for choice (A) it is not hard to see that $2^{\frac{\frac{1}{2}+12}{12}} = 2^{\frac{12.5}{12}}$ could not possibly be equal to 128.

(5) If we are allowed to use a calculator for this problem, we could use it to compute the answer choices quickly. For example, with $t = \frac{1}{2}$, choice (A) would give 2^((1 / 2 + 12) / 12) $\approx$ 2.0586. Clearly this is incorrect and so we can eliminate it.

(6) When using the strategy of picking numbers it is very important that you check every answer choice. It is possible for more than one choice to come out to the correct answer. You would then need to pick a new number to try to eliminate all but one choice.

Synthetic Division

We can divide any polynomial by a linear polynomial of the form $x - r$ by using a simple procedure called **synthetic division**. Let's illustrate this procedure with an example.

LEVEL 5: ADVANCED MATH

3. If the expression $\frac{x^3-5x^2+3x+9}{x-1}$ is written in the equivalent form $ax^2 + bx + c + \frac{d}{x-1}$, what is the value of d ?

* Solution using synthetic division: If we are dividing by $x - r$, then we begin by writing r in the upper left hand corner. In this case $r = 1$.

Next we make sure that the polynomial we are dividing by is written in descending order of exponents (which is it) and that every exponent is accounted for (which they are). We then write down the coefficients of this polynomial. So we have the following:

$$1\rfloor \quad 1 \quad -5 \quad 3 \quad 9$$

We begin by bringing down the first 1.

$$1\rfloor \quad 1 \quad -5 \quad 3 \quad 9$$
$$\overline{\quad 1 \quad\quad\quad\quad\quad}$$

We now multiply this number by the number in the upper left. So we have (1)(1) = 1. We place this number under the −5.

$$1\rfloor \quad 1 \quad -5 \quad 3 \quad 9$$
$$\quad\quad\quad 1 \quad\quad\quad$$
$$\overline{\quad 1 \quad\quad\quad\quad\quad}$$

Next we add −5 and 1.

$$1\rfloor \quad 1 \quad -5 \quad 3 \quad 9$$
$$\quad\quad\quad 1 \quad\quad\quad$$
$$\overline{\quad 1 \quad -4 \quad\quad\quad}$$

We repeat this procedure to get $(-4)(1) = -4$, then add 3 and −4 to get −1.

$$1\rfloor \quad 1 \quad -5 \quad 3 \quad 9$$
$$\quad\quad\quad 1 \quad -4 \quad$$
$$\overline{\quad 1 \quad -4 \quad -1 \quad}$$

Finally, we multiply $(-1)(1) = -1$, then add 9 and −1 to get 8.

$$1\rfloor \quad 1 \quad -5 \quad 3 \quad 9$$
$$\quad\quad\quad 1 \quad -4 \quad -1$$
$$\overline{\quad 1 \quad -4 \quad -1 \quad 8}$$

272

The bottom row gives the coefficients of the quotient (which is a polynomial of 1 degree less than the dividend) and the remainder.

So the quotient polynomial is $x^2 - 4x - 1$ and the remainder is 8.

We put the remainder over the linear divisor and add it to the quotient.

So we have $\frac{x^3 - 5x^2 + 3x + 9}{x-1} = x^2 - 4x - 1 + \frac{8}{x-1}$. In particular $d = 8$.

Notes: (1) There is no need to actually write down the quotient here. Once we write down the final row, we immediately see that $a = 1$, $b = -4$, $c = -1$, and $d = 8$. This question is asking for d, and so we grid in **8**.

(2) This problem can also be solved using long division. This procedure is more time consuming than synthetic division, so I will omit it here and leave it as an optional exercise for the interested reader.

Now try to solve each of the following problems. The answers to these problems, followed by full solutions are at the end of this lesson. **Do not** look at the answers until you have attempted these problems yourself. Please remember to mark off any problems you get wrong.

LEVEL 2: ADVANCED MATH

4. The value of x that will make $\frac{x}{3} - 2 = -\frac{11}{4}$ a true statement lies between which of the following numbers?

    (A) −3 and −2
    (B) −2 and −1
    (C) −1 and 0
    (D) 0 and 1

LEVEL 4: ADVANCED MATH

$$\frac{1}{x}+\frac{3}{x}=\frac{1}{2}$$

5. Dennis is helping Billy assemble his new computer desk. Billy can put the desk together three times as fast as Dennis, and together Billy and Dennis can finish assembling the desk in 2 hours. The equation above represents this situation. Which of the following describes what the expression $\frac{3}{x}$ represents in this equation?

   (A) The fraction of the job that would be completed by Billy in 1 hour.
   (B) The fraction of the job that would be completed by Dennis in 1 hour.
   (C) The time, in hours, that it takes Billy to complete one third of the job.
   (D) The time, in hours that it takes Billy to assemble the desk by himself.

$$y = (x + 7)(3x - 5)$$
$$x = 3y + 1$$

6. How many ordered pairs (x, y) satisfy the system of equations shown above?

   (A) None
   (B) One
   (C) Two
   (D) More than two

7. A radioactive substance decays at an annual rate of 17 percent. If the initial amount of the substance is 650 grams, which of the following functions h models the remaining amount of the substance, in grams, t years later?

   (A) $h(t) = 0.17(650)^t$
   (B) $h(t) = 0.83(650)^t$
   (C) $h(t) = 650(0.17)^t$
   (D) $h(t) = 650(0.83)^t$

LEVEL 5: ADVANCED MATH

8. The expression $\frac{3x-5}{x+2}$ is equivalent to which of the following?

    (A) $\frac{3-5}{2}$

    (B) $3 - \frac{5}{2}$

    (C) $3 - \frac{5}{x+2}$

    (D) $3 - \frac{11}{x+2}$

9. If the expression $\frac{9x^2}{3x+5}$ is written in the equivalent form $\frac{25}{3x+5} + k$, what is k in terms of x ?

    (A) $9x^2$
    (B) $9x^2 + 5$
    (C) $3x - 5$
    (D) $3x + 5$

10. The equation $\frac{54x^2+85x-32}{kx-3} = -27x - 2 - \frac{38}{kx-3}$ is true for all values of $x \neq \frac{3}{k}$, where k is a constant. What is the value of $|k|$?

11. Give one possible solution to the equation $\frac{1}{x^2+x} - \frac{x-6}{x+1} = \frac{x+5}{x^2+x}$.

12. * An arrow is launched upward with an initial speed of 70 m/s (meters per second). The equation $v^2 = v_0^2 - 2gh$ describes the motion of the arrow, where v_0 is the initial speed of the arrow, v is the speed of the arrow as it is moving up in the air, h is the height of the arrow above the ground, t is the time elapsed since the arrow was projected upward, and g is the acceleration due to gravity (approximately 9.8 m/s²). What is the maximum height from the ground the arrow will rise to the nearest meter?

Answers

1. 5	5. A	9. C
2. D	6. C	10. 2
3. 8	7. D	11. 1 or 4
4. A	8. D	12. 250

Full Solutions

5.

Solution by solving the equation: We can solve the given equation by first multiplying each side by $2x$ to get $2x \cdot \frac{1}{x} + 2x \cdot \frac{3}{x} = 2x \cdot \frac{1}{2}$, or equivalently $2 + 6 = x$. So $x = 8$. It follows that $\frac{3}{x} = \frac{3}{8}$.

It seems reasonable at this point that $\frac{3}{8}$ would represent the fraction of the job that Billy would complete in 1 hour.

Let's verify this. We assume that Billy can complete $\frac{3}{8}$ of the job in 1 hour. Since Billy can put the desk together three times as fast as Dennis, it follows that Dennis can complete $\frac{1}{8}$ of the job in 1 hour. So together they can complete $\frac{3}{8} + \frac{1}{8} = \frac{4}{8} = \frac{1}{2}$ the job in 1 hour, and therefore they can complete the whole job in 2 hours.

Since everything works out, the answer is choice (A).

Notes: (1) $\frac{1}{x}$ represents the fraction of the job that would be completed by Dennis in 1 hour. So Dennis can complete $\frac{1}{8}$ of the job in 1 hour.

(2) $\frac{1}{2}$ represents the fraction of the job that both Billy and Dennis, working together, can complete in 1 hour.

(3) The time it would take Dennis to complete the job himself is 8 hours.

(4) The time it would take Billy to complete the job himself is $\frac{8}{3}$ hours (or $2\frac{2}{3}$ hours).

* Direct solution: The right hand side of the equation, $\frac{1}{2}$, is the fraction of the job that both Billy and Dennis, working together, can complete in 1 hour.

On the left hand side of the equation we are expressing $\frac{1}{2}$ as a sum of two terms. Each term represents the portion of $\frac{1}{2}$ that each of Billy and Dennis contribute. Since Billy works three times as fast as Dennis, $\frac{3}{x}$ is the fraction of the job that Billy contributes, choice (A).

276

6.

Solution by substitution: We replace x by $3y + 1$ twice in the right hand side of the first equation to get

$$y = (3y + 8)(9y - 2) = 27y^2 + 66y - 16$$

Subtracting y from each side of this last equation yields

$$0 = 27y^2 + 65y - 16$$

This is a quadratic equation with $a = 27$, $b = 65$, and $c = -16$. We compute the discriminant of this equation to get

$$b^2 - 4ac = 65^2 - 4(27)(-16) = 65^2 + 4(27)(16) > 0$$

Since the discriminant is positive, the quadratic equation has **two** real solutions, choice (C).

Notes: (1) Recall that the quadratic equation $ax^2 + bx + c$ can be solved by using the quadratic formula

$$x = \frac{-b \pm \sqrt{b^2 - 4ac}}{2a}$$

The quantity under the square root, $b^2 - 4ac$, is called the *discriminant* of the quadratic equation. If the discriminant is positive, then the equation has 2 real solutions. If the discriminant is zero, then the equation has 1 real solution. And if the discriminant is negative, then the equation has no real solutions (the solutions are complex in this case).

(2) It was not necessary to finish computing the discriminant in this problem. We needed only to find out if it was positive, zero, or negative.

* Quick graphical solution: We can get a quick rough sketch of the parabola by plotting the two x-intercepts $(-7,0)$ and $(\frac{5}{3}, 0)$ and noting that the parabola opens upwards.

We can then plot the x-intercept of the line, $(1,0)$ and note that the slope of the line is $m = \frac{1}{3}$. A quick sketch will show that the line hits the parabola twice.

Notes: (1) To see that the slope of the line is $\frac{1}{3}$, we need to solve the second equation for y to get $y = \frac{1}{3}x - \frac{1}{3}$.

(2) If a calculator were allowed for this problem, we could also solve by graphing the two equations in our calculator, finding an appropriate window, and counting the points of intersection. Note that we would first have to solve the second equation for y. I leave the details of this solution to the reader.

7.

Solution using a general exponential function: Recall that a general exponential function has the form $P(t) = a \cdot (1 + r)^{ct}$, where $a = P(0)$ is the initial amount and r is the growth rate.

In this problem, $a = P(0) = 650$, and since the substance is decaying at an annual rate of 17 percent, $c = 1$, and the exponential rate is $r = -.17$. So we have $P(t) = 650(1 - .17)^t = 650(0.83)^t$, choice (D).

8.

Solution using synthetic division:

$$-2 \rvert \; 3 \quad -5$$
$$\underline{\qquad -6}$$
$$\quad\; 3 \quad -11$$

So $\frac{3x-5}{x+2} = 3 - \frac{11}{x+2}$, choice (D).

* Clever solution: $\frac{3x-5}{x+2} = \frac{3(x+2)-6-5}{x+2} = \frac{3(x+2)}{x+2} - \frac{11}{x+2} = 3 - \frac{11}{x+2}$, (D).

Notes: (1) We replaced x by $(x + 2)$ to match the denominator. By doing this we "accidentally" added $3 \cdot 2 = 6$ to the numerator. So we subtract 6 to "undo the damage" we caused.

(2) This problem can also be solved by picking numbers. I leave this solution as an exercise for the reader.

9.

* Quick algebraic solution: We have $\frac{9x^2}{3x+5} = \frac{25}{3x+5} + k$, so that

$$k = \frac{9x^2}{3x+5} - \frac{25}{3x+5} = \frac{9x^2-25}{3x+5} = \frac{(3x+5)(3x-5)}{3x+5} = 3x - 5, \text{ choice (C)}.$$

Solution using synthetic division: For this particular problem, this solution is a bit tricky. We first need to factor out the 3 in the denominator to get $\frac{9x^2}{3(x+\frac{5}{3})} = \frac{3x^2}{x+\frac{5}{3}} = \frac{3x^2+0x+0}{x+\frac{5}{3}}$.

Note that we need to add in the missing terms, each with a coefficient of 0. We are now ready to use synthetic division

$$-\frac{5}{3}\Big|\ \ 3\ \ \ \ \ 0\ \ \ \ \ \ 0$$
$$\underline{\ \ \ \ \ \ \ \ \ \ \ \ -5\ \ \ \ \ 25/3}$$
$$3\ \ \ -5\ \ \ \ \ 25/3$$

So $\dfrac{9x^2}{3x+5} = 3x - 5 + \dfrac{25}{3}\left(\dfrac{1}{x+\frac{5}{3}}\right) = 3x - 5 + \dfrac{25}{3x+5} = \dfrac{25}{3x+5} + 3x - 5.$

So $k = 3x - 5$ and the answer is choice (C).

10.
* Quick algebraic solution: We multiply each side of the equation by $kx - 3$ to get

$$54x^2 + 85x - 32 = (-27x - 2)(kx - 3) - 38$$

$$54x^2 + 85x - 32 = -27kx^2 + (81 - 2k)x + 6 - 38.$$

So we must have $-27k = 54$, and so $k = -2$. Therefore $|k| = \mathbf{2}$.

Note: We could also solve $81 - 2k = 85$ to get $k = -2$.

11.
* Algebraic solution: $x^2 + x = x(x + 1)$ is the LCD of the fractions that appear in the equation. So let's begin by multiplying each term by $x(x + 1)$:

$$x(x+1)\cdot\dfrac{1}{x^2+x} - x(x+1)\cdot\dfrac{x-6}{x+1} = x(x+1)\cdot\dfrac{x+5}{x^2+x}$$

$$1 - x(x - 6) = x + 5$$

$$1 - x^2 + 6x = x + 5$$

$$0 = x^2 - 5x + 4$$

$$0 = (x - 1)(x - 4)$$

So the two possible solutions are **1** or **4**.

Notes: (1) The LCD (least common denominator) of a set of fractions is the LCM (least common multiple) of the denominators.

In this problem the denominators are $x^2 + x = x(x + 1)$ and $x + 1$. So the LCD is $x^2 + x = x(x + 1)$.

(2) Multiplying each side of a rational equation by the LCD of the fractions that appear in the equation gives an equation without any fractions.

(3) Using the distributive property, we see that multiplying each side of an equation by an expression is the same as multiplying each term by that expression.

(4)
$$x(x + 1) \cdot \frac{1}{x^2+x} = x(x + 1) \cdot \frac{1}{x(x+1)} = 1$$

$$-x(x + 1) \cdot \frac{x-6}{x+1} = -x(x - 6) = -x^2 + 6x$$

$$x(x + 1) \cdot \frac{x+5}{x^2+x} = x(x + 1) \cdot \frac{x+5}{x(x+1)} = x + 5$$

(5) Remember to check that neither solution is extraneous at the end. To do these we need only check that 1 and 4 do not make any denominator zero in the original equation.

(6) If a calculator were allowed for this question, an alternative would be to put each side of the equation into your graphing calculator and then to use the intersect feature (see the graphical solution to problem 2 in Lesson 5 to see how to do this).

12.
* We are given that $v_0 = 70$ and $g \approx 9.8$ so that

$$v^2 = 4900 - 19.6h.$$

The maximum height occurs when $v = 0$. It follows that

$$4900 - 19.6h = 0^2 = 0, \text{ and so } 4900 = 19.6h.$$

We divide each side of this last equation by 19.6 to get

$$h = \frac{4900}{19.6} = \mathbf{250}.$$

280

LESSON 24
PROBLEM SOLVING

Reminder: Before beginning this lesson remember to redo the problems from Lessons 4, 8, 12, 16, and 20 that you have marked off. Do not "unmark" a question unless you get it correct.

Try to solve each of the following problems. The answers to these problems, followed by full solutions are at the end of this lesson. **Do not** look at the answers until you have attempted these problems yourself. Please remember to mark off any problems you get wrong.

LEVEL 1: PROBLEM SOLVING

1. A 770 gallon tank is filled to capacity with water. At most how many 14 ounce bottles can be filled with water from the tank? (1 gallon = 128 ounces)

2. The mean annual salary of an NBA player, S, can be estimated using the equation $S = 161,400(1.169)^t$, where S is measured in thousands of dollars, and t represents the number of years since 1980 for $0 \le t \le 20$. Which of the following statements is the best interpretation of 161,400 in the context of this problem?

    (A) The estimated mean annual salary, in dollars, of an NBA player in 1980.
    (B) The estimated mean annual salary, in dollars, of an NBA player in 2000.
    (C) The estimated yearly increase in the mean annual salary of an NBA player.
    (D) The estimated yearly decrease in the mean annual salary of an NBA player.

LEVEL 2: PROBLEM SOLVING

Paramecia present (in thousands) over twelve days

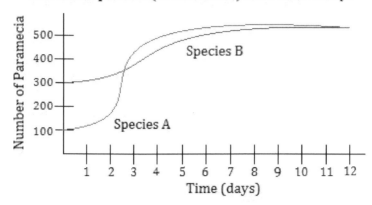

3. A small puddle is monitored by scientists for the number of *paramecia* present. The scientists are interested in two distinct species, let's call them "species A" and "species B." At time t = 0, the scientists measure and estimate the amount of species A and species B present in the puddle. They then proceed to measure and record the number of each species of *paramecium* present every hour for 12 days. The data for each species were then fit by a smooth curve, as shown in the graph above. Which of the following is a correct statement about the data above?

   (A) At time $t = 0$, the number of species B present is 150% greater than the number of species A present.

   (B) At time $t = 0$, the number of species A present is 75% less than the number of species B present.

   (C) For the first 3 days, the average growth rate of species B is higher than the average growth rate of species A.

   (D) The growth rate of both species A and species B decreases for the last 8 days.

282

4.   * A chemist has a supply of 5.2 liter bottles of a certain solvent that must be shipped to a central warehouse. The warehouse can accept the solvent at the rate of 3 hectoliters per minute for a maximum of 8 hours per day. If 1 hectoliter equals 100 liters, what is the maximum number of bottles that the warehouse could receive from the chemist each day?

   (A) 461
   (B) 462
   (C) 27,692
   (D) 83,200

LEVEL 3: PROBLEM SOLVING

5.   A mixture is made by combining a red liquid and a blue liquid so that the ratio of the red liquid to the blue liquid is 17 to 3 by weight. How many liters of the blue liquid are needed to make a 420 liter mixture?

6.   A certain exam lasts a total of 4 hours. Each part of the exam requires the same amount of time and 10 minute breaks are included between consecutive parts. If there is a total of 4 breaks during the 4 hours, what is the required time, in minutes, for each part of the test?

7.   A bus driver drove at an average speed of 45 miles per hour for 3 hours while the bus consumed fuel at a rate of 15 miles per gallon. How many gallons of fuel did the bus use for the entire 3-hour trip?

8.   * John, a United States resident, is on vacation in Spain and uses his credit card to purchase a souvenir for 184 euros. The bank that issues the credit card converts the purchase price at the foreign exchange rate for that day, and an additional fee of 6% of the converted cost is applied before the bank posts the charge. If the bank posts a charge of $212 to John's account, what exchange rate, in Euros per one U.S. dollar, did the bank use?

LEVEL 4: PROBLEM SOLVING

$$S = 25.33H + 353.16$$

9.   * The linear regression model above is based on an analysis of the relationship between SAT math scores (S) and the number of hours spent studying for SAT math (H). Based on this model, which of the following statements must be true?

   I. The slope indicates that as H increases by 1, S decreases by 25.33.
   II. For a student that studies 15 hours for SAT math, the predicted SAT math score is greater than 700.
   III. There is a negative correlation between H and S.

   (A) I only
   (B) II only
   (C) III only
   (D) I and II only

10.   A ball is dropped from 567 centimeters above the ground and after the fourth bounce it rises to a height of 7 centimeters. If the height to which the ball rises after each bounce is always the same fraction of the height reached on its previous bounce, what is this fraction?

   (A) $\frac{1}{81}$
   (B) $\frac{1}{27}$
   (C) $\frac{1}{9}$
   (D) $\frac{1}{3}$

284

11. Vincent must inspect electronic components that are arranged in a long line. The components are labeled numerically in order from 1 to 9, with the pattern repeating. For example, the tenth component is labeled with a 1 and the eleventh component is labeled with a 2. He must start with the first component and proceed in order, stopping when he encounters a defective component. If the first defective component he encounters is component 6, which of the following could be the total number of components that Vincent inspects, including the defective one?

(A) 103
(B) 105
(C) 107
(D) 109

LEVEL 5: PROBLEM SOLVING

12. A business is owned by 1 man and 5 women, each of whom has an equal share. If one of the women sells $\frac{2}{5}$ of her share to the man, and another of the women keeps $\frac{1}{4}$ of her share and sells the rest to the man, what fraction of the business will the man own?

(A) $\frac{9}{40}$

(B) $\frac{37}{120}$

(C) $\frac{2}{3}$

(D) $\frac{43}{120}$

Answers

1. 7040	5. 63	9. B
2. A	6. 40	10. D
3. D	7. 9	11. B
4. C	8. .92	12. D

Full Solutions

5.

* We can represent the number of liters of red liquid by $17x$ and the number of liters of blue liquid by $3x$ for some number x. Then the total amount of liquid is $20x$ which must be equal to 420. $20x = 420$ implies that $x = 21$. Since we want the number of liters of blue liquid, we need to find $3x$. This is $3(21) = \mathbf{63}$.

Important note: After you find x make sure you look at what the question is asking for. A common error is to give an answer of 21. But the amount of blue liquid is **not** equal to x. It is equal to $3x$!

Alternate solution: We set up a ratio of the amount of blue liquid to the total liquid.

blue liquid	3	x
total liquid	20	420

$$\frac{3}{20} = \frac{x}{420}$$
$$20x = 3 \cdot 420$$
$$x = 3 \cdot \frac{420}{20} = \mathbf{63}.$$

6.

* The exam lasts $4(60) = 240$ minutes. There are a total of $4(10) = 40$ minutes in breaks. So each part of the test lasts $\frac{200}{5} = \mathbf{40}$ minutes.

Note: Since there are 4 breaks, there must be 5 parts to the exam (breaks fall between consecutive parts). A common error is to mistakenly assume that there are only 4 parts to the exam.

7.

* The bus driver drove $d = r \cdot t = 45 \cdot 3 = 135$ miles, and so the amount of fuel that the bus used was $\frac{135}{15} = \mathbf{9}$ gallons.

Notes: (1) We used the formula "distance = rate × time" or $d = r \cdot t$.

In this problem the rate is $r = 45$ miles/hour and the time is $t = 3$ hours.

(2) The bus gets 15 miles for each gallon of fuel. So the bus can drive 15 miles on 1 gallon of fuel. The bus can drive $15 \cdot 2 = 30$ miles on two gallons of fuel. The bus can drive $15 \cdot 3 = 45$ miles on three gallons of fuel. And so on.

In general, the bus can drive $15x$ miles on x gallons of fuel.

So we have $15x = 135$, where x is the number of gallons of fuel needed to travel 135 miles. So $x = \frac{135}{15} = 9$.

8.
* If we let C be the original cost of the item in dollars, then we have $C + .06C = 212$, or equivalently $1.06C = 212$. So $C = \frac{212}{1.06} = 200$.

So we know that 184 euros corresponds to 200 dollars. We want to know how many euros correspond to 1 dollar. So we set up a ratio.

The two things being compared are "euros" and "dollars."

euros	184	x
dollars	200	1

Now draw in the division symbols and equal sign, cross multiply and divide the corresponding ratio to find the unknown quantity x.

$$\frac{184}{200} = \frac{x}{1}$$
$$200x = 184 \cdot 1$$
$$x = \frac{184}{200} = .92$$

So we grid in $.92$.

9.
* The slope of the line is $25.33 = \frac{25.33}{1}$. This indicates that as H increases by 1, S increases by 25.33. Also since the slope is positive, there is a **positive correlation** between H and S. So I and III are false, and the answer must be choice (B).

Notes: (1) We did not have to check II because once we determined that I and III were false, there was only one answer choice left that excluded both of them.

287

(2) For completeness let's check that II is true. To see this we just need to perform the following computation:

$$25.33(15) + 353.16 = 733.11 > 700.$$

10.

* Solution by starting with choice (C): Let's begin with choice (C). We divide 567 by 9 four times and get 0.0864197531 which is much too small. So we can eliminate choices (A), (B) and (C). We next try choice (D). If we divide 567 by 3 four times we get 7 so that (D) is the correct answer.

Note: We could have also multiplied 7 by 3 four times to get 567.

An algebraic solution: We want to solve the following equation.

$$567x^4 = 7$$

$$x^4 = \frac{7}{567} = \frac{1}{81}$$

$$x = \frac{1}{3}$$

Thus, the answer is choice (D).

11.

* We have a sequence which repeats in cycles of 9. Component 6 is in the 6th position in this cycle. So we are looking for a number that gives a remainder of 6 when divided by 9. Well, 99 is evenly divisible by 9. Therefore $99 + 6 = 105$ gives a remainder of 6 when divided by 9. So the answer is choice (B).

Solution by starting with choice (C): Let's compute the remainder when 107 is divided by 9. We do the long division by hand (or by using the Calculator Algorithm from Lesson 9). 9 goes into 107 eleven times with a remainder 0f 8. So if we just subtract 2 from 107 we will get a number that gives a remainder of 6 when divided by 9. So the answer is $107 - 2 = 105$, choice (B).

Remark: Notice that remainders have a very nice, cyclical pattern. The remainders when you divide ..., 97, 98, 99, 100, 101, 102,.. by 9 are ..., 7, 8, 0, 1, 2, 3,..

12.

Using the answer choices as a guide we will split the business into 120 parts, so that each person has $\frac{120}{6} = 20$ parts. We have $(\frac{2}{5})(20) = 8$ and $(\frac{3}{4})(20) = 15$. So after both sales the man has $20 + 8 + 15 = 43$ parts out of 120 parts total. Thus, the answer is choice (D).

Remark: The number 120 comes from multiplying the least common denominator of the two fractions $(5 \cdot 4 = 20)$ by the number of people (6).

* Direct solution: This is quick, but a bit tricky. Each of the 6 people begins with $\frac{1}{6}$ of the business. The first woman sells $(\frac{2}{5})(\frac{1}{6})$ of the business, and the second woman sells $(\frac{3}{4})(\frac{1}{6})$ of the business (if she keeps $\frac{1}{4}$, then she sells $\frac{3}{4}$). Therefore we can get the answer by doing the following single computation in our calculator:

$$\frac{1}{6} + (\frac{2}{5})(\frac{1}{6}) + (\frac{3}{4})(\frac{1}{6}) = \frac{43}{120}$$

This is choice (D).

Download additional solutions for free here:

www.thesatmathprep.com/28Les800.html

LESSON 25
HEART OF ALGEBRA

Try to solve each of the following problems. The answers to these problems are at the end of this lesson.

Full solutions to these problems are available for free download here:
www.thesatmathprep.com/28Les800.html

LEVEL 3: HEART OF ALGEBRA

1. If $4 - 3x = 2x + 11 - 7x$, what is the value of $x - 3$?

$$T = 25 + 3c$$

2. The equation above is used to model the number of chirps, c, made by a certain species of cricket in one minute, and the temperature, T, in degrees Fahrenheit. According to this model, what is the estimated increase in temperature, in degrees Fahrenheit, when the number of chirps in one minute is increased by 1?

   (A) 3
   (B) 5
   (C) 25
   (D) 28

$$2x - 5y = -28$$
$$y - x = -13$$

3. What is the solution (x, y) to the system of equations above?

   (A) $(5, -8)$
   (B) $(31, 18)$
   (C) $(-4, 4)$
   (D) $(0, -13)$

4. Which of the following numbers is NOT a solution of the inequality $5x - 7 \geq 6x - 4$

   (A) -6
   (B) -4
   (C) -3
   (D) -2

LEVEL 4: HEART OF ALGEBRA

$$\frac{5}{\sqrt{x-7}} = 6$$

5. For $x > 7$, which of the following equations is equivalent to the equation above?

    (A) $25 = 36(x - 7)$
    (B) $25 = 6(x - 7)$
    (C) $25 = 6(x - \sqrt{7})$
    (D) $5 = 36(x - 7)$

6. Last month Joe the painter painted many rooms. He used 3 coats of paint on one third of the rooms he painted. On two fifths of the remaining rooms he used 2 coats of paint, and he only used 1 coat of paint on the remaining 24 rooms. What was the total number of coats of paint Joe painted last month?

7. A carpenter spent a total of $5.44 for nails and screws. Each screw cost 2 times as much as each nail, and the carpenter bought 6 times as many nails as screws. How much, in dollars, did the customer spend on screws? (Disregard the $ sign when gridding your answer.)

8. If $i = \sqrt{-1}$, and $\frac{(7+5i)}{(-2-6i)} = a + bi$, where a and b are real numbers, then what is the value of $|a + b|$?

LEVEL 5: HEART OF ALGEBRA

9. If $xy = 22, yz = 10, xz = 55$, and $x > 0$, then $xyz =$

10. If $|-3a + 15| = 6$ and $|-2b + 12| = 4$, what is the greatest possible value of ab?

$$x = 36z$$
$$y = 36z^2 + 5$$

11. If $z > 0$ in the equations above, what is y in terms of x?

(A) $y = \frac{1}{36}x^2 + 4$

(B) $y = \frac{1}{36}x^2 + 5$

(C) $y = \frac{1}{36}x^2 + 36$

(D) $y = \frac{1}{6}x^2 + 4$

12. If $2a - 8b = 5$, what is the value of $\frac{3^a}{9^{2b}}$?

(A) 9^5

(B) 3^5

(C) $\sqrt{3^5}$

(D) The value cannot be determined from the information given.

Answers

1. 1/2 or .5	5. A	9. 110
2. A	6. 116	10. 56
3. B	7. 1.36	11. B
4. D	8. 3/10 or .3	12. C

LESSON 26
GEOMETRY AND TRIGONOMETRY

Try to solve each of the following problems. The answers to these problems are at the end of this lesson.

Full solutions to these problems are available for free download here:

www.thesatmathprep.com/28Les800.html

LEVEL 3: GEOMETRY AND TRIG

1. Which of the following equations represents a line that is perpendicular to the line with equation $y = -2x - 3$?

    (A) $2x + 3y = 1$
    (B) $2x + y = 1$
    (C) $4x - 8y = 1$
    (D) $6x - 3y = 1$

2. The height of a solid cone is 22 centimeters and the radius of the base is 15 centimeters. A cut parallel to the circular base is made completely through the cone so that one of the two resulting solids is a smaller cone. If the radius of the base of the small cone is 5 centimeters, what is the height of the small cone, in centimeters?

3. In a right triangle, one angle measures $x°$, where $\cos x° = \frac{2}{3}$. What is $\sin((90 - x)°)$

LEVEL 4: GEOMETRY

4. The length of each side of an equilateral triangle will be doubled to create a second triangle. The area of the second triangle will be how many times the area of the original triangle?

5. In triangle DEF, $DE = DF = 10$ and $EF = 16$. What is the area of the triangle?

6. The points $(0,4)$ and $(5,4)$ are the endpoints of one of the diagonals of a square. What is a possible y-coordinate of one of the other vertices of this square?

7. In the xy-plane, line k passes through the point $(0, -3)$ and is parallel to the line with equation $5x + 3y = 4$. If the equation of line k is $y = sx + t$, what is the value of st?

8. A container in the shape of a right circular cylinder has an inside base radius of 5 centimeters and an inside height of 6 centimeters. This cylinder is completely filled with fluid. All of the fluid is then poured into a second right circular cylinder with a larger inside base radius of 7 centimeters. What must be the minimum inside height, in centimeters, of the second container?

    (A) $5/\sqrt{7}$
    (B) $\dfrac{7}{5}$
    (C) 5
    (D) $\dfrac{150}{49}$

LEVEL 5: GEOMETRY

9. A sphere with volume 36π cubic inches is inscribed in a cube so that the sphere touches the cube at 6 points. What is the surface area, in square inches, of the cube?

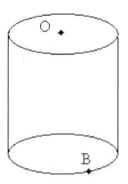

10. The figure above shows a right circular cylinder with diameter 4 and height 7. If point O is the center of the top of the cylinder and B lies on the circumference of the bottom of the cylinder, what is the straight-line distance between O and B ?

    (A) 3
    (B) 7
    (C) 11
    (D) $\sqrt{53}$

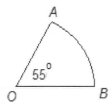

11. * In the figure above, AB is the arc of a circle with center O. If the length of arc AB is 7π, what is the area of region OAB to the nearest integer?

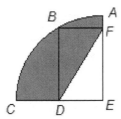

12. In the figure above, arc ABC is one quarter of a circle with center E, and radius 12. If the length plus the width of rectangle $BDEF$ is 16, then the perimeter of the shaded region is

(A) $16 + 6\pi$
(B) $20 + 6\pi$
(C) $28 + 6\pi$
(D) $2 + 12\pi$

Answers

1. C	5. 48	9. 216
2. 22/3 or 7.33	6. 1.5 or 6.5	10. D
3. 2/3, .666, or .667	7. 5	11. 252
4. 4	8. D	12. B

295

LESSON 27
PASSPORT TO ADVANCED MATH

Try to solve each of the following problems. The answers to these problems are at the end of this lesson.

Full solutions to these problems are available for free download here:
www.thesatmathprep.com/28Les800.html

LEVEL 3: ADVANCED MATH

$$h(x) = kx^3 - 7$$

1. For the function h defined above, k is a constant and $h(2) = 25$. What is the value of $h(-1)$

    (A) -18
    (B) -11
    (C) 0
    (D) 18

2. In the xy-plane, which of the following is an equation of a circle with center $(3,0)$ and a radius with endpoint $(2,\frac{3}{2})$?

    (A) $(x+3)^2 + y^2 = \frac{13}{4}$
    (B) $(x-3)^2 + y^2 = \frac{13}{4}$
    (C) $(x+3)^2 + y^2 = \frac{\sqrt{13}}{2}$
    (D) $(x-3)^2 + y^2 = \frac{\sqrt{13}}{2}$

$$16x^6 + 40x^3y^2 + 25y^4$$

3. Which of the following is equivalent to the expression above?

    (A) $(4x^3 + 5y^2)^2$
    (B) $(4x^2 + 5y)^4$
    (C) $(16x^3 + 25y^2)^2$
    (D) $(16x^2 + 25y)^4$

296

4. In the xy-plane, the graph of function g has x-intercepts at -5, -2, 2, and 5. Which of the following could define g ?

    (A) $g(x) = (x - 5)^2(x - 2)^2$
    (B) $g(x) = (x + 5)^2(x + 2)^2$
    (C) $g(x) = (x - 5)^2(x + 2)(x - 2)^3(x + 5)$
    (D) $g(x) = (x - 5)(x + 5)(x - 2)^2$

LEVEL 4: ADVANCED MATH

5. If $x \neq 0$ and x is directly proportional to y, which of the following is inversely proportional to $\frac{1}{y^2}$?

    (A) x^2
    (B) x
    (C) $\frac{1}{x}$
    (D) $\frac{1}{x^2}$

$$(x - n)(x - 9) = x^2 - 4nx + k$$

6. In the equation above, n and k are constants. If the equation is true for all values of x, what is the value of k ?

7. Let a, b, and c be numbers such that $-a < b < c < a$. Which of the following must be true?

    I. $c - b > 0$
    II. $b + c > 0$
    III. $|b| < a$

    (A) I only
    (B) III only
    (C) I and III only
    (D) I, II, and III

8. The function g has the property that $g(a) = g(b)$ for all real numbers a and b. What is the graph of $y = g(x)$ in the xy-plane?

    (A) A parabola symmetric about the x-axis
    (B) A line with slope 0
    (C) A line with slope 1
    (D) A line with no slope

9. For all numbers x, define the function h by $h(x) = 2x + 6$. Which of the following is equal to $h(6) + h(5)$?

    (A) $h(11)$
    (B) $h(14)$
    (C) $h(32)$
    (D) $h(34)$

LEVEL 5: ADVANCED MATH

10. If $x^2 + y^2 = k^2$, and $xy = 8 - 4k$, what is $(x + y)^2$ in terms of k?

    (A) $k - 4$
    (B) $(k - 4)^2$
    (C) $k^2 - 4k + 8$
    (D) $(k - 2)^2 + 4$

11. Let g be a function such that $g(x) = k(x - 5)(x + 5)$ where k is a nonzero constant. If $g(b - 3.7) = 0$ and $b > 0$, what is the value of b ?

12. Let Δa be defined as $\Delta a = a^2 - a$ for all values of a. If $\Delta b = \Delta(b - 2)$, what is the value of b?

Answers

1. B	5. A	9. B
2. B	6. 27	10. B
3. A	7. C	11. 8.7
4. C	8. B	12. 3/2 or 1.5

LESSON 28
PROBLEM SOLVING AND DATA ANALYSIS

Try to solve each of the following problems. The answers to these problems are at the end of this lesson.

Full solutions to these problems are available for free download here:

www.thesatmathprep.com/28Les800.html

LEVEL 3: PROBLEM SOLVING

1. Daniel and eight other students took two exams, and each exam yielded an integer grade for each student. The two grades for each student were added together. The sum of these two grades for each of the nine students was 150, 183, 100, 126, 151, 171, 106, 164, and Daniel's sum, which was the median of the nine sums. If Daniel's first test grade was 70, what is one possible grade Daniel could have received on the second test?

2. * During a sale at a retail store, if a customer buys one t-shirt at full price, the customer is given a 25 percent discount on a second t-shirt of equal or lesser value. If John buys two t-shirts that have full prices of $30 and $20, by what percent is the total cost of the two t-shirts reduced during the sale? (Disregard the percent symbol when you grid your answer.)

LEVEL 4: PROBLEM SOLVING

3. The average (arithmetic mean) of 17 numbers is j. If two of the numbers are k and m, what is the average of the remaining 15 numbers in terms of j, k and m?

(A) $\frac{k+m}{17}$

(B) $17j + k + m$

(C) $\frac{16j-k-m}{17}$

(D) $\frac{17j-k-m}{15}$

4. Which scatterplot shows a relationship that is appropriately modeled with the equation $y = ab^x$, where $a > 0$ and $b > 1$?

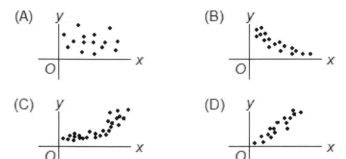

(A)

(B)

(C)

(D)

5. A farmer purchased several animals from a neighboring farmer: 6 animals costing $50 each, 10 animals costing $100 each, and k animals costing $200 each, where k is a positive odd integer. If the median price for all the animals was $100, what is the greatest possible value of k?

6. The average (arithmetic mean) age of the people in a certain group was 32 years before one of the members left the group and was replaced by someone who is 10 years younger than the person who left. If the average age of the group is now 30 years, how many people are in the group?

7. On a certain exam, the median grade for a group of 25 students is 67. If the highest grade on the exam is 90, which of the following could be the number of students that scored 67 on the exam?

    I. 5
    II. 20
    III. 24

    (A) I only
    (B) III only
    (C) I and III only
    (D) I, II, and III

8. * Jessica has two cats named Mittens and Fluffy. Last year Mittens weighed 12 pounds, and Fluffy weighed 19 pounds. Fluffy was placed on a diet, and his weight decreased by 20%. Mittens weight has increased by 20%. By what percentage did Mitten's and Fluffy's combined weight decrease, to the nearest tenth of a percent?

LEVEL 5: PROBLEM SOLVING

9. A group of students take a test and the average score is 90. One more student takes the test and receives a score of 81 decreasing the average score of the group to 87. How many students were in the initial group?

10. A scatterplot includes the points $(1,0)$, $(2,0)$, $(3,0)$, and $(0, -6)$. The data is fitted with a cubic curve whose equation has the form $y = x^3 + bx^2 + cx + d$. If the curve passes through all four of the given points, find the value of $b + c$.

11. * John, a United States resident, is on vacation in Spain and is trying to decide if he should use his own credit card from the U.S., or to purchase a prepaid credit card for 500 euros in Spain.

    The bank that issues John's U.S. credit card converts all purchase prices at the foreign exchange rate for that day, and an additional fee of 6% of the converted cost is applied before the bank posts the charge.

    If John decides to purchase the prepaid card, he can use this card spending dollars at the exchange rate for that day with no fee, but he loses any money left unspent on the card.

    Suppose that John does decide to buy the prepaid card. What is the least number of the 500 euros John must spend for the prepaid card to have been the cheaper option? Round your answer to the nearest whole number of euros.

12. At Brilliance University, the chess team has 16 members and the math team has 13 members. If a total of 7 students belong to only one of the two teams, how many students belong to both teams?

Answers

1. 80 or 81	5. 15	9. 2
2. 10	6. 5	10. 5
3. D	7. D	11. 472
4. C	8. 4.5	12. 11

ACTIONS TO COMPLETE AFTER YOU HAVE READ THIS BOOK

1. **Take another practice SAT**

   You should see a substantial improvement in your score.

2. **Continue to practice SAT math problems for 10 to 20 minutes each day**

   You may want to purchase *New SAT Math Problems arranged by Topic and Difficulty Level* for additional practice problems.

3. **'Like' my Facebook page**

   This page is updated regularly with SAT prep advice, tips, tricks, strategies, and practice problems. Visit the following webpage and click the 'like' button.

   ## www.facebook.com/SATPrepGet800

4. **Review this book**

   If this book helped you, please post your positive feedback on the site you purchased it from; e.g. Amazon, Barnes and Noble, etc.

5. **Claim your FREE bonuses**

   If you have not done so yet, visit the following webpage and enter your email address to receive solutions to all the supplemental problems in this book and other materials.

   ## www.thesatmathprep.com/28Les800.html

About the Author

Dr. Steve Warner, a New York native, earned his Ph.D. at Rutgers University in Pure Mathematics in May, 2001. While a graduate student, Dr. Warner won the TA Teaching Excellence Award.

After Rutgers, Dr. Warner joined the Penn State Mathematics Department as an Assistant Professor. In September, 2002, Dr. Warner returned to New York to accept an Assistant Professor position at Hofstra University. By September 2007, Dr. Warner had received tenure and was promoted to Associate Professor. He has taught undergraduate and graduate courses in Precalculus, Calculus, Linear Algebra, Differential Equations, Mathematical Logic, Set Theory and Abstract Algebra.

Over that time, Dr. Warner participated in a five year NSF grant, "The MSTP Project," to study and improve mathematics and science curriculum in poorly performing junior high schools. He also published several articles in scholarly journals, specifically on Mathematical Logic.

Dr. Warner has more than 15 years of experience in general math tutoring and tutoring for standardized tests such as the SAT, ACT and AP Calculus exams. He has tutored students both individually and in group settings.

In February, 2010 Dr. Warner released his first SAT prep book "The 32 Most Effective SAT Math Strategies," and in 2012 founded Get 800 Test Prep. Since then Dr. Warner has written books for the SAT, ACT, SAT Math Subject Tests and AP Calculus exams.

Dr. Steve Warner can be reached at

steve@SATPrepGet800.com

BOOKS BY DR. STEVE WARNER

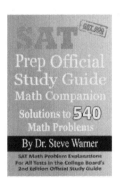

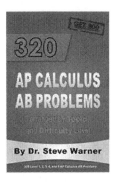
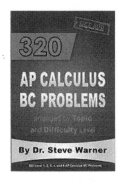
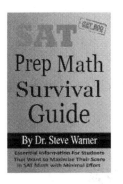